Japanese Management

We dedicate this book to one of our authors, Father Robert J. Ballon, Professor Emeritus of Sophia University, who passed away on 14 December 2004. We remain deeply indebted to Father Ballon for the generous way he freely shared his advice in the preparation of this book. His wise counsel, wit and the warmth of his personality will be sadly missed by the editors and the wider community of scholars in Japanese business studies.

René Haak and Markus Pudelko

Contents

Part I   Introduction

Part II   Contributions

Part III   Conclusion

List of Figures and Tables

Figures

Tables

List of Abbreviations and Acronyms

CNC	Computer Numerical Control
CPA	Certified Public Accountants
ESOP	Employee Share Ownership Program
EU	European Union
FANUC	Fujitsu Automatic Numerical Control
FDI	Foreign Direct Investment
FILP	Fiscal and Loan Program
FRI	Fujitsu Research Institute
FY	Fiscal Year
GATT	General Agreement on Tariffs and Trade
GDP	Gross Domestic Product
GNP	Gross National Product
HR	Human Resource
HRM	Human Resource Management
HQ	Headquarters
IMVP	International Motor Vehicle Program
IT	Information Technology
JETRO	Japan External Trade Organization
JMNC	Japanese Multinational Corporation
JPY	Japanese Yen
JUSE	Japanese Union Scientists and Engineers
LDP	Liberal Democratic Party (Japan)
M&A	Mergers and Acquisitions
METI	Ministry of Economy, Trade and Industry (Japan)
MIC	Mobile Internet Centre
MIT	Massachusetts Institute of Technology
MITI	Ministry of International Trade and Industry (Japan)
MNC	Multinational Corporation
MNE	Multinational Enterprise
MOF	Ministry of Finance (Japan)
NC	Numerical Control
NGO	Non-Governmental Organization
NIE	Newly Industrializing Economy
NRI	Nomura Research Institute
OECD	Organisation for Economic Cooperation and Development
OEM	Original Equipment Manufacturer
PDAC	Plan Do Check Act
POS	Point of Sales

PPP	Purchasing Power Parity
R&D	Research and Development
ROE	Return on Equity
SME	Small and Medium-sized Enterprises
TPS	Toyota Production System
TQC	Total Quality Control
TQM	Total Quality Management
TRIM	Trade-Related Investment Measures
TRIPS	Trade-Related Aspects of Intellectual Property Rights
TSE	Tokyo Stock Exchange
UNCTAD	United Nations Conference on Trade and Development
UK	United Kingdom
UN	United Nations
US	United States
USA	United States of America
USD	US Dollar
WTO	World Trade Organization

Notes on the Contributors

James C. Abegglen is Chairman of the Asia Advisory Service K. K., Tokyo, Japan.

Robert J. Ballon was Professor Emeritus at the Faculty of Comparative Culture, Sophia University, Tokyo, Japan.

Schon L. Beechler is an Associate Professor at the Graduate School of Business, Columbia University, New York, United States.

Caroline Benton is Professor, MBA Programme, validated by the University of Wales, UK.

Ronald Dore is Associate of the Centre for Economic Performance at the London School of Economics, London, United Kingdom.

René Haak is Head of the Business and Economics Section and Deputy Director of the German Institute for Japanese Studies, Tokyo, Japan.

David Methé is Professor at the Institute of Business and Accounting, Kwansei Gakuin University, Japan.

Luke Nottage is Senior Lecturer in Law at the University of Sydney, Australia, and Codirector of the Australian Network for Japanese Law.

Markus Pudelko is Lecturer at the University of Edinburgh Management School, Edinburgh, United Kingdom.

Yoshiya Teramoto is Professor at the Graduate School of Asia Pacific Studies, Waseda University, Tokyo, Japan.

Leon Wolff is Senior Lecturer in Law at the University of New South Wales, Sydney, Australia, and Codirector of the Australian Network for Japanese Law.

Foreword

Japanese management has been a subject of great interest to Western scholars and managers since the 1970s. Ten years ago, Western industry was at pains to master Japanese management concepts, hoping to share in the elements of success promised by the Japanese way of doing business. Topics such as Japanese human resource management, lean production and total quality management often formed part of training programmes for European and American managers. With the weakness of the Japanese economy in recent years, this has changed drastically. Now it increasingly seems that the Japanese management model is outdated. Numerous factors have contributed to this recent development: production has been moved to cheaper neighbouring countries; there have been crises in banking; companies have collapsed; unemployment has risen; domestic consumption has stagnated; socio-demographic problems have emerged and the state is massively in debt. Japanese management needs to change in order to respond to the combination of these factors which have precipitated this serious crisis. Today, scholars differ vastly in their description of the current state of Japanese management and where it is heading. This book presents analyses and evaluations of various aspects of Japanese management. By looking at strategy, organizational structure, globalization, organizational learning, corporate finance, corporate governance, human resource management, production management, innovation and other topics, this book will address a fundamental question about Japanese management: can it continue on its original track with minor adjustments or is major change required to regain competitiveness? It is hoped that the book will be a useful, if not an essential tool for scholars, students and managers with an interest in Japanese management.

The German Institute for Japanese Studies (DIJ) in Tokyo, founded in 1988, is one of Germany's foreign research institutes and is concerned with research on contemporary Japan. The Institute is thus a manifestation of the awareness in Germany of the need to obtain a better understanding of Asia, and of Japan in particular. To this end, the DIJ conducts research in the fields of social science, humanities, the economy of modern Japan and Japanese–German relations (see www.dijtokyo.org). In August 2002 the DIJ, in cooperation with the University of Edinburgh Management School, started to organize this book project entitled *Japanese Management: The Search for a New Balance between Continuity and Change*. We would like to thank those who have contributed to the book and made its publication possible. The majority of chapters are based on empirical research into Japanese management. Special thanks are due to Markus Pudelko, Lecturer at the University of Edinburgh Management School, and René Haak, Deputy Director and Head of the Business and Economics Section of the German Institute for Japanese Studies who conceived the original idea for this book and who efficiently oversaw the editing.

Tokyo, Autumn 2004   IRMELA HIJIYA-KIRSCHNEREIT
                                              Director, German Institute for
                                                   Japanese Studies (DIJ)

Part I
Introduction

1
The Current State of the Japanese Economy and Challenges for Japanese Management: An Overview

Markus Pudelko and René Haak

The success of Japanese companies in the world markets since the 1970s has attracted widespread attention. What became known as 'the Japanese management model' was the first non-Western model to question the supremacy of Western approaches to management, and its principles and practices were imitated in many ways in a number of other Asian countries, such as South Korea, Taiwan and Singapore. But 'learning from Japan' was not a phenomenon limited to Asian nations. Many Western corporations also adopted several aspects of Japanese management, particularly with regard to production processes, and 'Japanese management' developed into a subdiscipline of management studies.

It might be argued that until the early 1990s the Japanese management model was coherent and self-contained, possessing an inherent logic in which its various elements were mutually self-reinforcing, very much in tune with the Japanese societal context and well suited to success in world markets. At the same time this coherent and self-contained model was clearly distinguishable from Western management principles and practices. These factors, together with the circumstances prevailing in the world markets at that time, were major reasons for its success.

This favourable situation, however, has changed rather drastically over the last two decades. Most strikingly, what was once described by many as a highly successful alternative to Western-style management is now often considered to be a model of the past. Numerous factors have contributed to this, including the following:

- The long-lasting stagnation of the Japanese economy.
- Ill-advised macroeconomic policies.
- Delayed microeconomic reforms.
- Delayed corporate restructuring.
- The introduction of new technologies.
- Globalization-induced changes in the international competitive environment.

- The entry of new competitors that are aping Japanese management practices.
- Socio-demographic developments.
- Changes in the value system of Japanese society.

The long-lasting stagnation of the Japanese economy

During the phase of the 'bubble economy' the prices of real estate and corporate shares went into a mutually supporting upward spiral, while at the same time consumer prices remained fairly stable. When satisfaction with nominal wealth creation eventually turned into anxiety about uncontrollable asset inflation, the Bank of Japan raised its discount rate in order to curtail the money supply and stop the rise in asset prices. After hitting a record high of 38 915 at the end of 1989, investors lost confidence and the 225-share Nikkei average at the Tokyo Stock Exchange began to fall. In 2003 the Nikkei Index hit bottom, having lost about 80 per cent of its value. The real estate market took even heavier losses, and by the end of 2004 property prices had fallen by 90 per cent.

Most companies had fuelled their growth strategies with bank loans, for which they provided real estate as collateral, so the radical fall in the value of their shares and collateral brought many companies close to bankruptcy. In order to improve their balance sheets they had to pay back their debts, which meant cutting costs by halting capital investment (this was also aimed at reducing the manufacturing overcapacity inherited from the growth period), making supply chains more efficient, ceasing to hire new employees and replacing some of their better-paid core employees with lower-paid temporary ones. Employees' anxiety about (or *de facto*) job losses and wage cuts, the decline in the value of their assets and uncertainty about the health of financial institutions (due to the non-performing loan problem) resulted in their spending less. With falling domestic demand, consumer prices went down and capital investment was discouraged even more, further complicating the situation for companies. Consequently employment and income declined still further and a vicious cycle of low growth and deflation started. The average annual growth rate of real GDP, which had been 4.4 per cent during the 1970s and 4.1 per cent during the 1980s, fell to a mere 1.4 per cent during the 1990s. Over the same period the unemployment rate rose from 2.1 per cent to 5.4 per cent and the job opening to applicant ratio fell from 1.40 to 0.54. Particularly disconcerting was the youth unemployment rate, which at 9.9 per cent in 2002 was almost double the average. The number of bankruptcies peaked in 2003, with about 20 000 cases (in 1990 there had been fewer than 1000).

However there are currently encouraging signs of recovery that might put Japan, after the so-called 'lost decade' of the 1990s, back on the path of sustainable growth. (Actually the label 'lost decade' might be somewhat of a misnomer as at the micro level many structural changes were made during that time and these may have prepared the ground for revived growth.) Real GDP grew by 2.4 per cent in 2003 and is expected to expand by more than 4 per cent in 2004. The forecast figure for 2005 is, depending on the source, rather lower at around 2 per cent. The stock market is on the rise and there are indications that real estate prices are levelling out. A turnaround in property prices after more than a decade would certainly strengthen consumer confidence, and the resulting growth of consumer spending would help to sustain economic growth, which so far has been based almost exclusively on an impressive rise in exports over the past few years, mainly to China. Indeed there are early though conflicting signs that consumer prices might rise again, which would finally bring consumer price deflation to an end. Rising prices would also encourage companies to borrow money again, as many of them have succeeded in substantially reducing their debts. This would in turn help banks to increase their business after seven years of declining lending.

Japan still has the largest current account surplus in the world and the world's second largest trade surplus (next to Germany), it has been the world's largest creditor for 20 years, it has a high R&D expenditure rate (higher than the United States and Germany) and it has a top-ranking secondary education system (according to the PISA study, measuring the abilities of 15-year-old high school students, of all the OECD countries Japan ranks first in mathematics, second in science and eighth in reading comprehension). These are all necessary conditions for regaining a healthy economy, and indeed Japan is now in a good position to escape from the decade or more of economic stagnation and repeated recessions.

Ill-advised macroeconomic policies

It took the Japanese government a long time to understand and acknowledge the structural crisis of the economy during the post-bubble years. Believing it was dealing with just a cyclical downturn, the government introduced one public spending programme after another, while the Bank of Japan lowered the short-term (nominal) interest rate to zero and increased the money supply in order to encourage companies to invest again. However, because of the overcapacity in capital goods and continuing consumer uncertainty, these policies failed to jump-start the economy.

With growing deflation, real interest rates increased and GDP shrank. Deflation therefore put a severe constraint on monetary policy, as the Bank of Japan could not lower the nominal interest rate below zero. In Spring 2000, when the economy showed slight signs of improvement, the governor of the bank overoptimistically raised the interest rates which, in the midst of deflation, turned out to be a costly mistake. The economy went down again and the Bank of Japan had to return to the zero per cent interest rate policy.

With the immediate banking crisis now under control, the main problem is government debt. Because of falling tax revenue on the one hand and rising expenditure on the other, the annual budget deficit and cumulative government debt have increased sharply. The budget deficit amounts to approximately 9 per cent of GDP and the gross government debt level is a staggering 150–170 per cent, depending on the measurement used. This frequently reported figure is however misleading as it does not take into account the substantial amount of 455 trillion yen of assets owned by the government. When this is taken into consideration the net government debt is 60–80 per cent of GDP. The public work programmes with which the government tried, largely in vain, to stimulate growth have been blamed frequently for this situation. Between 1990 and 2000 the parliament passed no fewer than 21 supplementary budgets to provide for additional public work expenditure. Public work programmes peaked in 1997 but have significantly declined since. While these programmes have probably been over-emphasized as the cause of the government's debt problem, the issues of social security and local transfer expenditure have been underrated. Public awareness of the pension system crisis is, however, increasing. Whereas social security and retirement benefits were left largely to companies in times of high economic growth and a balanced population, with unemployment insurance hardly being an issue, now that there is low economic growth, an aging society and higher unemployment the state has to establish a satisfactory social security system, particularly with regard to pensions. This daunting task is still largely pending.

When in 1997 there was a slight improvement of the economic situation the government increased consumption taxes in order to reduce its deficit. However this measure was ill-timed as it immediately checked consumer spending, which had been just about to recover. With a reviving economy, taxes might rise again in the near future to close the government income gap. But this could result in a further reduction in consumer spending. Nonetheless there is little question that at some point higher tax revenues will be needed to reduce the deficit and cover the cost of social security and pensions. There is considerable scope for raising taxes as the tax level in Japan still is very low – at around 20 per cent it is lower than that in the United States and about half that in Europe. In view of the aggregate demand problem, however, timing will be crucial.

Delayed microeconomic reforms

Government mistakes also occurred at the micro level. In the 1950s and early 1960s the Ministry of Commerce and Industry, later renamed the Ministry of International Trade and Industry (MITI) and now the Ministry of Economy, Trade and Industry (METI), was rather successful in allocating scarce resources to the reconstruction of export-oriented industries (at the expense of domestic consumption). Between the late 1960s and the 1980s, with lack of capital no longer being an issue, it changed its focus to the guidance of mainly manufacturing firms. Relying purely on short-term market forces was not considered sufficient to foster long-term growth. Whether administrative guidance was ever a fruitful strategy was always a matter of much controversy; that is, were Japanese companies successful because of or despite administrative guidance? There are indications that in the early years administrative guidance had rather a positive effect on economic growth. However with the growing complexity of world markets, shorter product cycles, new technologies and the increasing sophistication and fragmentation of consumer demands the limitations of the bureaucracy's ability to pre-empt market outcomes became evident. Despite the numerous examples of ill-advised guidance given to domestic companies, it was not until the second half of the 1990s that METI shifted its attention to deregulation and structural economic reform.

Furthermore the government and its elite bureaucracy were slow to notice the worldwide increase in the relative importance of services *vis-à-vis* manufacturing. For too long their efforts went into improving the competitiveness of selected manufacturing sectors at the neglect of services. Even today, not least because of excessive regulation, protective measures against foreign competitors and an overly domestic focus, Japanese service industries continue to be comparatively uncompetitive. A lasting recovery of the economy will hardly be possible without a substantial strengthening of the service sector. For this to happen, thorough liberalization of the regulatory environment will be required.

The introduction of stricter guidelines for the banking sector, particularly with regard to non-performing loans, took a long time and arguably prolonged the banking crisis. While the situation of the largest banks, which have frequently been urged to merge with each other, has clearly improved, a large number of smaller regional banks are still burdened by non-performing loans and management problems. The government should step into recapitalize some, force others to merge and close down those which are beyond help. Privatization and reform of the Japanese postal service, considered to be the largest savings institution in the world, is still not under way. Separation of its postal, banking and insurance activities would allow for greater transparency and for regulation on the same terms as private competitors.

In the construction, wholesale, retail and utilities sectors, many companies are only surviving because of government protection, tax breaks and subsidies. The same goes for many small and medium-sized companies across a wide range of manufacturing and service sectors. This not only takes an enormous amount resources away from more productive uses, but also distorts competition, holds back productivity improvements and cements the lack of competitiveness of the beneficiaries.

Delayed strategic readjustments and corporate restructuring

Errors have been made not only by the government but also by the top managers of companies. Most companies, efficient or not, can do reasonably well in a growth economy, particularly if successful companies are not trying to drive weaker ones out of business, as was the case in Japan. In high-growth Japan, many companies received that share of the market which was regarded as 'fair' by means of administrative guidance or government procurement, for example in the construction sector. In this situation, less competitive companies did not have to work hard to improve their performance in order to survive, and as a result many industries are burdened by the presence of too many producers. Now that the economy has matured, companies can no longer count on receiving a share of an ever growing market, and because the government's budgets have become smaller they cannot indefinitely count on government support in the form of contracts or subsidies.

With a very strong focus on long-term growth, the short-term profit situation was not sufficiently considered. Even companies that triumphed globally in terms of market share during the years of high growth often had only very low profit margins. As a result they encountered financial problems when the economy went into decline.

Striving for growth also led some companies to overdiversify and enter markets in which they had no specific competitive advantage. During the years of high growth they were able to sell their products and thus continue their growth, but shrinking markets and a tougher competitive environment created problems for them. In order to concentrate on their core competences, some companies are now pulling out of markets where they have encountered losses, selling off or closing down divisions that are not part of their more focused strategy, and starting to acquire companies whose activities fit into their strategic concepts. These moves imply a quite significant paradigm shift as the members of the core workforce, rather than the shareholders, have always been regarded as the prime stakeholders in Japanese companies, so the selling off of company divisions entails the selling off the company's main stakeholders.

Cross-shareholdings and stable shareholdings have long limited the potential for radical restructuring through mergers and acquisitions, and takeovers by foreign companies have been hardly possible (and even at the end of 2004 foreign companies were only able to acquire Japanese firms that had major financial problems). Cross-shareholdings (still about 10 per cent) and stable shareholdings (about one third) are, however, in the process of being reduced. In particular foreign stock holding is almost five times as high as it was 20 years ago, although unfriendly takeovers by foreign or domestic companies are still virtually impossible to stage in Japan.

Supply chain management has become a competitive disadvantage for many Japanese companies. Major manufacturers simply have too many suppliers and are too tightly bound to them. This has increased costs, and not enough pressure has been put on suppliers to become more cost efficient themselves. Vertical *keiretsu* networks have been particularly affected by this problem. Nissan, under Carlos Ghosn, has set a highly publicized example of how to streamline a company's supply chain successfully.

Japanese companies have all too often focused their efforts on the efficient manufacturing of products, which in the companies' attempts to gain market share have been developed to appeal to the highest possible number of customers. This has invariably led to the adoption of 'me-too' strategies and learning from best practice activities, whereby companies try to copy competitors' products and successful production processes. However when products are regarded by customers as rather interchangeable in terms of features, design and quality, the only factor of importance for them becomes the price. This leads to a self-destructive spiral of margin cutting. Consequently companies should differentiate their products more from those of their competitors. A more differentiated product might appeal to a smaller group of potential customers, but its perceived uniqueness will allow for higher profit margins.

The need for differentiated products and bolder strategies in turn requires more unconventional and less *status-quo*-oriented top managers. In order to streamline the decision-making process at the top while at the same time increasing the scope for new ideas and expertise, several companies have reduced the size of their boards of directors by up to 50 per cent and for the first time have invited outside directors to join their boards. Japanese corporations have recently been given a legal choice between the traditional corporate governance structure or a more American-style one, and a growing number have opted for the latter. While top managers, who are ultimately responsible for the survival of the company, often recognize the necessity of reform and change, middle managers tend to hold on to old values and practices and serve as a brake on structural reforms.

The introduction of new technologies

Japanese businesses took a long time to adapt to new information technologies and could not provide the environment required for the knowledge-intensive economy. For example Japan still lags behind in the use of the internet and has not embraced the organizational restructuring made possible by the internet and other IT applications. While the invention of new IT products has often been dominated by small but highly specialized start-up companies, particularly in the United States, Japan still relies on its major conglomerates. The number of companies starting up, especially in high value added industries such as IT, has been very low over the last two decades. With deregulation, lowered minimum capital requirements, changes in the tax system and easier access to venture capital, however, this problem is now being addressed.

Cultural factors also play a significant role here. While starting a new venture is always and everywhere a risky business, the American business environment is legally and socially tolerant of failure and bankruptcy. In Japan, in contrast, a businessman who goes bankrupt might not only lose his house and the savings of his entire family, but also the stigma of bankruptcy will prevent him from being given a second chance.

Globalization-induced changes in the international competitive environment

In the last two decades global trade has grown at twice the rate of global production. Lower-value-added and labour-intensive production activities are steadily shifting to countries that have a cost advantage. Although Western Europe outsources much of its labour-intensive production to Eastern Europe and American companies' preferred production location is Mexico, geographic proximity has become less important. More and more East and South East Asian countries, and particularly China, have emerged as successful production bases. Even though these countries are close to Japan, making them ideal locations for labour-intensive production, for a long time Japanese companies were rather reluctant to embrace the idea of outsourcing. Strained relations with its neighbours, going back to colonial and war periods, were one reason; another was their reluctance to cut jobs in Japan and transfer them abroad. However, this has changed substantially over the last decade, and more and more companies are integrating other Asian countries into their production networks. In this cross-border value-adding process based on the division of labour, Japanese firms are generally shifting the production of semifinished goods to other Asian countries for which the technology and capital comes mainly from Japan. High-value-added activities such as R&D and the production of more sophisticated products are mostly kept in Japan. In 2003 China accounted for about 40 per cent of all Japanese overseas production, other Asian countries for 40 per cent and Western countries for 18 per cent. Almost half of overseas production was for the local markets, but an increasing share was for export to Japan (about a third) and to third countries (about a quarter).

Globalization not only implies the transfer of labour-intensive, low-value-added production processes so as to reduce costs, it also affects the location of more advanced activities in the value chain. In order to ensure that each activity, ranging from R&D to marketing, is conducted in the most suitable place, activities are outsourced to specialized suppliers, joint ventures are formed and companies are acquired across the world. Japanese firms that have relied heavily on their horizontal and vertical relations within their *keiretsu* and that are known for employing a rather insular approach to management, have often found it difficult to engage in flexible cross-cultural cooperation. Globalization poses a particular challenge for Japanese SMEs as they are often not in a position to exploit the benefits of globalization. Problems arise in assuring that the foreign work force has the necessary qualifications, and with how best to divide up the value added chain and establish the various units in different locations.

Entry of new competitors that are aping Japanese management practices

East and South East Asian countries have already been mentioned in the context of production sites for Japanese corporations. But obviously these countries also possess successful indigenous companies that are competing directly with Japanese firms. These countries often employ very similar competitive strategies to those pioneered by Japan. For example South Korea and Taiwan, and to some extent China, concentrate on the production of a limited range of middle-tech products that can be successfully exported to the world markets if their quality is sufficiently high and their price is low. Both these requirements can be achieved through production efficiency, as Japanese companies have demonstrated. Businesses cooperate closely with their government, which gives preferential treatment to a few major companies. Smaller companies, the production of goods for domestic consumption and the service sector are comparatively neglected. Chinese companies especially are emerging as competitors of Japanese firms. Chinese products are competitive not only in traditional light manufacturing industries such as textiles and toys, but increasingly in labour-intensive assembly industries such as electronics, communication equipment and optical goods. These industries are still important for Japan in terms of employment and global market position, and it maintains a formidable manufacturing and supplier base.

Despite Japan's strong position in technology-intensive, high-value-added product segments, the revenue and profits generated from high-volume, cost-sensitive market segments still have a significant influence on the overall economic performance of many Japanese companies in industries such as consumer electronics, office and communication equipment, agricultural machinery and heavy goods vehicles.

As long as Japanese companies continue to rely heavily on the efficient production of high-quality but interchangeable goods that are comparatively easy to copy, companies from other Asian countries will be able to take market share away from them. The relative decline in Japan's competitiveness *vis-à-vis* other Asian countries is due not only to the latter's labour cost advantage but also to improvements in their management ability, product quality and productivity. This may well lead to head-on rivalry with Japanese companies in Asian markets and the Japanese home market alike. As outlined above in the context of domestic competition, the arrival of new Asian competitors means that Japanese companies should pay more attention to differentiating their products, offering unique value to their customers and building up stronger brand images.

Socio-demographic developments

Japan, like most European countries (but unlike the United States), is burdened with an increasingly ageing society. This is the result of a steeply declining fertility rate and an increase in life expectancy (the highest in the world). The government has to adapt to this situation and make provision for the soaring costs of pensions and medical care. For companies too, pension payments constitute a growing financial burden. Demographics also have a direct influence on management, specifically on two of the three main pillars of Japanese human resource management: lifetime employment and the seniority principle (the third being company unions). If, hypothetically, all new members of the core workforce of a large company are to have secure jobs for their entire working lives and are guaranteed to rise up the ranks, then the company must constantly grow in size. This requires a growing economy and an increasing number of new recruits, which can only be provided by population growth. As both conditions are no longer met, lifetime employment and the seniority principle can no longer function as before and consequently they are on the decline. This is particularly true of the seniority system.

Although the decline in the number of people of working age is not currently a problem as there is a comparatively high unemployment rate and therefore it is not difficult to recruit new personnel, it will be a considerable problem once the Japanese economy returns to sustainable growth. With the male workforce in decline, companies could tap one source of employees that has been almost completely neglected, at least for higher positions: the substantial pool of well-qualified women, many of whom would be eager to build up a career. Indeed a growing number of young Japanese women are not keen on adopting the traditional role of wife and mother and have decided not to marry. Giving women the same career opportunities as men would, however, constitute a substantial change to the employment practices of Japanese companies, and with all the other changes that are currently taking place, this is one of the aspects so far least subject to any modification.

Changes in the value system of Japanese society

Japanese are frequently depicted as highly collectivist and relationship-oriented. As employees they are usually described as loyal to the company (to which they have a family-like attachment), strongly motivated, self-sacrificing and patient with regard to the realization of their own aspirations. While characteristics and attitudes that are deeply embedded in cultural and social values are not easy subjects for fundamental transformation, change is occuring also in this area. Greater affluence has resulted in a tendency for the Japanese to become more individualistic, materialistic, short-term oriented, market-driven and less willing to sacrifice leisure time and holidays for the sake of the company. Companies can therefore no longer assume the same loyalty from their employees as they could two decades ago. This is even more the case as companies are not keeping their part of the implicit social contract between employers and employees – for example they are stepping back from the tradition of lifetime employment and the seniority principle. As a consequence companies must find new ways of motivating their workforce.

Despite the above mentioned changes to Japanese social values, it would be wrong to expect a profound Westernization of Japanese society. Japanese society will certainly retain its uniqueness, not by choice but as a historical imperative.

It should be stressed that the factors outlined above are not mutually exclusive – rather in many ways they reciprocally affect and reinforce each other. It is the combination of these factors that brought about a serious crisis for the Japanese management system. The degree to which management practices need to be changed in order to overcome this predicament, and the extent to which Japanese management can continue in its present guise, are currently highly disputed. A further complication is that fundamental changes to some aspects of an otherwise unchanged system would lead to internal inconsistencies, which could put the entire system in jeopardy. Consequently authors differ vastly in their proposals for which directions it should take.

* * *

This volume brings together up-to-date research by a number of renowned American, Asian, Australian and European scholars of Japanese management with the objective of disentangling some of the confusion that characterizes the current debate on continuity and change in Japanese management.

David Methé in his chapter 'Continuity through Change in Japanese Management: Institutional and Strategic Influences' addresses the question of how Japanese corporations adjust to variations in their environment. According to him, the principal task of the Japanese management system is to ensure the corporation's continuing existence and safeguard the jobs of its core workforce. Given the difficult economic environment that currently prevails, Japanese companies are under mounting pressure to change in order to survive. Methé identifies three drivers of change for the Japanese management system: The entrepreneurial activities of start-up firms, foreign companies entering the Japanese market, and changes already introduced by established major companies. As entrepreneurial start-up companies and foreign entrants are still rather weak, Methé considers it unlikely that major changes to the Japanese management system will be provoked by them. This leaves only the major companies as initiators of change. Evidence is given that change in such companies tends to be largely homeostatic, that is, it resynchronizes the corporation with its environment without changing its fundamental character. However the gravity of the economic problems calls for heterodynamic changes that will radically alter basic elements of the organization. Consequently some pillars of the traditional Japanese management system are being significantly transformed or even abandoned. This is particularly true of the seniority system and cross-shareholding. The rationale for these heterodynamic changes, however, remains the survival of the company and the preservation of its identity as an economic community. At the moment companies are experimenting with a combination of various aspects of the traditional Japanese management system and new elements. The economic environment will determine which of these combinations will succeed.

Robert J. Ballon had stressed over many decades the particular qualities and merits of the Japanese managerial system. A leitmotiv of his work is explaining the Japanese business system in the context of Japan's unique cultural and social environment, and it is from this perspective that he approaches his contribution in Chapter 3 on 'Organizational Survival'. Since the Meiji period and their confrontation with the West, economic success and organizational survival has been for the Japanese 'not so much an action to decide than a reaction to [the] urgent necessity' to 'safeguard [their] nationhood'. Private companies have thus been entrusted with the public mission of ensuring the survival of Japan as a nation. Ballon starts his analysis by discussing the specific socio-economic environment of the Japanese firm. He suggests that this can best be described as a complex of close, interdependent interactions between the public and private spheres and among large and small companies. These interactions are based on competitive strategies and cooperative structures. Next the author focuses on the viability of the company itself. He discusses three key issues: how the company fits into its environment, how it manages its human and financial resources, and how it interacts with its stakeholders. Ballon suggests that the Japanese perceive a business organization as a living organism. Accordingly, Japanese employees do not just work for a company, they are the company. In an argumentation which is very similar to Methé's, he concludes that for any living organism, and that includes in this context the Japanese corporation, continued existence is what matters most. Consequently the question of whether to strive for continuity or pursue change is close to irrelevant. As internal change is required for survival in a changing environment, organisms and organizations need to ensure their survival, or their continuity, through change. According to Ballon, for the Japanese 'continuity is through change'.

Schon L. Beechler has published extensively on Japanese multinationals, specifically on their human resource management and globalization practices. In her contribution entitled 'The Long Road to Globalization: In Search of a New Balance between Continuity and Change in Japanese MNCs' she addresses both these issues beginning with the difficulty that Japanese multinationals have with 'both thinking and acting globally'. Beechler suggests that the 'challenges of global management are essentially challenges not of structure or strategy but of management philosophy and approach'. Japanese multinationals might be global in their international investment strategies and structures, but they lack what Beechler calls a 'global mindset'. Headquarter-dominated control systems and decision making dominated by Japanese nationals are particularly problematic. Beechler makes several recommendations, including the greater involvement of non-Japanese managers in decision making at overseas subsidiaries, which would improve collaboration with Japanese expatriates and increase local responsiveness. Another important objective should be to attract and retain highly qualified local managers with global skills and train them in such a way that they are able to perform effectively in global integration roles. In short, 'Japanese MNCs must simultaneously be locally responsive and globally integrated, taking advantage of resources around the globe, both Japanese and non-Japanese.' Beechler concludes that while Japanese corporations have to change and adapt in order to globalize successfully, Japanese cultural and societal values and norms will continue to have a significant influence on corporate culture. Therefore the notion that Japanese corporations might lose their 'Japaneseness' in the process of globalization is deeply flawed.

Ronald Dore has been known over many decades for explaining the characteristics and specifically the merits of the Japanese business model to his readers. In his most recent book *Stock Market Capitalism, Welfare Capitalism: Japan and Germany versus the Anglo-Saxons* he describes convergence tendencies of the Japanese management model towards Anglo-Saxon stock market capitalism, but at the same time questions the value of this development for Japanese society. In Chapter 5 of the present volume, 'Innovation for Whom?', he continues in much the same vein, focusing in particular on intellectual property rights. By referring to a widely publicized court case he highlights how inventors' right to 'proper' recompense is becoming greater than their employing companies' right to exploit their inventions. For Dore this is a clear indication that the entire Japanese business model is shifting towards a higher degree of market individualism. Other manifestations of this shift are the current discussion on ending lifetime employment, the replacement of the seniority system with performance-related remuneration and promotion and the growing importance of shareholder value. Dore ascribes this 'market-individualist syndrome' to cultural influences from the Anglo-Saxon countries, constraints arising from the globalization of financial markets, and most importantly to a growing individualism in Japanese society.

Yoshiya Teramoto and Caroline Benton focus in their chapter, entitled 'Organizational Learning Mechanisms for Corporate Revitalization', on the relationship between institutions and organizational learning processes. Drawing on institutional economics their starting point is an analysis of institutions, defined as a 'self-sustaining system of beliefs', and their effect on economic growth. They conclude that a number of institutionalized practices that have previously promoted growth in Japan are becoming a liability in the context of the global market and are therefore being subjected to fundamental change. Examples are lifetime employment, the seniority principle, the main bank system, the *keiretsu* system, cross-shareholding and government-led intra-industry cooperation. As institutions affect how organizations learn, a change of institutions implies new rules for and methods of learning. According to the authors, the limited range of persons involved in knowledge acquisition and the limited diversity of knowledge interpretation are fundamental weaknesses of traditional organizational learning in Japan. Although they are well suited to incremental innovation, the traditional learning processes do not promote radical, non-linear types of innovation. Based on this analysis the authors develop a new model for organizational learning that addresses complexity, diversity and the dynamics of change. This model is designed to help companies to access more diverse and richer sources of individual and organizational knowledge.

Luke Nottage and Leon Wolff bring, with their chapter 'Corporate Governance and Law Reform in Japan: From the Lost Decade to the End of History?', a legal perspective to this publication. They argue that Japan's sluggish economic performance contrasts starkly with the eruption of activity in law reform. They compare the scale of ongoing legal innovation with that of the Meiji restoration and the allied occupation and speak of a '"third wave" of legal and regulatory reform'. The need to restore economic competitiveness is described as the main driving force of the process. In their analysis the authors focus on the influence of various stakeholders under the new corporate governance framework on management. Next to the shareholders, also creditors, employees, government, consumers, suppliers, and NGOs are considered. They conclude that under the new corporate governance regime, shareholders have gained the most influence, followed by consumers and to some extent NGOs. On the other hand there are clear losers in the struggle for corporate control. First and foremost are those who were once considered to be the real 'owners' of Japanese companies – the employees. With the banking crisis, the deterioration of the main bank system and the decline of loans as the main instrument of corporate finance, creditors might even be evicted from the inner circle of stakeholders in Japanese corporations. The government will also be less able to guide and influence corporate decision making, and its role will shift to *ex post* control. One leitmotiv that runs through the entire chapter is the degree to which the current legal reforms constitute 'Americanization', particularly with regard to convergence towards a shareholder-oriented model of corporate governance. Overall Nottage and Wolff accept there is movement towards an American-type corporate governance model, but they make several important qualifications.

James C. Abegglen, whose book *The Japanese Factory* (1958) was arguably the first thorough analysis of the Japanese business model to appear in the West, is known to Japanese management scholars for his rather sympathetic view of Japanese business principles and practices. In Chapter 8 of this volume, 'A Perfect Financial Storm', Abegglen describes the turmoil the Japanese financial system has endured over the last one and a half decades. According to Abegglen, 'companies have weathered the storm', though 'at considerable cost, made necessary by a brutally difficult economic environment and changed regulations'. He explains the means by which Japan progressed from a capital-short, developing, postwar economy to a 'bubble economy' with extraordinary rises in real estate and share prices in the 1980s, and describes how Japan was drawn after the bursting of the 'bubble' in the 1990s into a vicious cycle of low growth and deflation. He then discusses how Japan has largely overcome its financial crises, which regulatory reform steps have been taken to increase transparency, and how recent developments have changed the nature of corporate finance in general and the role of the main bank in particular. The most lasting change the financial debacle has triggered is the shift away from bank lending and towards direct debt and equity, but the institution of the main bank will continue to exist in a modified form. While Abegglen acknowledges fundamental changes in the Japanese financial system, as in many other areas, the Japanese will continue, in his view, to hold firmly on to those aspects that are strongly based on cultural values and social norms.

Markus Pudelko examines in his contribution 'Japanese Human Resource Management: From Being a Miracle to Needing One?', the management of the human factor. Much of the reported findings from his empirical work suggest that rather comprehensive changes are taking place in Japanese HRM, and that there is a clear move towards Western, or more specifically American practices. However comparative data gathered by Pudelko in Japan, the United States and Germany put this claim into perspective. For example it might be true that the traditional Japanese focus on seniority in respect to promotion and remuneration is to some extent being replaced by Western-style performance-related criteria (the change argument); but the comparative data indicate that Japanese companies are *still* significantly more seniority oriented than their American and German counterparts and are likely to continue to be so in the future. This argument justifies the sustained validity of the continuity argument. Whereas all articles take on a time perspective which might lead to zooming in on change (change over time), this article in particular highlights the importance of what might be called the location perspective, which tends to underline the continuity argument (despite changes over time, overall patterns between countries continue to persist).

René Haak's chapter on 'Japanese Production Management: Organizational Learning at the Confluence of Knowledge Transfer, Technology Development and Work Organization' shows that Japanese production management is associated with specific forms of work organization, logistics, manufacturing processes, personnel deployment and education. Its main characteristics have been strongly influenced by the Toyota production system and are expressed in the philosophy of continuous improvement, that is, incremental changes based on evaluation of the current production process. It is the task of Japanese managers to determine which parts of the production process should be maintained as is and which should be altered. Haak argues that the highly regarded *kaizen* concept – the Japanese leadership philosophy that has remained valid even during the years of low economic growth, has proven to be an effective means of individual, organizational and interorganizational learning, particularly in the area of production. While several chapters of this book stress the changes that have taken place in Japanese management, Haak finds a considerable degree of continuity. This should come as little surprise as production management has arguably been the area of management in which Western companies could learn most from Japan.

Finally, in the concluding chapter Markus Pudelko attempts in 'Continuity versus Change. The Key Dilemma for Japanese Management' to summarize the arguments put forward for a fundamental change to the Japanese management model in order to regain competitiveness, and those which speak against change. One key claim is that it is not so much that Japanese management practices have changed for the worse and caused a decline in the competitiveness of Japanese companies, rather that the global business environment has altered in a way that happens to favour the strengths of the American management model and goes against the strengths of the Japanese one. According to Pudelko's interpretation, the inherent strengths and weaknesses of various management models remain quite constant over time; what does vary is the relative relevance of those strengths and weaknesses. The challenge for the Japanese management model is therefore to balance continuity and change in such a way that the evolving demands of the global business environment can be met.

Part II
Contributions

2
Continuity through Change in Japanese Management: Institutional and Strategic Influences

David Methé

Introduction

This chapter examines the Japanese management system and the changes it is undergoing. In the 1980s this system was touted as a viable alternative to, if not better than, the US model of management. Recently this thinking has been called into serious question. Japan has been called 'the system that soured' (Katz, 1998) and its ability to change has been described as arthritic (Lincoln, 2001), leading some to wonder whether it really can change (Carlile and Tilton, 1998).

Because of space limitations this chapter can only touch lightly on the many aspects of the Japanese management system and the way it is changing. It is hoped that this does not result in too superficial a treatment of a profound subject. The discourse is derived from the author's observations as an outsider living and working in Japan, from primary interviews and from secondary sources. It is hoped that the study will stimulate discussions on the topic of change in Japanese business enterprises and lead to more systematic studies. Such studies would be particularly relevant in that for 15 years or more Japanese firms have not only been confronted with an extended period of slow growth, punctuated by recessions, but have also had to contend with deflation. This is also occurring as the Japanese population is ageing, fewer people are marrying and having children and new centres of technological and market opportunity and competition are opening up around the world.

A central issue of the chapter is how organizations adjust to variations in their environment. We shall look at business organizations and how they contend with perturbations in their economic environment. The change phenomenon is filled with apparent paradoxes. Change means that something new is created, yet change is a common process of life. The creation of something new implies movement from one stable state to another stable state, yet at various levels of an entity and over various timeframes everything is in flux. Engaging in change may end in failure, but not changing risks getting out of step with your environment, which can also result in failure. Change implemented to solve problems creates a starting point for new problems that may be more difficult to solve than the first set. Random change can result in complex structures that function purposefully. Purposeful change requires choices about what to throw away, what to keep, which innovations to incorporate and how to reconcile our identity with what we keep, throw away and incorporate. Through change, organizations alter and are able to survive. We continue through change.

Although many have viewed the 1990s as a lost decade for Japanese business and management, at that time and subsequently Japanese organizations have been engaged in these paradoxes of change. It has been a period of experimentation when the choices of what to keep, what to throw away and which innovations to incorporate have been made more explicit and visible. Japanese management has been evolving and changing throughout its postwar history. The combination of slowing economic growth and deflation has served to increase the variety and intensity of experimentation in management systems in order to survive. This is not to say that it is in chaos and that no patterns exist. Patterns do exist and we shall discuss some of them, but the patterns that can be observed at one time or in one organization are only approximations of the range of changes that are occurring across organizations and over time. In order to facilitate understanding of the changes occurring in Japanese organizations we shall adopt simplifying assumptions or stereotypes as shorthand ways of discussing these organizational changes, but it should be remembered that the manifestations of the changes vary among the organizations.

What is Japanese-style management?

What is meant by the traditional Japanese management model? There have always been variations in this model, and the definition of Japanese-style management as a social science concept and as a coherent practice depends on when and where the researcher encounters it (Yonekawa, 1985; Hayashi, 2002). Many of the early writings on Japanese-style management emphasized its sociological and organizational–behavioural aspects (Abegglen, 1958; Cole, 1972; Hatvany and Pucik, 1981; England, 1983; Manchus, 1983), while later writings tended to focus on the external structure and internal workings of the Japanese firm (Dunphy, 1987; Ito, 1995; Lin and Hui, 1999), plus the economic rationale underpinning its workings (Aoki, 1988; Aoki and Dore, 1994). More recently others have begun to provide institutional explanations (Aoki, 2001; Hall and Soskice, 2001). Thus management takes a variety of forms in Japanese organizations. That variety derives as much from our current observational filters as from the types of firm we observe and when and where we observe them. To illustrate this we shall look at Japan's dual economic structure.

The dual structure of the Japanese economy

Observations of Japan in the mid 1970s often emphasized that one part of the Japanese economy was made up of large firms that were engaged in international trade and economic activities, while the other consisted of firms that were small or medium sized and were engaged in domestic economic activities. By the mid 1980s talk of the dual economy had all but vanished and had been replaced by discussions of Japanese management, as practised by large firms. By the mid 1990s the dual structure discussion had re-emerged, this time focusing on Japanese firms that were globally competitive and those that were not. The latter were mostly small or medium sized, and a key distinction was the economic sector they were in. The construction and distribution sectors were seen as uncompetitive and a major hindrance to the recovery of the Japanese economy as a whole and the financial sector in particular.

It is important to recognize that the Japanese economy has always consisted of small and medium-sized firms coexisting in a dual structure with large firms. Ballon and Honda (2000) estimate that in 1997 there were about 2.5 million incorporated firms in Japan, of which about 35 000 were large in terms of capitalization. The large firms accounted for about 1.4 per cent of the total. In 1985 about 1.6 million incorporated firms had existed (about 1.2 per cent of the total), about 19 000 of which were large. Thus between 1985 and 1997 large firms increased in terms of number and as a proportion of incorporated firms, but not substantially. The more important issue to recognize is the shift in our perspective of the meaning of the dual structure phenomenon and the role of small and large firms.

Small and medium-sized firms not only account for the largest proportion of total firms, but also employ most of the workforce in Japan (Ballon and Honda, 2000; Sugimoto, 2003). Sugimoto (2003) estimates that in 2000 about 78 per cent of the total workforce was employed by firms with fewer than 300 employees. Most of them operate in the retail, distribution and construction industries, but they also play important roles in industrial sectors such as car manufacture and electronics, either as supplier firms in *keiretsu* or as subcontracting firms or *shitauke*. Some of those which started out as small or medium-sized supplier firms have become large in their own right. For example Denso, which belongs to the Toyota *keiretsu* (*Nikkei Weekly*, 3 May 2004), has grown in terms of both its size and the scope of its customer base.

Some of these firms are very successful and are independent of any subcontracting or *keiretsu* supplier relationships (*Nihon Keizai Shimbun*, 17 February 2004). Firms such as Mabuchi Motors, Nidec and Shimadzu are examples of such successful players (Marsh, 2003). In the semiconductor industry Rohm, Omron and Sharp remained profitable throughout the 1990s and we still so today, while the giants of the industry – NEC, Toshiba, Hitachi, Mitsubishi Electric and Fujitsu – have all incurred losses (Methé, 2005). However there has been little systematic study by Western scholars of small and medium-sized firms as most have concentrated on the largest firms in the most globally competitive sectors, such as the automotive and electronics industries.

One outcome of the focus on large firms is that what we have come to know as the Japanese management system relates primarily to these firms. Less is known about the management systems of smaller firms, including their employment practices, product-market composition and governance structure. Some studies suggest that small and medium-sized firms model their human resource practices on those of the large firms (Hashimoto, 1993). In spite of the lack of systematic academic study, it safe to say that a more active labour market exists among these firms and that lifetime employment is more an ideal to strive for than the reality it is in the large firms. Furthermore their governance structure is different because often they are headed by the owner-operator or members of the owner-operator's family (Hamabata, 1990). Bankruptcy, running at about 16 000 or more enterprises per year, predominantly relates to small and medium-sized enterprises.

Thus when investigating how the Japanese economy has shifted over time and considering overall economic trends, such as unemployment rates or changes in management practices, it should be remembered that small and medium-sized firms play a crucial role by sheer weight of numbers (*Nikkei Weekly*, 14 April 2003). The large firms garner the attention and in some respects set the trends for the smaller firms to follow, but much of the experimentation in and variety of management practices is generated by these smaller firms. In order to facilitate our discussion we shall draw upon stereotypical images of the Japanese management system as these have evolved in the larger firms, but as the above discussion indicates it is important to bear in mind that the actual application of these stereotypes varies from organization to organization.

Defining traditional Japanese management

From studies conducted over the years we can identify stereotypical elements of the traditional Japanese management model. These elements are often described as the 'pillars' of the management system. There are six basic pillars and these can be divided into three internal and three external pillars (Noguchi, 1998). The external pillars are the main bank system, cross-shareholding and stable shareholding. The internal ones are lifetime employment, seniority-based promotion and remuneration, and company unions. From the first mention of these pillars, especially lifetime employment, there has been debate on their definition and the extent to which they are practised (Abegglen, 1958; Marsh and Mannari, 1971; Cole, 1972, 1973).

As early as the 1970s researchers were calling into question the permanence of lifetime employment and debating whether it was based on Japanese culture or supported by an economic rationale (Cole, 1972). Marsh and Mannari (1971) reported labour turnover rates of 26–30 per cent in 1963–68, not much different from the 27–32 per cent reported by the Japan Labour Institute for the period 1991–2001 (JIL, 2001, 2002). Employees were observed to be expressing a desire to leave and were putting this desire into practice (Marsh and Mannari, 1971), usually by moving from one large company to another (Cole, 1972). The changes in the economic and social systems in the early 1970s were seen as putting so much pressure on the permanent employment system that its long-term viability was being called into question (ibid.)

Some thirty years later scholars and business people alike are still debating whether lifetime employment will last or is breathing its last (Hirakubo, 1999). It can be argued that part of the explanation for the practice's longevity lies in the vagueness with which it is applied. But it can also be explained by the economic, organizational and social benefits that it generates, which appear to exceed the costs associated with it. During periods of rapid and sustained economic growth the benefits did indeed outweigh the costs, but now confronted with the twin problems of slow growth and deflation it is not clear that this is still the case.

The definition of lifetime employment is elastic because there is no official or government classification of it and no enterprise offers a contract that stipulates permanent employment. Employees who are considered 'permanent' have been given tacit assurance that they will not lose their jobs during cyclical downturns in the economy, that the company will attempt to keep them on the payroll until the economy recovers. A distinction is made between regular employees and temporary employees (Hashimoto, 1993). Regular employees currently account for about 70 per cent of the total workforce, but not all members of the regular workforce are considered permanent employees. Most of the people who work for small and medium-sized firms and many regular employees of large firms are not placed in the permanent category. The elasticity of the definition accounts for the fluctuating number of employees included in the category, with estimates ranging from 20 per cent to 30 per cent (Cole, 1972; Hashimoto and Raisian, 1985; Hashimoto, 1993). Thus the meaning of *shusin koyo* or permanent employment is open-ended in practice.

In terms of economic benefits, the lifetime employment system creates a sense of commitment to the firm, and because of this a willingness to accept changes that are necessary to keep up with advances in technology and adjust to the market. The system allows for training and the development of company-specific skills and knowledge, but it locks in employees since their skills are tied to one company. The costs flow from the fact that the lifetime employment system cannot easily adjust to extended economic downturns. Labour costs are not as flexible under this system as they are in the more open labour market in the United States. Hence if an economic downturn is short a company can use other mechanisms to adjust costs, but if the downturn is long the pressure will build to reduce labour costs in some way that could include changes in the management system.

With the seniority-based remuneration system, or *nenko joretsu*, salaries and wages are based on the number of years of experience or the age of the employee rather than on specific skills, abilities or specialization (Tachibanaki, 1982; Inohara, 1990). The monthly salary is usually determined by years with the company or age, plus factors such as marital status and number of dependants. A bonus payment is usually given twice a year. The bonus is also based on several factors, including the financial health of the organiza- tion, the position of the individual employee and merit. Promotion is based on education as well as age (Tachibanaki, 1982; Sakamoto and Powers, 1995). Promotion is a key means of directing change in an organization because it affects the existing leadership patterns, which in turn affect the stability of the organization. Favouring years of experience with the organization over other criteria would tend to bias organizations towards maintaining a steady course even in the face of substantial environmental changes (Sakano and Lewin, 1999).

Company unions have received less attention in the literature but they play an important role in shaping the company as an economic community (Chao, 1968; Oh, 1976). Each union is tied directly to its enterprise and represents the workers of that enterprise (Noguchi, 1998). As the primary representative of the employees, the union represents not only blue-collar but also white-collar workers. Employees join the union upon entering the company and remain members until they leave the company or are promoted into a management position, usually at the *kacho* or *bucho* level when they reach their late thirties or early forties. Thus even the highest managers have belonged to the union at some time (Ballon and Honda, 2000). For both management and workers, union membership can forge a sense of common experience, and at its strongest a sense of solidarity in terms of being a part of an economic community. Unions also play a crucial part in gatekeeping and pacing change in the wage system and in the diffusion of technological and managerial innovations in general (Manchus, 1983; Mansfield, 1989).

The main bank system was once seen as central to the governance of Japanese firms because the main banks were the major source of their investment funds (Aoki and Patrick, 1994). Governance by these banks was credited with the turnaround of Mazda and Asahi Beer in the late 1970s and early 1980s. However their influence has declined because of the changes in the institutional environment surrounding the financial market regulations (Ito, 1996). Financial market liberalization began in the 1970s when the Japanese government opened up its financial markets to the world, and it picked up momentum in the mid 1980s with the liberalization of interest rates on deposits (Sato, 1999). In addition, when some Japanese firms became successful they were able to finance their investments through sources other than their main banks. Conversely, towards the end of the 1990s unsuccessful firms made increasing use of main banks as lenders of last resort. This not only kept a number of uncompetitive firms in business, but also caused a worsening of the debt crisis in Japan during the 1990s (Miyajima, 1998).

Cross-shareholding and stable shareholding are external pillars that limit the control exerted by the financial markets. These equity-based pillars are utilized to maintain control of the company through friendly firms, many of which are part of the company's *keiretsu* (Okumura, 2000). The combined effect of these two pillars and the main bank pillar is to leave the management of the company free from financial market discipline to pursue its management policies. This freedom can be seen in the make-up of the board of directors, which is chosen from the ranks of company managers (*Asahi Shinbun*, 22 May 2002). Only when the company runs into trouble does the main bank step in; equity holders rarely move to take over the management of a company, and few shareholders play a part in shaping the governance of the company (*Asahi Shinbun*, 24 May 2002).

These pillars support numerous practices that relate to governance, decision making, superior–subordinate relationships, labour–management relations, supplier relationships, innovation, technology management and other managerial activities. These activities or organizational routines are the surface manifestations of the embedded processes and underlying values that comprise the core of the Japanese management system.

The core of the Japanese management system

At the core of any system, be it a society or a business organization, is a set of values or assumptions that define the identity of the organization and how its members represent themselves to others. The identity of a system is part of the institutional environment and provides the conditions that form what some scholars have referred to as its deep structure (Gersick, 1991); that is, the accumulated decisions about its fundamental parts and how these relate to each other and the environment. As we have seen with the discussion of the pillars of the Japanese management system, these parts can be both tangible and intangible and give the organization form (Baron, 2004). The core of a system can thus be defined in terms of its institutional identity and the basic arrangement of parts for carrying out a set of activities.

It regulates organizational routines such as consensus decision making, total quality management and employee rotation, and it shapes the identity of the organization and its members (Baron, 2004) as well as intangibles such as the organization's reputation or legitimacy (Elsbach and Sutton, 1992; Aldrich and Fiol, 1994; Suchman, 1995; Baum and Oliver, 1996). As in the case of the Japanese management system, the legitimacy bestowed on the organization by society results in part from the perceived coherence between the organization's identity and the pillars that give it form. Consequently organizational routines are presented to the members of the organization as conventions or natural ways of carrying out an activity, and they act without questioning the underlying values or assumptions (Gomez and Jones, 2000).

The goals of the system we also related to its identity and conventions and are influenced by the values present in the system. One overriding goal is the survival or preservation of the system. Another, as we shall see, is maintaining the institutional identity of the company as an economic community rather than an economic vehicle for the preservation of the shareholders' wealth.

Strategic orientation

The system we shall look at in this chapter is the business organization, and the terms enterprise, firm, company and business organization will be used interchangeably to denote an entity that provides a service or produces a product. Most Western readers, especially those who have obtained an MBA from a US business school, will argue that the business organization exists to maximize the long-term wealth of the shareholders. The standard view put forward by the American business school model is that the shareholders are the *raison d'être* of the firm and that generating a maximum return on the shareholders' investment is the most important measure of managerial effectiveness. Thus the identity of the firm lies primarily with the shareholders and other stakeholders play secondary roles, if any.

In Japan the business organization exists for a larger number of stakeholders, but paramount importance is placed on the employees. The organization exists because of the employees and for the employees. This is not to imply that the employees reap the lion's share of the benefits of the organization's activities as the other stakeholders (shareholders, suppliers and so on) are compensated, but it is recognized that without the employees there is no organization (Aoki, 1988; Ballon and Honda, 2000).

Institutional identity is reflected in the strategic orientation of firms as they compete in industries. Strategic orientation is essential in reconciling the often conflicting pressures for maintaining the institutional identity of organizations and meeting the demand for survival placed on organizations by a turbulent environment. Alterations to strategy are an important factor in how a firm adjusts its institutional identity to the vicissitudes of environmental change. For this reason we need to discuss the strategic orientation of Japanese managers who balance these elements.

Part of the Japanese manager's strategic orientation in the context of the company as an economic community has been towards self-sufficiency in technologies and products, resulting in expansion and integration along the value chain. This is most evident in the vertical *keiretsu* (Miyashita and Russell, 1994). Vertical *keiretsu* and their horizontal counterparts resemble clubs in that inclusion is not based on some hereditary or kinship tie but on selection criteria founded on economic rationality. The structure within these clubs is a complex network of hierarchical arrangements that include cross-shareholding, personnel transfer and main bank affiliation (Lincoln *et al.*, 1992). Peripheral firms that can contribute to the economic well-being of the central firm or firms join the club as affiliated firms (Okumura, 2000). Once firms have joined the club it is often difficult to eject them. However affiliates that do not contribute to the well-being of the central firm will be absorbed or in some way altered, and new ones will be allowed to enter (Ballon and Honda, 2000). This process tends to be slow, and as part of the economic rationality is connected to the reputation of the firm as a faithful supplier, contracts tend to be relational and not spot-market based. As the relational aspect expands and deepens the affiliated firms also become a mechanism for preserving employment, in that surplus employees from the central firm are be sent to affiliated firms. This practice has also been used to preserve the lifetime employment pillar of the management system when adjusting to short-term economic downturns.

Another strategic consideration for Japanese managers is profits. This is not about rates of return for the absentee shareholder, but rather a gauge of how well the organization is faring in supporting its community of stakeholders. Profits are built on meeting the demands of customers, but it is recognized by Japanese managers that in the long run profits flow from market share so they often sacrifice current profits in order to build and maintain market share. The larger the market share the more work there is for the employees, thus in the case of maintaining the company as an economic community it is better to be a larger company in terms of market share than a more profitable but smaller company. This can be seen in many markets, including beer (the battle between Asahi and Kirin), retailing (the battle between Aeon and Ito Yokado), semiconductors (NEC and Toshiba) and personal computers (NEC and Fujitsu). These are often discussed in terms of which firm has the largest market share and therefore the dominant position in the industry, rather than which firm is the more profitable and hence earning the highest rates of return for the shareholders.

The company as an economic community is not the same as the company as a family. Recruits are screened and selected to carry out the tasks needed to provide goods and services to customers and make a profit. The company as an economic community does not necessarily mean it is benevolent to its stakeholders and inherently honest, nor that the managers are kind and trusting souls and their employees are happy and satisfied with their position in the company. Some employees leave voluntarily – about 30 per cent of newly hired employees leave within the first three years of their employment (*Nikkei Weekly*, 17 May 2004) – and some are dismissed. However maintaining the institutional identity of the company as an economic community means there are reciprocal obligations between the company and its employees and these have to be observed in both good times and bad (Methé, 1982). For example when Yamaichi Securities went bankrupt in the late 1990s its president made an emotional televised appeal – but not for himself or the shareholders. Rather he took responsibility for the bankruptcy and pleaded for other companies to hire his employees because they were not to blame for the failure of the firm. Few if any Western executives would do the same on national television.

Vectors of change in the Japanese economic system: entrepreneurial entry, foreign entry and change by incumbent firms

In the remainder of this chapter we shall examine how Japanese firms have responded to changes in their environment and the implications of their responses for the continuity of the Japanese management system. In particular we shall examine whether they have changed their organizational forms in terms of the deep structure that gives meaning to their identity (Carroll, 1994; Freeman, 1995). We shall draw most of our examples from technology-intensive industries such as electronics, plus a few observations from firms in other industries.

It can be expected that entrepreneurial start-ups, foreign firms entering Japan and changes undertaken by incumbent Japanese firms will have an impact on the economic structure of Japan and therefore on the Japanese management system. Different organizational forms are sources of different types of change (Methé *et al.*, 1996), and incumbent firms experiment with different strategies when confronted with similar environmental conditions (Methé *et al.*, 1997). Thus variety is brought to the overall economic system by entrepreneurial start-ups, foreign entrants and the changes made by incumbent firms.

Given the difficult economic environment that has existed in Japan over the past decade, Japanese firms are under growing pressure to change in order to survive. Change is occurring, but in a way that tends to preserve the broader institutional aspects of Japanese-style management, and in particular the identity of the company as an economic community. In this chapter we are particularly interested in how changes at the firm level support continuity at the institutional identity level. In the following subsections we shall examine the three vectors of change – entrepreneurial entry, foreign entry and change by incumbent firms – in turn, but first we shall investigate how change is characterized in organizational studies as it is important to understand how the mechanisms of change and the types of change are related.

There are many studies of change in and its implications for organizations (for example Argyris, 1976, 1992; March, 1981; Ford and Ford, 1994; Van de Ven and Poole, 1995; Barnett and Carroll, 1995; Methé *et al.*, 2000). At the risk of oversimplifying a rich stock of research literature, for ease of presentation only some of the main points will be summarized here.

Systems attempt to maintain themselves in the face of environmental perturbations by matching the level of variety in the environment with the level of variety in the organization (Ashby, 1952). Organizations change in order to survive. Part of that survival depends on protecting their core from being overwhelmed by the external environment. The core of the organiza- tion is bound up with the identity of the organization and its members. However if that identity itself is seen to be threatening the chance of survival, then the organization is faced with the dilemma of whether to preserve itself or its identity. How an organization reconciles this dilemma and emerges with a new identity is a key aspect of understanding the process of organizational change.

Following Argyris (1976, 1992) we distinguish between two types of change. The first is what we term homeostatic change, which is aimed at resynchronizing the organization with its environment while preserving its fundamental character. The second type of change we term heterodynamic change, which radically alters the fundamentals of the organization, thus changing its current identity to a new one. In essence the basic form of the organization is transformed in such a way that forces the organization to recreate itself.

It is difficult to say *a priori* whether there is a one-to-one relationship between a vector of change and the type of change that will result. However research indicates that heterodynamic change is more likely with new entrants (Hannan and Freeman, 1984; Tushman and Romanelli, 1985; Singh *et al.*, 1986; Haveman, 1992; Romanelli and Tushman, 1994) and homeostatic change more likely with incumbents (Delacroix and Swaminathan, 1991; Kelly and Amburgy, 1991; Fox-Wolfgramm *et al.*, 1998).

We shall examine these vectors in terms of their potential for generating either homeostatic or heterodynamic change. Following the discussions of the vectors and their effects on the Japanese management system we shall explore the implications of those effects at the strategic and institutional levels. Homeostatic and heterodynamic changes have consequences that feed back into the organization itself and affect its chances of survival, and they also feed back into the environment in a manner that may affect the ability of the organization to survive in the future.

Entrepreneurial entry

One source of potential change in an economic system consists of the entrepreneurial activities of start-up firms. Japan cannot be claimed to be a hotbed of entrepreneurial activity, but it has gone through periods of interest in venture businesses. At the end of World War II, some firms that are currently household names in Japan, such as Kyocera, Sony, Honda and Ito Yokado, have their entrepreneurial roots in that period. Entrepreneurial activity declined thereafter, and although there were occasional bursts of entrepreneurial activity, the rate at which new companies were founded year on year remained at around 6 per cent during the 1970s and falling to about 4 per cent by 1990 (Small and Medium Enterprise Agency, 1998). Even more significant was that the high technology start-ups most associated with the Silicon Valley phenomenon in the United States did not catch on in Japan (Feigenbaum and Brunner, 2002). These high-risk, high-return ventures were likely to create new industrial subfields if not whole new industries and to introduce or take advantage of new management systems. However in Japan the motives for starting a business were different and the environment was not conducive to the rapid growth of start-ups (Methé and Bracker, 1994; Bracker and Methé, 1994; JSBRI, 2002).

In the United States the production of integrated circuits, personal computers, software and so on was pioneered, developed and dominated by start-ups, while in Japan it was dominated by established incumbents and large firms that diversified into it from related business activities. Japanese entrepreneurial activity remained relatively weak despite government measures to foster the development and growth of start-ups in high technology fields. The rate at which new companies were founded continued to decline throughout the 1990s, falling to 3.1 per cent in 1999–2000. Even more distressing to the small and medium-sized segment of the Japanese economy, the number of closures increased and remained high from the early to the mid 1980s. In 1999–2000 the closure rate stood at 4.5 per cent (METI, 2003). Thus more companies were closing down than were being founded. This trend has continued until today.

The establishment of new financial markets such as Mothers and Hercules (formerly Nasdaq Japan) and Jasdaq has relaxed the listing requirements but done little to push start-up activities to the economic forefront. It is still difficult to found a company in Japan, with upwards of six legally required steps compared with one in the United States and costing eight times more than in the United States (JSBRI, 2002). The average time between foundation and listing on one of the exchanges has fallen from 26 years in 1997 to 18 years today, but this is still substantially longer than it is in the United States. Moreover the interorganizational networks and institutional support required for listing (Stuart *et al.*, 1999) are not as strong as in the United States.

There are also large institutional hurdles for would-be Japanese entrepreneurs to overcome and the number of financing options is limited. Many start-ups are financed with the entrepreneurs' own savings or those of relatives or friends. Borrowing from banks is also quite common, but the strings attached to this with respect to collateral, can have a drastic impact on the individual entrepreneur should the venture fail. (We shall consider this in greater detail below.) Although investorment angels do exist in Japan, their number is small compared with the United States and they usually do not invest such large amounts as their American counterparts (METI, 2003).

In addition start-ups confront an environment that is unsupportive in terms of the basic resources needed for a company to survive and grow. They have trouble attracting employees and customers, as well as obtaining financial resources (Methé and Bracker, 1994; Small and Medium Enterprise Agency, 1999; JSBRI, 2002). With any start-up activity there is a risk that the venture will fail, and working for or with such a company carries the prospect of having to start one's career anew or find a new supplier. The employment risk is compounded by the low social status accorded to entrepreneurs and small and medium-sized business owners in Japanese society. For example in one survey a question on the social value of entrepreneurs only produced a positive response by 8 per cent of the Japanese respondents compared with 91 per cent in the United States, 88 per cent in Canada and 38 per cent in the United Kingdom (METI, 2003). The very low social standing of entrepreneurs can be partly explained by the way that social status is determined in Japan. Social status depends heavily on the attributes of the company a person works for, and in particular its size and age (Sugimoto, 2003), while technological virtuosity and potential for profit are not considered as important. By definition start-ups are small and very young and therefore convey little status.

The social and economic problems that arise from business failure and the difficulty of re-entering the workforce after such a failure are consistently identified as significant reasons for not attempting to start up a new business in Japan (Small and Medium Enterprise Agency, 1999; JSBRI, 2002; METI, 2003). Comments by Tadashi Yanai of the firm Fast Retailing are telling. When asked about the state of entrepreneurship in Japan by the *Nikkei Weekly*, Yanai stated that 'In Japan, you are attacked if you fail even once, as I did, and as Masayoshi Son, president of Softbank Corp. has done. The way Japanese society impedes young entrepreneurs from becoming successful is really absurd' (Nagaoka, 2004). The impact of this attitude towards business failure is illustrated by the fact that only one in ten entrepreneurs who have failed have been able to restart their businesses, compared with 50 per cent in the United States (*Nihon Keizai Shimbun*, 7 April 2003).

The difficulties encountered when starting and even more so when restarting a venture business also include the securing of finance. As noted above, funding for entrepreneurs often comes from banks, and banks tend to impose very strict loan conditions on entrepreneurs (*Nikkei Weekly*, 5 May 2003). As a result, about 75 per cent of those who fail have to sell their houses and about 43.4 per cent declare personal bankruptcy. The implications of failure extend beyond the entrepreneur and may also include family members and friends, since they are often needed to secure funds through the loan guarantee system at Japanese banks (*Nihon Keizai Shimbun*, 16 May 2003). Furthermore banks regard business failure very severely in Japan, with 41.9 per cent indicating that borrowers' past records of business failure is the most critical factor in whether to lend to entrepreneurs (*Nikkei Weekly*, 22 September 2003).

Likewise buying supplies from a start-up company carries risks should the company go out of business. Many established companies in Japan place stringent requirements on would-be suppliers that go beyond the usual product-related characteristics such as price, quality and delivery time. For example a supplying company has to have a reputation for consistent performance before it is viewed as a legitimate supplier, and this reputation can only be built over time. This has led some Japanese start-ups to enter global markets first in order to establish a reputation among the foreign competitors of the domestic companies they would like to supply. Thus reputation and cognitive and social legitimacy are essential to start-up success, especially in new industrial environments (Aldrich and Fiol, 1994). This may be one reason why it is people in their fifties and sixties rather than in their forties or younger who are behind start-ups in Japan, that is, they have had time to build up a reputation and establish a network of contacts.

Even in relatively supportive environments such as that in the United States, entrepreneurial start-ups are confronted with many difficulties. These difficulties are collectively termed the liability of newness (Singh *et al.*, 1986). In order to reduce the liability of newness a start-up may approach its entrepreneurial activities in ways that conform to the prevailing management and business systems. Hence it is not surprising that Japanese entrepreneurial companies that have survived long enough to become large, such as Softbank and Rakuten, have implemented organizational practices that closely resemble the traditional practices of their established counterparts. For example the founder of Rakuten, Hiroshi Mikitani, has drawn on the *zaibatsu* system of organization as a model for expanding his online trading empire (Utsunomiya, 2003).

This is not to say that entrepreneurial start-ups are not having an effect on the Japanese management system and the Japanese economic structure as a whole. However at the moment it is unlikely that entrepreneurial start-ups will serve as vectors of revolutionary change in either the management system or the economy.

Foreign entry

A second way in which change is introduced into an economic system is when firms outside the system establish a presence within the system, either through direct entry, merger or acquisition, or an alliance such as a joint venture (Methé *et al.*, 1996). Like entrepreneurial start-ups, foreign firms face a whole range of difficulties that have been termed the liability of foreignness (Zaheer, 1995; Zaheer and Mosakowski, 1997). Foreign entrants are confronted with the problem of how best to adapt to the local economic conditions and whether to adopt a substantial proportion of local manage-ment practices. The question is, which approach will yield the foreign entrant an advantage over its local competitors? In some cases this question is moot since the host country government regulates the form of entry that foreign firms can take. This has not been the case in Japan for quite some time. In spite of this, and the fact that the Japanese economy is the world's second largest, the amount of foreign direct investment is comparatively small. This in itself tends to minimize the vector of change role that foreign firms can play in the Japanese economy and management system, and the liability of foreignness limits it even further.

When confronting the liability of foreignness an entering company must decide on its management style. In a study of this topic Khan and Yoshihara (1994) found that only about 3 per cent of firms used a Western management style and 15 per cent used the parent company style with a few Japanese features. The remaining 82 per cent had adopted a Japanese or predomi-nantly Japanese style. Thus in terms of being a vector for change, foreign companies have been rather weak in bringing alternative management methods to Japan. Khan and Yoshihara also found that while there was no substantial correlation between management style and success, the slightly more successful companies had adopted the Japanese style and had Japanese CEOs heading the company (ibid.)

In the case of merger or acquisition, the external pillars of cross-shareholding and stable shareholding make foreign entry difficult if the target Japanese enterprise is financially healthy. Although the amount of cross-shareholding has been declining since the 1980s, the amount of stable shareholding has held fairly steady (Okabe, 2002) and this can be a signi-ficant barrier to the acquisition of Japanese firms (*Nikkei Weekly*, 22 March 2004). Only about 40 per cent of the shares traded on the Tokyo stock exchange are openly traded. Stable shareholders have held some 60 per cent since the 1970s. Although it is not impossible to mount a hostile takeover, the likelihood is low and for the most part is confined to companies that are in deep financial difficulty.[1]

Both the number of foreign enterprises in Japan and the number of employees that work for them is small. In 2003 it was estimated that about 1.6 million full-time regular employees were working for foreign enterprises

(JIL, 2003). Given that the total number of full-time regular employees in Japan was about 43.2 million (ibid.), employees working for foreign enterprises only accounted for 2.3 per cent of the total workforce. As noted earlier in this chapter, Ballon and Honda (2000) estimate that in 1997 there were about 2.5 million incorporated firms in Japan. The estimated number of foreign firms in 2002 was about 6000 (JIL, 2003), or about 0.24 per cent of the total number of incorporated firms.

Even a small number of firms can be a major source of change if they are large or dominate their sectors of the economy. However most foreign enterprises are small or medium sized (ibid.), and although they include well-known names such as Dell, IBM, Merrill Lynch, Goldman Sachs, Siemens and Daimler-Chrysler, they tend not to dominate their respective economic sectors. While cases differ by industrial sector and by firm, on the whole foreign firms usually occupy specialized niches in the Japanese market and only a few have come to dominate those niches; fewer still have moved into the broad mainstream of the Japanese economy. Nonetheless foreign firms tend to be profitable and the number of entrants continues to grow.

For firms that enter Japan through the establishment of a wholly owned subsidiary, attracting and keeping qualified employees is a major hurdle (ACC, 2001). Again, workers' aversion to risk and their desire for high status is part of the reason for this. It is a common perception among Japanese workers that foreign enterprises will pack up and leave if there is an economic downturn in Japan or they suffer a decline in their own fortunes. The recent withdrawal of Daimler-Chrysler from Mitsubishi Motors (*Nihon Keizai Shimbun*, 23 April 2004; *Nikkei Weekly*, 26 April 2004, p. 2) is but one example in a long list of companies that have lost interest in Japan (Debroux, 1993). As a result Japanese workers, and especially school graduates, tend to shy away from them.

Another factor is the lack of flexibility in the Japanese labour market (Aoki, 1988). A major reason for this inflexibility is the pension system, which makes it very difficult for workers to collect pension benefits if they change employers (JETRO, 2001). As a result many stay with their firms until the mandatory retirement age, even if better employment opportunities present themselves. Changes to the pension system are slow in coming so in the near future it is unlikely that Japanese workers will be able to transfer to foreign companies in mid career without losing their pension rights (Shimada, 2003).

Foreign firms could be a source of change if they successfully transferred substantial portions of their home management systems to Japan. As noted above, some foreign firms have adopted a hybrid of the Japanese and their own management systems, and this has affected how they handle change. For example the recent turnaround at Nissan, engineered by Carlos Ghosn, was done without a massive lay-off of workers and with careful pruning of the *keiretsu* supplier base (Ghosn, 2002). The turnaround was the result of finding a delicate balance between the economic and business reality of lowering the operating costs and debts of the nearly bankrupt carmaker, while functioning in a business environment where the mass lay-off of employees was not considered an acceptable strategy. Ghosn's achievement in this regard earned him the top position in the *Nihon Keizai Shimbun* list of top managers of the *Heisei* era (*Nihon Keizai Shimbun*, 14 January 2004). However this does not mean that the turnaround was without ill effect. The subsequent consolidation in the steel industry was in part triggered by Nissan dropping a long-standing supplier relationship with a steel company. This consolidation later affected Nissan's ability to acquire steel when demand for cars began to pick up.

The course followed by IBM Japan at its Yasu production facility, which was used for the fabrication of integrated circuits and liquid crystal displays (*Nikkei Industrial Daily*, 7 July 2003) further illustrates the hybrid approach to change. Because IBM was moving away from commodity products the Yasu facility was to be closed, but the managers of IBM Japan worked hard to secure employment for their workers through a number of joint ventures with Japanese, US and Taiwanese companies. 'As a result ... Yasu was turned into an industrial park housing a number of different firms', thus saving most of the jobs (*Nikkei Industrial Daily*, 7 July 2003). The restructuring of IBM's operations impacted differently on IBM Japan compared with the rest of IBM. In the mid 1990s IBM cut its workforce of 400 000 to 220 000. IBM Japan was part of that exercise, but its workforce was only reduced from a peak of about 25 000 to around 20 000 in 2003. IBM Japan was able to adapt both to the external environment created by a decade of slow growth and deflation and to the internal environment of being a subsidiary of a large multinational enterprise, and still maintain the core of the company as an economic community.

Hence as with entrepreneurial firms, foreign firms entering Japan do have some influence on the Japanese management system, and this influence has increased over the past few decades as the number of foreign firms has increased and more Japanese workers have been attracted to them. However it is unlikely that they will wield sufficient influence radically to change the Japanese management system or the structure of the Japanese economy in the near future.

Change by incumbent firms

We shall now look at the last vector of change for the Japanese management system. When considering change in incumbent organizations it is important to remember that the way in which the Japanese management system is defined will affect our interpretation of the types of change the system is undergoing and its chance of survival. If the Japanese management system is viewed as static with each pillar rigidly defined, then it may be on its last legs. But if it is interpreted as a more elastic system that can be altered to meet the exigencies of its environment, then it may be around for a long time. The latter interpretation allows us to move beyond considering whether or not the system is dead or alive and to look at how it is changing, which components are being kept, which are being eliminated, what new ones are being introduced and how they are affecting the core of the management system, that is, the extent to which the changes are altering the identity of the company as an economic community.

An examination of one pillar of the Japanese management system – lifetime employment – can provide some insights. Some have declared that lifetime employment is dead (for example Hirakubo, 1999). However in a 2003 survey of large firms (more than 1000 employees) conducted by the Ministry of Health, Labour and Welfare, about 40 per cent of the companies surveyed indicated that their lifetime employment system would be maintained as it was and another 40 per cent said they would make partial modifications. Only about 10 per cent intended to make drastic changes (Ministry of Health, Labour and Welfare, 2003). In the same survey, more than 75 per cent of workers stated that the lifetime employment system was good or good on balance. The percentage was higher for older workers, but even in the case of those in the 20–29 age bracket, over 60 per cent considered it was good or good on balance.

The same applied to the seniority-based remuneration and promotion systems. About 50 per cent of the companies surveyed had introduced some form of performance evaluation (ibid., Section 4). Of these companies, about 88 per cent were having difficulties with implementing the system. Most of the difficulties reflected the inherent problem of rating employees who performed different jobs. Other problems were lack of training for evaluators and overly generous evaluations. Nonetheless about 30 per cent of the firms surveyed were increasing the weighting given to merit-based pay (ibid., Section 3).

Thus while the seniority system may be on its way out, the changes made so far have not been drastic and have been phased in over a long time. Some firms are having so much difficulty with the new merit system that they are considering scrapping it and trying something else or returning to the seniority system (*Japan Times*, 31 March 2004). Fujitsu has had a lot of difficulty with its merit system, which was initiated in 1993 and completely replaced the seniority system in 1998. Under the new system the targets had been set too low and Fujitsu's overall performance dropped relative to that of domestic competitors who did not have a comprehensive merit system (*Nihon Keizai Shimbun*, 7 January 2004). Fujitsu's system has already been revised once and further revisions are being considered. Even where the merit system has had a relatively positive impact on productivity and creativity, such as at Canon, it is still experiencing teething problems. Some 20–30 per cent of Canon's employees are not satisfied with the system

(*Nihon Keizai Shimbun*, 26 February 2004). Toyota, on the other hand, kept much of its seniority-based wage system intact and posted record profits of over one trillion yen in fiscal year 2003 (*Nihon Keizai Shimbun*, 26 February 2004).

With regard to promotion, some companies intend to accelerate the rate of promotion and base more promotions on merit (Mizuno, 2004). There appears to be some correlation between the age of top managers and the performance of firms. In a survey of 2258 companies (Kato, 2004), those whose top managers were in their forties and early fifties performed better than those whose CEOs were in their early sixties. However these better performing companies made up only about 15 per cent of the total; 60 per cent had CEOs in their early sixties and about 24 per cent had CEOs in their late sixties. Only 1 per cent of CEOs were in their thirties.

The deflationary price spiral has had a profound effect on Japanese firms' ability to maintain the seniority system. With downward price pressure in most goods markets, costs have to be reduced, and these include labour costs. Possession of an ageing workforce paid according to length of service has placed many Japanese firms in a severe 'cost crunch'. Performance-related pay is supposed to be aimed at improving productivity, but it appears that many Japanese firms are putting it in place as a way around the seniority system in order to lower costs.

Company unions are playing a major role in these changes. Adaptations to lifetime employment and performance-related pay are of obvious importance to unions since they directly affect their members (*Nihon Keizai Shimbun*, 14 February 2003: *Nihon Keizai Shimbun*, 7 February 2004). The unions have pushed for employment stability over wage increases (*Nihon Keizai Shimbun*, 16 January 2004) and so far have been flexible about the introduction of performance-related pay. While they have been carefully tracking complaints about the new pay system, the reality of deflation and the need to stay competitive have stayed their hand. However they have drawn the line at job cuts (*Nikkei Weekly*, 17 February 2003).

Surprisingly the unions are also playing a role in mergers and acquisitions. Because of changes to the Commercial Code and institutional regulations on cross-shareholding and merger and acquisition activity, it is now more likely that consolidation and rationalization will take place. About 12 000 merger and acquisition deals have taken place since 1993; mergers within *keiretsu* add another 8000 or so, bringing the total to about 20 000 over a ten-year period (*Nikkei Weekly*, 9 February 2004). The introduction of the holding company law has also helped companies to reorganize their structure. However unions have a strong voice in how mergers and acquisitions proceed. Recently, for example, the decision of whether to merge the companies Kanebo and Kao or move Kanebo's activities to the Industrial Revitalization Corporation of Japan hinged on the union's acceptance of the various proposal (Nakamoto, 2004; Pilling and Nakamoto, 2004). The fact that the union had such an influence on the two companies' merger plans shows the strength of the part unions play in maintaining companies as economic communities.

A look at how the Japanese management system has been readjusted in a well-established firm can give us a better understanding of the changes that are being made or are likely to be made in the future. Sony is in many respects closer to its Western than to its Japanese counterparts. Beginning with its governance system, Sony has a Board of Directors that in terms of the number of board members and the use of external board members and committees is much like a board found in a US company. It adopted this system in the mid 1990s, when other Japanese electronics companies had not even begun to consider such a change. The reform was enabled by an amendment to the Commercial Code that permitted, but did not mandate, the adoption of US-style board structures (Hashimoto, 2002). Although other Japanese companies are now reducing the number of board members and adding external members, this does not necessarily constitute a swing towards the US model as real in many cases there is only one outside director, and often this director comes from a related company in the same group (*Nikkei Weekly*, 13 October 2003). Sony on the other hand has adhered to the spirit as well as to the letter of governance reform and has a much more active board.

Foreign influence is also evident in share purchases. A larger percentage of Sony's equity shares are owned by foreigners than is the case with most Japanese companies – about 38.6 per cent in 2003–4 compared with 29.7 per cent for NEC, 31.3 per cent for Hitachi, 18.8 per cent for Toshiba, 14.6 per cent for Mitsubishi Electric and 20.1 per cent for Fujitsu (*Nikkei Financial Daily*, 6 January 2004.) Foreign ownership of equity is a growing trend not only in the case of Japanese electronic firms but also for Japanese industry as a whole (Okabe, 2003). These foreign investors are not as passive as equity shareholders in the past, but it remains to be seen how much influence they can actually exert (*Nihon Keizai Shimbun*, 28 April 2004). If they are in it for the long haul they may simply become another form of stable investor, albeit less predictable than the traditional investors. Alternatively if they actively trade on the same basis as they would on the New York Stock Exchange they might exert some influence on the Japanese management system. Sony has attracted foreign shareholders for a longer time and at a higher percentage than other Japanese firms, so it serves as an indicator of how other Japanese firms might respond as foreign ownership increases or as they adopt US governance structures.

One of the reasons why Sony has attracted so much foreign shareholder attention is that it has a strong presence in the US consumer electronics market. Thus it is less dependent on the sale of its products in the Japanese market than are its Japanese competitors. However it is also more exposed to market and financial market discipline.

Some Japanese executives have confided in private that they do not view Sony as a typical Japanese company because of its governance structure and strategic orientation; a telling remark. Moreover Sony has hired employees in mid-career and has promoted younger, more capable managers over those with longer service. In spite of these differences, Sony is like its large Japanese counterparts in two respects: it has been under pressure from aggressive competitors and has had to adjust its competitive strategy, but it is also concerned with maintaining the identity of the company as an economic community, despite some indications to the contrary.

In an attempt to affect a turnaround in the face of growing competition, in October 2003 Sony announced a three-year plan to reduce costs by as much as US $3 billion by 2006. This included laying off some 20 000 workers. To US managers this was well within the purview of acceptable management actions to preserve the equity value of the company, but in Japan it could have been seen as a weakening of the company as an economic community. However the lay-offs were to be spread over three years, which would lessen the blow and only 7000 of those laid off would be in Japan. It is not clear how Sony will accomplish this reduction, but at about 2300 workers per year this downsizing could be accomplished by reducing the hiring of new recruits, introducing early retirement and transferring workers to subsidiaries, methods that have often been used to reduce employee numbers in large companies while preserving the benefits of lifetime employment (Sullivan and Peterson, 1991; Hashimoto, 1993) during economic slowdowns.

Even Sony's more drastic plan to cut its number of suppliers from 4700 to 1000 by 2006 may not constitute real abandonment of traditional management principles. While a large number of Sony's vertical *keiretsu* suppliers will be eliminated, thus disrupting the broader community of the *keiretsu* club, not all the affiliated firms in question will be real members of the supplier *keiretsu*. For example when Nissan began to unbundle its *keiretsu* suppliers it found that many of the affiliated firms were linked only through financial transactions and had no real supplier function. Another factor to consider is the way in which the number of affiliated firms will be cut. For example Toyota reduced its number of *keiretsu* suppliers by merging several firms into one, thus preserving jobs and the fundamental structure of the arrangement. Should Sony's current position improve it can always revise the number upwards, much as Hitachi did recently when it reversed its decision to divest itself of certain operations (accounting for 20 per cent of its total sales) because its market and financial position had improved. The focus would henceforth be on turning around the operations before restructuring continued (*Nikkei Weekly*, 9 February 2004).

The sense of the company as an economic community has never applied to all workers or to all firms, but where it has existed it still does.[2] The community itself may be redefined from time to time, but it is preserved.

The use of spin-offs has been another organizational practice used by Japanese business organizations to adjust to expansions and contractions in markets, industries and the economy (Ito, 1995). Large Japanese enterprises have often set up subsidiary companies and moved employees from the main company to the subsidiaries, thus preserving employment. The joint establishment of Elpida by NEC and Hitachi, and Renesas by Hitachi and Mitsubishi Electric may appear to have ended the lifetime employment commitment to those transferred, but their jobs were preserved and the primary stockholders of each company were the parent companies in each case. It may not be immediately clear which *keiretsu* club Elpida and Renesas belong to or whether they will become truly independent, but in time this will be sorted out.

In order to put these changes into perspective and gain some additional insights we need to look at the impact they have had on the Japanese management system.

Impact of changes on the Japanese management system

What type of change is going on in Japan? In general the vector for hetero-dynamic change is most likely to be a new organizational form entering an existing system, such as an entrepreneurial start-up or an entrant from another business field or country (Methé *et al.*, 1996). In the case makes sense of company structure and institutional identity, a start-up has the freedom to choose an identity that differs from the prevailing one, and as it is new it does not have to undo or unlearn a previous organizational routine. To a lesser extent this is also true of a foreign entrant. As we saw earlier, the influence of both entrepreneurial start-ups and foreign entries is rather weak in Japan and it is unlikely that changes emanating from either of these two sources will significantly alter the Japanese management system. This leaves us with changes initiated by incumbent firms. Studies indicate that such change tends to be homeostatic or first order (ibid.; Fox-Wolfgramm *et al.*, 1998).

In the case of homeostatic change, organizations often have strategic routines in place that allow managers to make adjustments to the organizational environment. These routines are usually based on past experiences and reflect the success an organization has had. Hence organizations tend to make incremental changes to their routines that propel them along a certain path or trajectory (Kelly and Amburgey, 1991) while maintaining the identity of the organization or system.

In the case of Japanese companies many of these routines began to develop in the 1950s. They were put to the test by the oil price rises in the 1970s and the hike in the value of the yen following the Plaza Accord in the 1980s. Changes to the routines included shifting workers from production to sales or maintenance during slow times, temporarily shutting down facilities, transferring workers to affiliated companies and cutting bonuses. These measures helped to maintain the pillars of the management system and the company as an economic community until the economy resumed its growth. Many companies also used these measures when confronted with the economic slowdown that followed the bursting of the bubble economy.

When environmental changes overwhelm the customary change routines and cause managers to examine the core values that guide these routines, heterodynamic change is necessary. This occurred in Japan when the traditional approaches to change no longer worked and the economy failed to return to growth. Japanese managers were forced to manipulate the pillars that formed the structure of the organization in order to allow new means of change to be tried.

This type of change is often associated with the punctuated equilibrium model of change (Tushman and Romanelli, 1985; Romanelli and Tushman, 1994), in which the organization alters its core elements in one fell swoop, thus moving the organization on to an entirely different path and a new identity (Gersick, 1991). However, as will be discussed below the changes to the Japanese management system have not amounted to sweeping change. Instead heterodynamic changes have been used selectively and combined with ongoing homeostatic change to maintain continuity in terms of the firm as an economic community.

As we noted earlier, many companies in Japan have retained and reinforced some aspects of the Japanese management system while paying less attention to others. Over the years scholars and practitioners alike had come to view the six pillars of the Japanese management system as essential and self-reinforcing. During the period of high growth the success of Japanese companies reinforced this view among practitioners and scholars alike. Nonetheless companies such as Toyota, Honda, (Nishioka, 2003) Canon, Sharp, Rohm, Omron (Maruyama, 2004), Pioneer (Suzuki, 2004) and others refined and adjusted the system in response to changes in the economic environment. They focused their strategies on products, technologies and markets, and were not afraid to close down unprofitable operations even when this went against the traditional strategic goal of maintaining market share. However they remained concerned to maintain their identity as an economic community and therefore lifetime employment, or at least in the case of the core employees, has remained a central feature of these companies and an important part of their identity.

During the difficult years Canon has relentlessly focused on profitability, which has required constant restructuring and withdrawal from unprofitable market segments such as typewriters, personal computers and optical cards (Koyama, 2002a). The restructuring has been accomplished without lay-offs. Redundant engineers and workers have been shifted to other operations, taking with them the experience gained from their previous activities. According to Canon's CEO, Fujio Mitarai, 'Our engineers who used to design computers brought dramatic improvements to our laser printer products' (ibid.) Mitarai has addressed the need to maximize profits and maintain market share by developing new products based on new technology that command premium prices and help the market to grow. These products are less susceptible to the price and margin erosion that occurs at the commodity end. This has been done with the traditional commitment to lifetime employment but with greater attention to employee performance.

At Canon and the other successful Japanese companies, product development has been based on an information-exploiting approach that incorporates problem-solving knowledge accumulated over many generations of product development (Methé, 1995). Redundancy, in the form of engineers with overlapping product development experience, can be turned into an effective and efficient tool if properly organized (Mansfield, 1989). Lifetime employment, with the proper performance incentives, can create a core of committed and actively loyal employees where learning can be transferred across product and technology generations. The seniority system may be impeding motivation, so Canon, Sony, Pioneer and others are making changes in this area (*Nikkei Weekly*, 8 December 2003; Suzuki 2004), including the introduction of performance-related pay and more rapid promotion. Performance-related pay, as long as it is directed at improving creativity and productivity rather than simply being used as a cost-reduction tool, can aid company survival. The more rapid promotion of managers, based on merit, may have a greater overall impact on the Japanese management system because competent people will rise quickly to a position where they can introduce appropriate changes (*Nikkei Weekly*, 8 March 2004; Mizuno, 2004).

With regard to the external pillars of the Japanese management system, cross-shareholding has been dropped on a selective basis, with only firms with a good product market rationale being retained, while stable shareholding continues to be part of the system (Okabe, 2002). The thinking continues to be that stable shareholding allows managers to plan for the long term and not risk exposure to the whims of the financial markets. Finally, as noted earlier the main bank system has been less essential to successful firms for some time and will continue, in its present form, to decline in importance.

Implications of change at the strategic and institutional levels

The relationship between the strategic and institutional levels has interested scholars for some time (Hrebiniak and Joyce, 1985), but it is attracting renewed interest in respect of the ways in which it affects the change process (Lewin *et al.*, 1999). Change can occur at all levels of a system, ranging from the individual level, company level, institutional level and societal level (Kieser, 1989). When an individual leaves an incumbent Japanese firm to pursue a career in a Japanese start-up or a foreign firm, this has an impact that reverberates up from the individual level through the firm level and into the institutional level. Likewise a firm-level change, such as changing to performance-related pay, reverberates down to the individual level and up to the institutional level; and changes at the institutional level, such as giving firms the legal right to adopt US style governance practices, reverberate down into the firm, influencing individual employees. The magnitude of such changes can vary according to whether, for example, one individual employee or many decide to change, or whether the institutional change is mandatory or simply an option. It can be a homeostatic change that results in the preservation of the system at that level, or it can be a heterodynamic change that results in fundamental alterations to the system at that level (Watzlawick *et al.*, 1974; Argyris, 1992).

Sometimes change at one level can fundamentally alter the system at that level but preserve the system at a second level; that is, the change that takes place at the second level is homeostatic, even though the change that occurred at the initial level was heterodynamic (Argyris, 1992). For example Japanese firms are attempting to introduce this form of heterodynamic change at one level in terms of redefining the pillars of the Japanese management system while maintaining the firm as an economic community at the institutional level. Their efforts to alter cross-shareholding, abolish the seniority system or redefine lifetime employment are examples of heterodynamic alterations to main pillars of the system that also preserve the core workforce and therefore the institutional identity of the company as an economic community.

Some of the changes occurring in the pillars of the management system at the strategic level are more difficult to classify according to the punctuated equilibrium model. Changes in recruitment practices such as mid-career hiring and reducing the number of young recruits have not fundamentally replaced the lifetime employment pillar in that only the number and category of employees have been altered. In this sense the changes could be considered homeostatic. However, over the long term the effects of these firm-level changes are generating pressures at other levels that may make it impossible to maintain the lifetime employment pillar and the company as community. This can be illustrated by considering the unemployment rate for younger and older people and the growing number of temporary employees in Japan. In 1985 the unemployment rate for the economy as a whole was 2.2 per cent but for younger workers it was about 4.4 per cent. This difference of 2.2 percentage points held for ten to twelve years but, by 2001, the unemployment rate for the economy as a whole was running at about 5.4 per cent, and for younger workers it was 9.9 per cent (METI, 2003). Overall, the rate for younger workers rose fastest, especially from 1997, when the gap had widened from 2.2 percentage points to 4.5 percentage points.

Also during this period there was a rise in the number of workers holding temporary or non-regular jobs, many in the service and retail sectors of the economy. The proportion of temporary to regular employees grew from 19.1 per cent in 1989 to about 27.2 per cent in 2002 (ibid.) The emergence of the 'freeter' phenomenon – young workers who took on a series of temporary positions while living at home, rather than joining a company with the expectation of staying for the rest of their working lives – was recognized as a serious economic and social issue, especially given the declining birth rate.

As discussed above, firms have been reducing their recruitment of school graduates following a homeostatic change in the permanent employment pillar. They are attempting to retain their current core of permanent employees in order to preserve their institutional identity as an economic community. Is it possible that this could generate conditions that will force a heterodynamic change to the institutional identity of the firm in the long term?

By not hiring young people as regular employees large firms are excluding the possibility of their becoming permanent employees, thus setting up a vicious circle. For young people in this situation the institutional identity of the firm as an economic community does not exist. Those working as non-regular employees do not receive the training and mentoring that existed in the past. They have been forced to choose jobs that have limited opportunities for development and learning and that will not offer them a significant improvement in pay over time. Living at home reduces their expenses and increases their disposable income. This may boost consumption and lift the economy in the short term, but it is weakening the foundation upon which firms have based their identity.

In the long term the lack of training and promotion will limit both the employment prospects of young people and their contribution to the economy, and it will further weaken the institutional identity of the firm as an economic community. Although accurate figures are difficult to obtain, a very disturbing aspect of the 'freeter' phenomenon is that many of these young workers are college graduates who would normally have been quickly absorbed into the regular workforce. Between the 1960s and the 1980s graduates often received several job offers, ensuring a 100 per cent acceptance rate for those graduating from college. That rate fell to a low of 82.1 per cent in 2003–4 (*Japan Times*, 2 April 2004). College graduates should be the future elite of Japan, but the current hiring practices mean that an ever-growing proportion of them no longer accept the idea of the firm as an economic community. This raises troubling questions about how Japan can maintain social stability and improve economic growth.

Conclusions

The Japanese management system has been evolving continually since the end of World War II. The 1990s have been characterized as a 'lost decade'. In our view, while it was a period of great challenge because of the twin forces of slow growth and deflation, rather than a lost decade it was a period of experimentation in which Japanese firms introduced variety to the Japanese management system, and this continues today. Some of the pillars of the system appear to be falling by the wayside, such as the seniority system and cross-shareholding. Some are still in existence but losing their influence, such as the main bank system. Others, such as lifetime employment and company unions, have remained more or less intact. So that companies can maintain their commitment to workers in their forties to sixties, however, young employees are faced with a more restricted definition of lifetime employment. With over one third of all workers now classified as non-regular, the percentage of those who have a job for life has shrunk. It can only be guessed what effect this will have on the future of the Japanese management system and the economy in general, but one need only remember that many of the homeless in Tokyo today were non-regular employees during the economic boom of the 1970s and 1980s to see the dark side of this trend.

However the forces unleashed by the attempts to preserve the Japanese management system may bring about opportunities that will mitigate the potentially darker outcome. Changes to the institutional framework that will support entrepreneurial firms are slow but under way. In the wake of the regulatory and financial market changes, employees are questioning the appropriateness of working all their life for a single company (Methé and Miyabe, 2005). At the same time there is growing interest in working for foreign firms. The biggest source of change, however, is still the established Japanese firm. Here aspects of the old Japanese management system, such as lifetime employment and stable shareholding, are being combined with less concern with self-sufficiency and a more focused approach to products, technologies and markets, and a concern for profits over market share. This may offer a template for continued experimentation. The economic environment will determine which of the various experiments will succeed and which will fail. It is too soon to tell what the ultimate identity of the Japanese management system will be, but it can be said with confidence that the features that are selected and retained will be a function not only of the economic environment but also of the imagination and insight of practising managers.

This will place greater importance on the attitudes, abilities and skills of managers, especially top managers in Japan. The challenge is to develop and train more managers that exhibit the leadership abilities necessary to identify and keep the elements of the traditional management system that are useful, and to creatively develop and blend them with innovative elements. As we have observed, there has been much experimentation, and some managers have been able to find the proper balance and their companies have prospered. However, a few successful companies cannot offer a base broad enough to support a stable society and economic growth. Further, it is unlikely that the successful companies will offer systematic training of such managers in a way that would offer broad-based support. This will require efforts on the part of government, education and society to accomplish. The emergence of business schools in Japan is one potential avenue to meet this need. The success of these schools in developing the required managerial talent is intricately bound to the organizational and institutional changes discussed above. It will be important to monitor the success of these new schools as a way to understanding the direction and pace of change.

The ultimate direction and pace of those changes will be determined by these new managers and they will build upon what currently exists. Continuity will be seen even as the management system changes. The key to their success will be in knowing what to keep, what to throw away and what to modify. This is at once simple to say and difficult to do, but Japanese society and managers have a lot of experience in wrestling with the paradoxes of change and it would be wise not to underestimate their resilience. For managers of non-Japanese firms one lesson is clear. In order to avoid being blindsided as they were in the 1980s, they need to continue to be engaged in Japan and not to misinterpret Japanese managers' attempts at balancing the paradoxes of change with an inability to change.

Notes

1. The recent attempted takeover of Nippon Broadcasting by Livedoor is an exception. The implications of this event for the Japanese management system are less clear in that, although the takeover did occur, the final result looks more like a cross-sharing holding agreement than a real hostile takeover. Further, the reactions of the business community and government to the takeover event has been to delay the implementation of new regulations that would have facilitated mergers and acquisitions. It appears that one of the reasons for this delay is to make it easier for the managers of Japanese firms to develop defences against such activities. This will make it more difficult to engage in merger and acquisition activities, especially for the foreign firms that wish to engage in them.
2. An interesting twist on who is included and who is not is offered by Sony's recent announcement by Sir Howard Stringer, its first foreign chief executive. This move, some have speculated, was designed to further increase the diversity of thinking in the still troubled electonics maker. This same motivation may also be seen in two other turnaround attempts with the announcements of Ms. Fumiko Hayashi and Ms. Mariko Nonaka to take over top positions in Daiei and Sanyo respectively. We look at these issues in greater detail in Methé and Miyabe (2005).

References

Abegglen, J. (1958) *The Japanese Factory* (Glencoe, Ill.: Free Press).

Aldrich, H. E. and C. M. Fiol (1994) 'Fools Rush In? The Institutional Context of Industry Creations', *Academy of Management Review*, 19 (4), pp. 645–70.

American Chamber of Commerce (ACC) (2001) *Finding the Perfect Match: Recruiting, Developing, and Retaining Employees in Japan* (Price Water House Coopers).

Aoki, M. (1988) *Information, Incentives, and Bargaining in the Japanese Economy* (Cambridge: Cambridge University Press).

Aoki, M. (2001) *Toward a Comparative Institutional Analysis* (Cambridge, Mass.: MIT Press).

Aoki, M. and R. Dore (1994) *The Japanese Firm: Sources of Competitive Strength* (New York: Oxford University Press).

Aoki, M. and H. Patrick (1994) *The Japanese Main Bank System: Its Relevance for Developing and Transforming Economies* (New York: Oxford University Press).

Argyris, C. (1976) 'Single- and Double-loop Models in Research on Decision-Making', *Administrative Science Quarterly*, 21 (3), pp. 363–75.

Argyris, C. (1992) *On Organizational Learning* (Cambridge, Mass.: Blackwell).

Ashby, W. R. (1952) *Design for a Brain* (New York: Wiley).

Ballon, R. J. (1992) *Foreign Competition in Japan: Human Resource Management* (London: Routledge).

Ballon R. and K. Honda (2000) *Stakeholding: The Japanese Bottom Line* (Tokyo: Japan Times).

Barnett, W. P. and G. R. Carroll (1995) 'Modeling Internal Organizational Change', *Annual Review of Sociology*, 21, pp. 217–36.

Baron, J. N. (2004) 'Employing Identities in Organizational Ecology', *Industrial and Corporate Change*, 13 (1), pp. 3–32.

Baum, J. A. C. and C. Oliver (1996) 'Toward An Institutional Ecology of Organizational Founding', *Academy of Management Review*, 39 (5), pp. 1378–427.

Bracker, J. and D. T. Methé (1994) 'A Cross-National Study of Planning Characteristics of U.S. and Japanese Entrepreneurs', *International Journal of Management*, 11 (2), pp. 634–40.

Carlile, L. and M. C. Tilton (eds) (1998) *Is Japan Really Changing its Ways? Regulatory Reform and the Japanese Economy* (Washington, DC: Brookings Institution).

Carroll, G. R. (1994) 'The Specialist Strategy: Dynamics of Niche Width in Populations of Organizations', *American Journal of Sociology*, 90, pp. 126–283.

Chao, K. (1968) 'Labor Institutions in Japan and her Economic Growth', *Journal of Asian Studies*, 28 (1), pp. 5–17.

Cole, R. E. (1972) 'Permanent Employment in Japan: Fact and Fantasies', *Industrial and Labor Relations Review*, 26 (1), pp. 615–30.

Cole, R. E. (1973) 'Functional Alternatives and Economic Development: An Empirical Example of Permanent Employment in Japan', *American Sociological Review*, 38 (4), pp. 424–38.

Debroux, P. (1993) *The Foreign Employer in Japan*, Bulletin no. 140 (Sophia: Sophia University Institute of Comparative Culture).

Delacroix, J. and A. Swaminathan (1991) 'Cosmetic, Speculative and Adaptive Organizational Change in the Wine Industry: A Longitudinal Study', *Administrative Science Quarterly*, 36 (4), pp. 631–61.

Dunphy, D. (1987) 'Convergence/Divergence: A Temporal Review of the Japanese Enterprise and its Management', *The Academy of Management Review*, 12 (3), pp. 445–59.

Elsbach, K. D. and R. Sutton (1992) 'Acquiring Organizational Legitimacy Through Legitimate Actions: A Marriage of Institutional and Impression Management Theories', *Academy of Management Review*, 35 (4), pp. 699–738.

England, G. W. (1983) 'Japanese and American Management: Beyond Theory Z', *Journal of International Business Studies*, 14 (2), pp. 131–42.

Feigenbaum, E. A. and D. J. Brunner (2002) 'The Japanese Entrepreneur: Making the Desert Bloom', unpublished monograph, Stanford University.

Ford, J. D. and L. W. Ford (1994) 'Logics of Identity, Contradiction and Attraction in Change', *Academy of Management Review*, 19 (4), pp. 756–85.

Fox-Wolfgramm, S. J., K. B. Boal and J. G. Hunt (1998) 'Organizational Adaptation to Institutional Change: A Comparative Study of First-Order Change in Prospector and Defender Banks', *Administrative Science Quarterly*, 43 (1), pp. 87–126.

Freeman, J. (1995) 'Business Strategy from the Population Level', in C. Montgomery (ed.), *Resource-Based and Evolutionary Theories of the Firm: Towards a Synthesis* (Boston, Mass.: Kluwer).

Gersick, C. J. (1991) 'Revolutionary Change Theories: A Multilevel Exploration of the Punctuated Equilibrium Paradigm', *Academy of Management Review*, 16 (1), pp. 10–36.

Ghosn, C. (2002) 'Saving the Business Without Losing the Company', *Harvard Business Review*, January, pp. 3–11.

Gomez, P.-Y. and B. C. Jones (2000) 'Conventions: An Interpretation of Deep Structure in Organizations', *Organization Science*, 11 (6), pp. 696–708.

Hall, P. A. and D. Soskice (eds) (2001) *Varieties of Capitalism: The Institutional Foundations of Comparative Advantage* (New York: Oxford University Press).

Hamabata, M. M. (1990) *Crested Kimono: Power and Love in the Japanese Business Family* (Ithaca, NY: Cornell University Press).

Hannan, M. T. and J. Freeman (1984) 'Structural Inertia and Organizational Change', *American Sociological Review*, 49 (4), pp. 149–64.

Hashimoto, M. (1993) 'Aspects of Labor Market Adjustments in Japan', *Journal of Labor Economics*, 11 (1), pp. 136–61.

Hashimoto, M. (2002) *Commercial Code Revisions: Promoting the Evolution of Japanese Companies* (Tokyo: Nomura Research Institute).

Hashimoto, M. and J. Raisian (1985) 'Employment Tenure and Earnings Profiles in Japan and the United States', *American Economic Review*, 75 (4), pp. 721–35.

Hatvany, N. and V. Pucik (1981) 'An Integrated Management System: Lessons from the Japanese Experience', *The Academy of Management Review*, 6 (3), pp. 469–80.

Haveman, H. A. (1992) 'Between a Rock and a Hard Place: Organizational Change and Performance under Conditions of Fundamental Transformation', *Administrative Science Quarterly*, 37 (1), pp. 48–75.

Hayashi, M. (2002) 'A Historical Review of Japanese Management Theories: The Search for a General Theory of Japanese Management', *Asian Business & Management*, 1 (2), pp. 189–207.

Hirakubo, N. (1999) 'The End of Lifetime Employment in Japan', *Business Horizon*, 42 (6), pp. 41–6.

Hrebiniak, L. G. and W. F. Joyce (1985) 'Organizational Adaptation: Strategic Choice and Environmental Determinism', *Administrative Science Quarterly*, 30, pp. 336–49.

Inohara, H. (1990) *Human Resource Development in Japanese Companies* (Tokyo: Asian Productivity Organization).

Ito, K. (1995) 'Japanese Spinoffs: Unexplored Survival Strategies', *Strategic Management Journal*, 16 (6), pp. 431–46.

Ito, T. (1996) *Japan and the Asian Economies: A 'Miracle' in Transition*, Brookings Papers on Economic Activity 2 (Washington, DC: Brookings Institution), pp. 205–60.

JETRO (2001) *The Survey on Actual Conditions Regarding Access to Japan* (Tokyo: JETRO).

JIL (2001) *Recent Statistical Survey Reports* (Tokyo: JIL, August).

JIL (2002) *Recent Statistical Survey Reports* (Tokyo: JIL, August).

JIL (2003) 'Number of Full-time Employees at Foreign-affiliated Firms Tops One Million', *Japan Labor Bulletin*, 42 (1).

JSBRI (2002) *White Paper on Small and Medium Enterprises in Japan: The Age of the Local Entrepreneur-birth, Growth and Revitalization of the National Economy* (Tokyo: Japan Small Business Research Institute).

Kato, T. (2004) 'Mid-life Managers Boost Earnings – Older CEOs Dominate; Presidents in 40s Rank Highest in Performance', *Nikkei Weekly, Nihon Keizai Shimbun*, 8 March, p. 21.

Katz, R. (1998) *Japan the System that Soured: The Rise and Fall of the Japanese Economic Miracle* (New York: M. E. Sharpe).

Kelly, D. and T. L. Amburgey (1991) 'Organizational Inertia and Momentum: A Dynamic Model of Strategic Change', *Academy of Management Journal*, 34 (3), pp. 591–612.

Khan, S. and H. Yoshihara (1994) *Strategy and Performance of Foreign Companies in Japan* (Westport, Conn.: Quorum Books).

Kieser, A. (1989) 'Organizational, Institutional, and Societal Evolution: Medieval Craft Guilds and the Genesis of Formal Organizations', *Administrative Science Quarterly*, 34 (4), pp. 540–64.

Koyama, T. (2002a) 'Strong Leadership, Top Tech Means Healthy Canon IC–East–West fusion. CEO Fujio Mitarai blends Western Ideas with Japanese Management Mentality, and Reaps Benefits', *Nihon Keizai Shimbun*, 18 March, p. 1.

Koyama, T. (2002b) 'Culture is "Core Competence"', *Nikkei Weekly, Nihon Keizai Shimbun*, 18 March, p. 1.

Lewin, A. Y., C. P. Long and T. N. Carroll (1999) 'The Coevolution of New Organizational Forms', *Organization Science*, 10 (5), pp. 535–50.

Lin Z. and C. Hui (1999) 'Should Lean Replace Mass Organizational Systems: A Comparative Examination from a Management Coordination Perspective', *Journal of International Business Studies*, 30 (1), pp. 45–79.

Lincoln, E. J. (2001) *Arthritic Japan: The Slow Pace of Economic Reform* (Washington, DC: Brookings Institution).

Lincoln, J. R., M. L. Gerlach and P. Takahashi (1992) 'Keiretsu Networks in the Japanese Economy: A Dyad Analysis of Intercorporate Ties', *American Sociological Review*, 57 (5), pp. 561–85.

Manchus, G. (1983) 'Employer–Employee Based Quality Circles in Japan: Human Resource Policy Implications for American Firms', *The Academy of Management Review*, 8 (2), pp. 255–61.

Mansfield, E. (1989) 'Technological Change in Robotics: Japan and the United States', *Managerial and Decision Economic*, 10 (special issue), pp. 19–25.

March, J. C. (1981) 'Footnotes to Organizational Change', *Administrative Science Quarterly*, 26 (4), pp. 563–77.

Marsh, P. (2003) 'Japan's Smaller Manufacturers Engineer a Carefully Protected Advantage', *Financial Times*, 21 April, p. 9.

Marsh, R. M. (1992) 'The Difference between Participation and Power in Japanese Factories', *Industrial and Labor Relations Review*, 45 (2) pp. 250–7.

Marsh, R. M. and H. Mannari (1971) 'Lifetime Commitment in Japan: Roles, Norms, and Values', *American Journal of Sociology*, 76 (5), pp. 795–812.

Maruyama, H. (2004) 'Omron Eyes All-time High Net Profit – Control Equipment Maker's Command of Local Market Keeps Sales Humming', *Nikkei Weekly, Nihon Keizai Shimbun*, 22 March, p. 24.

Methé, D. T. (1982) 'The Japanese Way of Management: Does it Make Sense for U.S. Firms?' in S. M. Lee and G. Schwendiman (eds), *Management by Japanese Systems* (New York: Praeger), pp. 506–20.

Methé, D. T. (1995) 'Basic Research in Japanese Electronic Companies: An Attempt at Establishing New Organizational Routines', in J. K. Liker, J. E. Ettlie and J. C. Campbell (eds), *Engineered in Japan: Japanese Technology-Management Practices* (New York: Oxford University Press), pp. 17–39.

Methé, D. T. (2005) 'Institutional, Technological, and Strategic Factors in the Global Integrated Circuit Industry: The Persistence of Organizational Forms', in Y. Okada (ed.), *Struggles for Survival: Institutional and Organizational Changes in the Japanese High-tech Industries* (Tokyo: Springer).

Methé, D. T. and J. Bracker (1994) 'A Cross-National Study of Perceptions of the Business Environment by U.S. and Japanese Entrepreneurs', *International Journal of Management*, 11 (1), pp. 599–603.

Methé, D. T. and J. Miyabe (2006) 'Employment Practices in Japanese Firms: Can "Mikoshi" Management Survive?', in R. Haak (ed.), *The Changing Structure of Labor in Japan. Japanese Human Resource Management between Continuity and Innovation* (Basingstoke and New York: Palgrave).

Methé, D. T., A. Swaminathan and W. Mitchell (1996) 'The Underemphasized Role of Established Firms as the Sources of Major Innovations', *Industrial and Corporate Change*, 5 (4), pp. 1181–203.

Methé, D. T., R. Toyama and J. Miyabe (1997) 'Product Development Strategy and Organizational Learning: A Tale of Two PC Makers', *The Journal of Product Innovation Management*, 14, pp. 323–36.

Methé, D. T., D. Wilson and J. L. Perry (2000) 'A Review of Research on Incremental Approaches to Strategy', in J. Rabin, G. J. Miller and W. B. Hildreth (eds), *Handbook of Strategic Management*, 2nd edn (New York: Marcel Dekker), pp. 31–66.

METI (2003) *Challenges and Directions of Economic and Industrial Policy in Japan* (Tokyo: METI).

Ministry of Health, Labour and Welfare (2003) *White Paper on the Labour Economy 2003: Economic and Social Change and Diversification of Working Styles* (Tokyo: Ministry of Health, Labour and Welfare).

Miyajima, H. (1998) 'The Impact of Deregulation on Corporate Governance and Finance', in L. E. Carlile and M. C. Tilton (eds), *Is Japan Really Changing its Ways? Regulatory Reform and the Japanese Economy* (Washington, DC: Brookings Institution).

Miyashita, K. and D. Russell (1994) *Keiretsu: Inside the Hidden Japanese Conglomerates* (New York: McGraw-Hill).

Mizuno, Y. (2004) 'Young Talent New Face of Industry: "Under-49" Business Leaders not Constrained by Shackles of Tradition, Personal Ties', *Nikkei Weekly, Nihon Keizai Shimbun*, 10 May, p. 21.

Nagaoka, F. (2004) 'CEOs Map out Growth Strategies – Powerful Leadership Playing Pivotal Role in Recovery of Companies and Nation', *Nikkei Weekly, Nihon Keizai Shimbun*, 5 April, p. 21.

Nakamoto, M. (2004) 'Union delays Kao/Kanebo deal', *Financial Times*, 16 February, p. 13.

Nishioka, K. (2003) 'Management Skills have left Hitachi far behind Toyota', *Nikkei Weekly, Nihon Keizai Shimbun*, 15 September, p. 28.

Noguchi, Y. (1998) 'The 1940 System: Japan under the Wartime Economy', *American Economic Review*, 88 (2), pp. 404–7.

Oh, T. K. (1976) 'Japanese Management – A Critical Review', *Academy of Management Review*, 1 (1), pp. 14–25.

Okabe, M. (2002) *Cross Shareholdings in Japan: A New Unified Perspective of the Economic System* (Cheltenham: Edward Elgar).

Okumura, H. (2000) *Corporate Capitalism in Japan* (New York: St Martin's Press).

Pilling D. and M. Nakamoto (2004) 'Japan Chooses Cosmetic Change', *Financial Times*, 5 March, p. 8.

Romanelli, E. and M. L. Tushman (1994) 'Organizational Transformation as Punctuated Equilibrium: An Empirical Test', *Academy of Management Journal*, 37 (5), pp. 1141–66.

Sakamoto, A. and D. A. Powers (1995) 'Education and the Dual Labor Market for Japanese Men', *American Sociological Review*, 60 (4), pp. 222–46.

Sakano, T. and A. Y. Lewin (1999) 'Impact of CEO Succession in Japanese Companies: A Co-evolutionary Perspective', *Organization Science*, 10 (5), pp. 654–71.

Sato, M. (1999) 'Big Bang Results get Mixed Reviews. Deregulation Increases Options for Companies, Investors, but Deep-seated Social mores Inhibit Fundamental Change', *Nikkei Weekly*, 5 April, p. 11.

Shimada, H. (2003) 'Koizumi's Pledge to Double Inward Investment in Five Years', *Journal of Japanese Trade*, 1 September.

Singh, J. V., D. J. Tucker and R. J. House (1986) 'Organizational Legitimacy and the Liability of Newness', *Administration Science Quarterly*, 31, pp. 171–93.

Small and Medium Enterprise Agency (1998) *White Paper on Small and Medium Enterprises in Japan* (Tokyo: Small and Medium Enterprise Agency).

Small and Medium Enterprise Agency (1999) *White Paper on Small and Medium Enterprises in Japan* (Tokyo: Small and Medium Enterprise Agency).

Stuart, T. E., H. Hoang and R. C. Hybels (1999) 'Interorganizational Endorsements and the Performance of Entrepreneurial Ventures', *Administrative Science Quarterly*, 44 (2), pp. 315–49.

Suchman, M. C. (1995) 'Managing Legitimacy: Strategic and Institutional Approaches', *Academy of Management Review*, 20 (3), pp. 571–610.

Sugimoto, Y. (2003) *An Introduction to Japanese Society*, 2nd edn (Cambridge: Cambridge University Press).

Sullivan, J. J. and R. B. Peterson (1991) 'A Test of Theories Underlying the Japanese Lifetime Employment System', *Journal of International Business Studies*, 22 (1), pp. 79–97.

Suzuki, K. (2004) 'Fine-tuning Pays off for Pioneer: Ito Drives Profit by Shifting to Digital Products Before Rivals', *International Herald Tribune*, 14 May, p. B3.

Tachibanaki, T. (1982) 'Further Results on Japanese Wage Differentials: Nenko Wages, Hierarchical Position, Bonuses, and Working Hours', *International Economic Review*, 23 (2), pp. 447–61.

Tushman, M. L. and E. Romanelli (1985) 'Organizational Evolution: A Metamorphosis Model of Convergence and Reorientation', in L. L. Cummings and B. M. Staw (eds), *Research in Organizational Behavior*, vol. 7 (Greenwich CT: JAI Press), pp. 171–222.

Utsunomiya, Y. (2003) 'Shopping Site Rakuten Thinks Empire: Portal's Owner Recalls the Days of the Zaibatsu in Pointing to his Future', *The Japan Times*, 15 October, p. 14.

Van de Ven, A. H. and M. S. Poole (1995) 'Explaining Development and Change in Organizations', *Academy of Management Review*, 20 (3), pp. 510–40.

Watzlawick, P., J. Weakland and R. Fisch (1974) *Change: Principles of Problem Formation and Problem Resolution* (New York: W. W. Norton).

Yonekawa, S. (1985) 'Recent Writing on Japanese Economic and Social History', *Economic History Review*, 38 (1), pp. 107–23.

Zaheer, S. (1995) 'Overcoming the Liability of Foreignness', *Academy of Management Journal*, 38 (2), pp. 341–63.

Zaheer, S. and E. Mosakowski (1997) 'The Dynamics of Liability of Foreignness: A Global Study of Survival in Financial Services', *Strategic Management Journal*, 18 (6), pp. 439–63.

3
Organizational Survival
Robert J. Ballon

Introduction

When the Japanese started full-fledged industrialization in the mid nine-teenth century, Japan's survival was at stake. Safeguarding nationhood meant catching up with the Western powers and being the first non-Western nation to industrialize. It was not so much an action to decide than a reaction to urgent necessity. Thus Western methods were subsumed in the Japanese web of values and practices *'wakon yôsai'*.[1]

During the 250 years of Japan's relative seclusion imposed by the Tokugawa regime (1632–1868), the Japanese had developed a vibrant commercial economy dominated by merchants and their associations. There was 'An elaborate system of payment based on trust, fostered by the inward-looking nature of a society untrammelled by alien inputs and promoting interdependence among its members. This tradition was put at the core of Japan's industrialization, with a bank being the first joint-stock company' (Ballon and Matsuzaki, 2000, p. 107). A new breed of industrialists was fostered by government subsidies (Takeuchi, 1999; Aoki, 2001), while the newly established compulsory education system produced white- and blue-collar workers (Patrick, 1976). The private sector was thus entrusted with the public mission of safeguarding the nation's survival, which required heavy industry and world trade. After the Pacific War (1941–45) there was a renewed effort to restore Japan's society and economy, and eventually the age-old subsistence income was metamorphosed into discretionary income and affluence. It took exactly 100 years (1868 to 1967) to raise Japan's gross domestic product (GDP) to number three in the world and later, with the demise of the USSR, to number two (Table 3.1).

The instrument used to catch up was the business organization, a Western form of business that came to be loaded with native traditions. For the Japanese a business organization is a living organism, and in order to survive it must respond to two intimately related elements: a specific historical and societal context that nurtures at the national level the interdependence of

Table 3.1   Gross domestic product in major countries, 2000 (US dollars)

GDP	United States	Japan	Germany	France	United Kingdom
At current prices and current exchange rates	9 810.2	4 765.3	1 866.1	1 294.2	1 429.7
Per capita	35 619.0	37 546.0	22 704.0	21 361.0	23 925.0
At current prices using PPPs*	9 810.2	3 295.8	2 127.5	1 463.4	1 460.3
Per capita	35 619.0	25 968.0	25 885.0	24 152.0	24 437.0

* PPPs = purchasing power parities.
Source: OECD (2003).

the public and private sectors, and at the private level the interdependence of large and small firms; and the business firm itself (large or small), which seeks to maintain and develop its viability by entrusting it to its members. Ideally, the Japanese do not *work* for an organization; they *are* the organization, and organizational survival spells their own survival. The viability of both the business environment and the business organization result from their social embeddedness. It creates a network of stakeholders spurred on by mutual contribution and benefit.

Survival of the business environment and organizations is predicated on constant interchange. Any change in the environment affects the organizations, and *vice versa*. But as with any living organism, continuity is achieved not by adding changes or replacing it by change; continuity is *through* change, a change that works not so much as an action on reality as a reaction to reality.

Calling on Japanese perceptions, the following section outlines the Japanese business organization environment. Since the nation's survival – its society and its economy – is at stake the public and private sectors constantly interact in an interdependent fashion. A similar interdependence exists among large and small firms; it promotes competitive strategies and supports cooperative structures. In the subsequent section the viability of the firm itself is considered: how it fits into the environment, how it manages resources, and how it interacts with its stakeholders. Finally, in the conclusion the challenge of business organization is described as continuity *through* change; constant change is the key to survival. The behaviour of large and small firms is fundamentally similar: both are manned by well-educated, relatively homogeneous Japanese.

Viability of the business environment

The viability of the Japanese business environment is determined by a specifically Japanese social context in which mutual interdependence among the actors is paramount: public realm and private interests are intimately related; firms of all sizes are integrated into a system of competition and cooperation where self-regulation prevails; and in order to survive the economy has to balance people and assets.

The public and private sectors

To the Japanese, the distinction between public and private is clear only at the extremes of the continuum; in between many functions overlap. Constant relations are nurtured by trade and industry associations, business federations, deliberation councils (*shingikai*, see Noble, 2003) and numerous formal and informal occasions at which bureaucrats, politicians and business people meet again and again at all levels, national and local. After early retirement officials sit on the boards of large private companies (*amakudari*) and/or public corporations (*yokosuberi*); such assignments are often repeated (*wataridori*) and beneficiaries succeed each other (Colignon and Usui, 2003). In addition one-to-one discussions are held in the context of administrative guidance (*gyôsei shidô*), a largely paralegal practice featuring rewards and punishments. Hence 'the tendency for regulations to undo what is intended at the outset as well as the complexity of the legislative system, with the government having to deal with LDP [Liberal Democratic Party] policy councils before submitting a bill to the Diet' (OECD, 2003, p. 122). 'What Japan's tripartite elite (bureaucracy, business, and the Liberal Democratic Party) has tried to accomplish, and what they have in large part succeeded in achieving, is the maintenance of the policy formation that emphasizes bureaucratic leadership exercised through informal processes' (Upham, 1987, p. 21). Their role has been described as 'authority without power': 'Formal law-making and law-enforcing processes – whether legislative, bureaucratic, or judicial – function in large measure as consensus-building processes rather than avenues for command and coercion' (Haley, 1991, p. 198).

Involved in these activities is a surprisingly small government sector that employs less than 8 per cent of the labour force, namely about one million civil servants in the central government and over three million in local governments (Table 3.2). Relations between the central and local governments are very close (Muramatsu *et al.*, 2001). In particular, public corporations – beneficiaries of the Fiscal and Loan Programme, which is largely financed by postal savings and pension funds (Cargill and Yoshino, 2003) – are focal points of central–local government interaction. In March 1999, of the 10 000 or so local public companies about 58 per cent were established in cooperation with the private sector.[2]

The private sector plays its role in public–private interdependence primarily through self-regulation, commonly exercised by trade and industry associations (*gyôkai dantai*), of which there more than 15 000 (Table 3.3). There are also 26 000 organizations under the Civil Code, many of which

Table 3.2   Employment in the public sector (per cent)

	1988	1993	1997
Canada	7.4	7.8	6.5
France	29.4	31.0	31.8
Germany	n.a.	17.7	17.1
Italy	22.9	23.1	22.9
Japan	8.0	7.2	7.0
United Kingdom	23.9	19.5	n.a.
United States	15.8	15.8	14.4

Note: Producers of government services as a proportion of total employees.
Source: OECD (2000, p. 145).

Table 3.3   Trade associations by type and industry

	All	Of which nationwide
Total	15 391	3 127
By type of association		
Voluntary (*nin-l dantai*)	9 655	1 987
Incorporated (*shadan hojin*)	2 107	715
Foundation (*zajdan hojin*)	116	78
Cooperatives (*kyodo kumiai*)	3 513	347
By industry		
Agriculture, fisheries, forestry Mining, construction	1 524	341
Manufacturing, food, etc.	4 433	1 793
Wholesaling	6 383	514
Retailing	3 051	479

Source: JFTC (1996).

are industry associations. In 1999 small-business associations were permitted to become limited or joint-stock companies, 'thus allowing them to make uninterrupted use of their business achievements and facilities' (JSBRI, 2001, p. 81):

> Protective self-regulation differs from a cartel by being a continuous process nested in the trade association and connected to other, long-term industry activities, such as lobbying... Self-regulation includes also the self-enforcement of rules by the association. Having outlined the competitive behaviour for their industry, companies often negotiate business plans, or divide markets either by territory or product category. They may agree to refuse to deal with companies that are not association members, and monitor their members' behaviour by requesting trade statistics from each member. (Schaede, 2000, p. 8)

The prevalence of self-regulation by associations has had a remarkable consequence, established by official fiat: two professions, attorneys at law and certified public accountants, play only a minor role in regulation. Currently Japan has fewer than 20 000 lawyers (*bengoshi*), and the judiciary has some 2000 judges and 3000 prosecutors (Ramseyer and Nakazato, 1998).[3] As can be expected, the rates of litigation are low.[4] 'Accounting and audit is another crucial business service activity hamstrung by restrictive practices and regulation. Japan has only 14 000 certified public accountants' (OECD, 2003, p. 122).[5] However, in line with internationally accepted accounting standards, the recent introduction of new measures to improve financial transparency has increased the need for professional accountants, if not lawyers as well. For tax reporting the millions of small and medium-sized enterprises (SMEs) may turn to some 50 000 certified tax agents (*zeirishi*).[6] However for the numerous small firms situated outside the major cities, legal and accounting expertise is hard to find.

Cohesion between the public and private sectors is kept alive in every Japanese mind by the broadly respected mass media, and in particular by a handful of national daily newspapers with a circulation of millions. They promote middle-class values and tend to reinforce the popular support for production-oriented policies that promise to overcome economic uncertainty and result in social development. In true Japanese fashion, however, this is done in a cartel-like fashion: 'institutionalized rules and relationships [guide] press relations with their sources and with each other . . . [They] limit the types of news that get reported and the number and makeup of those who do the reporting' (Freeman, 2000, p. 160).

Competition and cooperation

The business environment offers a context of interdependence that determines the dynamics of competition and cooperation. Fruin (1992) has described the Japanese enterprise system as 'competitive strategies and co-operative structures': firms compete for market share and cooperate in self-regulation through associations and other groupings. The system embraces the 47 400 large business establishments (of which 12 300 are incorporated and employ 13.5 million full-time regular employees) and the six million SMEs (of which 1.6 million are incorporated and employ 22.7 million regular employees) (Table 3.4). In all industries 99 per cent of the incorporated firms are SMEs (JSBRI, 2003, supplementary tables 3.1 and 3.3).

Competitive ranking among Japanese firms has traditionally been on the basis of market share. The Japanese term for competition, *kyôsô*, was coined in the early years of industrialization and is usually combined with an adjective (*katô*). *Katô kyôsô* (excessive competition) is the common expression for open markets and is illustrated by an exceptional phenomenon: firms stampeding to enter a product line as soon as it emerges (Table 3.5). To this day, more often than not, this excess results in a clamour for regulation that bureaucrats are keen to heed; it also puts into motion the self-regulation

Table 3.4   Number of firms and workers in non-primary industries, 2001[1]

	Small and medium	Small-scale	Large	Total
Business establishments[2]				
Number	6 071 654 (99.2)	4 688 360 (76.6)	47 407 (0.6)	6 119 061 (100)
Workers	43 704 264 (79.9)	15 453 922 (28.3)	10 976 327 (20.1)	54 660 591 (100)
Enterprises[3]				
Number	4 689 609 (99.7)	4 102 169 (87.2)	13 430 (0.3)	4 703 039 (100)
Regular employees	25 600 984 (66.9)	7 236 406 (18.9)	12 676 116 (33.1)	38 277 100 (100)
Companies only				
Number	1 595 493 (99.2)	1 154 034 (71.8)	12 317 (0.8)	1 607 810 (100)
Regular employees	21 249 910 (62.9)	4 426 618 (13.1)	12 555 860 (37.1)	33 805 770 (100)

Notes:
1. Percentage of total in brackets.
2. After the amendments of the Small and Medium Enterprises Basic Law in 1999, small and medium-sized business establishments have been defined as having 300 or fewer workers (100 or fewer in wholesaling and services, and 50 or fewer in retailing and food services). Small-scale business establishments are defined as having 20 or fewer workers (five or fewer in wholesaling, retailing, food service and services).
3. SMEs are defined as sole proprietors and companies with 300 or fewer regular employees (100 or fewer in wholesaling and service industries, and 50 or fewer in the retailing and food service sectors) or with capital stock of 300 million yen or less (100 million yen or less in wholesaling and 50 million yen or less in retailing, food service and services). Small-scale enterprises are companies with 20 or fewer regular employees (five or fewer in the wholesaling, retailing and service sectors) and individual proprietorships with 20 or fewer employees (five or fewer in the wholesaling, retailing and service sectors).
Source: JSBRI (2003, supplementary tables 1 and 3).

Table 3.5   Estimated number of Japanese rivals in selected industries, 1987 and 1997

Industry	1997	1987	Industry	1997	1987
Air conditioners	20	13	Large computers	5	6
Audio equipment	14	25	Fork-lift trucks	15	8
Cars	9	9	Personal computers	9	16
Cameras	13	15	Robotics	190	280
Carbon fibres	13	7	Steel	8	5
Construction equipment	30	20	Synthetic fibres	10	8
Copiers	15	14	Truck and bus tyres	6	5

Source: Adapted from Porter *et al.* (2000, p. 111).

practices mentioned earlier. One consequence of the uncompetitive nature of large segments of the market, especially construction and distribution, has been an extraordinarily high cost of living. Japanese workers' high wages are offset by the high cost of necessities, including food, housing, gasoline, apparel, consumer-packaged goods and services in general' (Porter *et al.*, 2000, p. 6).

Another form of self-regulation prevails in firm organized into groups. Two major forms of grouping (*keiretsu*) are well known (Flath, 2000; Shimotani, 1997). First, the horizontal *keiretsu* is a bank-centred grouping. The Japan Fair Trade Commission regularly surveys the six major horizontal groupings. Its survey in 2001 covered a total of 180 companies (a few companies belong to more than one group):

> Led by both banks that provide financing and *sogo-shosha* (general trading companies) that co-ordinate business deals, the six major corporate groups are made up of leading companies representing key industries of Japan. They are said to be maintaining tight-knit relations through cross-share holdings and exchanges of executive officers within their groups. (JFTC, 2001, p. 1)

Second, the vertical *keiretsu* consists of related firms (*kankei-gaisha*) that orbit around a large company (often a member of a horizontal *keiretsu*) referred to as the parent company (*oya-gaisha*). Related firms, usually of smaller size, are subsidiaries and affiliates (Table 3.6), plus subcontractors, suppliers, distributor and so on. These firms meet regularly in supplier associations in order to ensure that information and technology flow not only from and to the parent company but also among themselves. According to Whittaker (1997, p. 98), 'Supplier association members might be in a strong position to get new orders, and may at times apply subtle pressure to discourage parents from placing orders with outside companies, but they do not bargain collectively.'

Many small firms are clustered in the industrial districts (*jiba sangyô*) that can found in most large cities, and in the vicinity of plants owned by major manufacturers. In these locations small establishments in the same branch of industry, such as textiles, machine tools, and printing, cooperate among themselves and are often members of production cooperatives (also formed

Table 3.6 Number of subsidiaries and affiliates, selected major companies, 1955–95

	1955	1960	1970	1981	1991	1995
Toyota Motors	26	16	28	68	200	335
Nissan Motors	20	24	86	209	590	700
Mitsui	28	37	88	488	723	742
Itochu	17	33	113	312	728	1 061
Matsushita	70	187	562	476	671	670
NEC	8	19	49	121	235	320

Note: In the case of subsidiaries the parent company's equity is over 50 per cent; for affiliates it is 20–50 per cent.
Sources: Shimotani (1997, p. 8); JFTC (1995).

to gain access to government loans or to reduce taxes). 'Small factories accept orders for which they do a limited number of processes and farm out the rest, or take on more work than they can cope with, and farm out the extra to other small factories' (Whittaker, 1997, p. 109). A similar policy supports retailing where shopping districts are established (JSBRI, 2002).

These agglomerations are actively encouraged by local governments and provide the human contact required to establish new small firms. A traditional illustration of this is the practice of *norenwake*, whereby 'a trusted employee parts with his employer and, with that same person's help, sets up his own firm in the same line of business' (SMEA, 1997, p. 126). In 2001, notwithstanding the steady decline in the start-up rate, this amounted to 16.1 per cent of the total (JSBRI, 2002, p. 53). However since the 1990s business start-ups have been hampered by the scarcity of risk capital, the rigid legal structure, lengthy administrative processes and a non-pliant labour market, not to mention the social stigma that is often attached to business failure (Callen and Ostry, 2003).

In general the business relationship between Japanese firms, large or small, tends to overrule the business contract (if one is used). Supervening events are interpreted in the broader context of the relationship rather than in the narrow context of the contract. Such contracts are written by employees, consist of a few pages, and repeat several times the mantra 'in good faith'. The final clause usually reads as follows: 'Should matters arise that are not provided for herein or should some doubt arise as to the matters provided herein, X.Co and Y.Co shall resolve the same upon consultation with each other, to be conducted in a co-operative manner and in good faith' (Yanagida *et al.*, 1994, p. 249). Flexibility in performance is taken for granted.

Opportunistic behaviour is restrained not so much by litigation as by social control in the context of interdependence. 'The more a business limits its deals to contracts with a universe of firms subscribing to a common code of honourable behaviour and subject to the sanctions of others within this universe, the less cost-effective an investment in contractual draughtsmanship becomes' (Ramseyer, 1986, p. 522). In particular the subcontracting relationship thrives on subjectivity. It manifests a preference for long-term, ongoing relationships. Placing or filling orders involves a limited number of firms, and transactions are regulated by mutual understanding rather than by formal contracts. Small subcontractors readily relinquish some control of their internal management in the hope of obtaining more business.

Not surprisingly, competition law and policy is viewed guardedly. Its watchdog, the Japan Fair Trade Commission (FTC), offers a typical example of Japanese-like enforcement: it generally favours administrative processes over criminal prosecution. Over the years steady but slow progress has been made in introducing more regulatory balance and autonomy, and a more user-friendly system (Visser 'T Hooft, 2002; Taylor, 2003).[7] 'Despite increased resources, the FTC's activities remain limited in scope' (OECD, 2004, p. 122).

People versus assets

The specific nature of Japan's industrialization (for a century the only Asian nation to industrialize, the island syndrome, ethnic homogeneity, educated labour force, shortage of natural resources, access to world markets and so on) has meant heavy dependence – not by choice but by necessity – on human resource development. Japan's survival through industrialization has been put squarely into the population's hands:

> Population growth has been a central feature of modern Japan. At the start of the modern period in 1868, Japan had approximately 30 million people; in 1945, the year of Japan's wartime defeat, it had 72 million people; by the end of 1990 the population had reached 123 million, and by about 2010 it is projected to peak at 130 million. (Traphagan and Knight, 2003, p. 10)

Production is sought; consumption follows. The production function is stressed not only in terms of physical rewards such as daily necessities, income and international trade, but also, if not more, in terms of intangible social benefits such as solidarity, social esteem and occupational satisfaction. Quality of life (*iki-gai*) comes from quality of work (*hataraki-gai*). A network of trust is appreciated and defended as the way to control risk, uncertainty and opportunism at the individual and collective levels. The business firm is the clue:

> Japan is the most extreme case of separation of ownership and control in any country in the world. Management controls; shareholding is dispersed. Japanese management has two fundamental, interrelated goals. The first is to maintain management independence and autonomy in a self-selected, self-perpetuating management system. The second is to ensure the independent survival of the firm in perpetuity. Bankruptcy and liquidation are the worst possible managerial outcome, selling the firm (usually termed merger) is the second worst. (Patrick, 2003, p. 329)

Even Japanese unions, in their postwar form of enterprise-wide organization and mostly active in large firms, soon found that their own survival depended on the survival of the company whose workers they organized, and they progressively came to share the views of management. Today their *raison d'être* is evolving more and more from collective bargaining to labour–management consultation. Meanwhile the rate of unionization is steadily declining.[8]

The social embeddedness (Aoki, 2001) of Japan's enterprise system hampers productivity growth in many ways, ranging from the owner-managers of smaller firms being unable to find a successor or promising young employees, to unyielding seniority in larger firms. Due to the inefficiency and shortcomings of the welfare system, labour-market participation by older people (aged 55 or over) remains high (Debroux, 2003; Yashiro, 2003).

Moreover there is reluctance among Japanese people to dissociate the firm's financing from the human factor. For example there is a lack of interest in dealing at arm's length and transparency as this would deny the subjectivity of human rapport. Financial difficulty is a traditional feature of SMEs and is grudgingly accepted as such. In general the smaller the enterprise, the greater the proportion of borrowing and the less the experience of or interest in using direct financing (Table 3.7).

The financial system is embodied in the so-called main-bank system, which 'owes a lot to regulations that cartelized and protected the banks and ensured that they would be the primary source of external funds for Japanese corporations' (Flath, 2000, p. 301). In the case of larger firms the main bank is commonly a significant stockholder and the leading supplier of loans; it handles the largest preportion of routine banking needs and may have seconded directors to the firms. It is also expected to play a leading role in the event of financial difficulties (Ballon and Matsuzaki, 2000). Smaller firms expect main-bank patronage from local financial institutions, which are heavily involved in indirect financing and anxious to play a part in regional development (Table 3.8).

Table 3.7   Financing structure by number of employees, 2000

	<20	*20–100*	*101–300*	*>300*
Short-term bank borrowings	18.2	18.3	19.2	10.1
Short-term other borrowings	10.4	4.1	2.4	1.4
Long-term bank borrowings	30.0	21.8	17.6	11.4
Long-term other borrowings	10.4	8.6	2.2	0.8
Bonds	0.0	3.0	2.2	8.9
Amount of notes receivable, discounted	0.1	0.7	1.1	0.4
Trade liabilities	3.7	9.3	16.7	13.7
Others	16.3	16.8	14.8	20.2
Equity	10.5	17.4	24.8	33.1

Source: Adapted from JSBRI (2002, p. 143).

Table 3.8   Type of main bank for SMEs by number of employees, 2001

	<20	*20–100*	*101–300*	*>300*
City bank	21.8	28.2	46.6	59.4
Long-term credit bank/trust bank	0.4	0.6	2.3	7.7
Regional/second-tier regional bank	51.0	52.3	40.3	25.2
Credit union/association	19.0	11.3	3.2	0.2
Government-affiliated financial institution	1.6	2.5	3.0	0.6
Agricultural cooperative, etc.	1.2	1.1	1.3	0.9
None	5.0	4.1	3.2	6.0

Source: Adapted from JSBRI (2002, p. 146).

Viability of the firm

Japanese firms ensure their viability by adopting the norms that prevail at the national level. Three key aspects of this will be reviewed: (1) Sole proprietorships and other unincorporated firms are the majority; less than half of the firms adopt the incorporated form. (2) For all business organizations, whatever their size, survival is rooted in their human resources while financing practices are largely handled vicariously. (3) Business functions are then distributed among stakeholders.

Organizational form

The Commercial Code of 1899 confirmed the joint stock company (*kabushiki kaisha*) as the vehicle for establishing larger enterprises. Smaller enterprises were regulated by the Civil Code of 1898; it was only in 1938 that a special law established the better suited limited liability company (*yûgen kaisha*). However, many small firms, even small shops – for reasons of prestige and easier access to financial institutions – opted for the joint stock form while conveniently overlooking most of the legal requirements (Oda, 1992). In 1990 the minimum capital required for incorporation was raised. For joint stock companies it rose from 300 000 yen to 10 million yen, and for limited liability companies it rose from 100 000 yen to one million yen. Soon afterwards limited liability companies started to outnumber joint stock companies. By 2000, 2.4 million enterprises had been incorporated: 1.0 million joint stock companies and 1.4 million limited liability companies (Table 3.9). According to tax law, a family corporation (*dôzoku kaisha*) is defined as one in which 50 per cent or more of the total outstanding shares are held by no more than three (legally qualified) shareholders, their relatives or other persons connected to them. In 1999, 94.6 per cent of all companies were

Table 3.9 Number of companies by capitalization, 1990 and 2000

Capitalization (yen)	Joint stock companies		Limited liability companies	
	1990	*2000*	*1990*	*2000*
5 million	413 383	–	670 638	–
5–10 million	241 390	–	231 277	1 302 027
10–100 million	373 088	1 023 662	68 242	95 630
100–1000 million	22 501	28 706	1 184	1 072
1 billion plus	4 129	6 772	53	56
Total	1 054 491	1 059 140	971 394	1 398 785
Percentage	50.7	41.7	46.7	55.1

Note: There are also about 35 000 limited and unlimited partnerships, plus 35 000 'others', such as mutual companies, cooperatives and medical institutions.
Source: National Tax Administration (1991, 2002).

family corporations, and 54 per cent of them were capitalized at over 10 billion yen (National Tax Administration, 2001).

In addition to companies there are over three million sole proprietorships and unincorporated business establishments. Many Japanese are interested in starting a business on their own, but this is still easier for men than for women. More than half of start-ups are by people in their twenties or thirties.[9] The know-how required for starting a business has usually been acquired through prior occupational experience and calls on prior contacts. However since the mid 1990s the exit rates have exceeded the entry rates for both incorporated and unincorporated business organizations (JSBRI, 2002).

Human resources and financing

The social dimension of the Japanese firm tends to dominate its economic dimension. This reflects the importance that a society ruled by interdependence gives to human relations (*ningen kankei*).[10] Ideally the firm attempts to combine people and assets less by adding people (whenever needed, drawn from and returned to the labour market) to assets than by increasing people's capacities by means of assets. The epitome of this social dimension are the full-time, regular employees (*sha-in*, company members) in larger firms, where their status is supported by hiring temporary and part-time employees. *Sha-in*, mostly male, have been the beneficiaries of the much talked about lifetime employment and its determination of careers.[11] In Japan they identify themselves not by what they do – their occupation – but by where they do whatever has to be done at the workplace:

> There is no differential treatment of white-collar and blue-collar [regular] workers. The same wage and promotion systems are applied across both groups and everybody can be promoted up the status ladder. The departmental offices are open plan and even the chief of department's desk is located in the communal office. Everybody eats in the same canteen. On the manufacturing front, all staff members and workers wear the same uniform suits and managers visit the shop floor quite frequently. (Kono and Clegg, 2001, p. 26)

A vital consequence of the primacy of human resources is that the flow of information is handled not so much in terms of processing but as long-term proprietary creation of practical knowledge. Hence the importance of tacit knowledge in human resource development and the building of organizational memory:

> Japanese companies ... recognize that the knowledge expressed in words and numbers represents only the tip of the iceberg. They view knowledge as being primarily 'tacit' – something not easily visible and expressible.

Tacit knowledge is highly personal and hard to formalize, making it difficult to communicate or to share with others. Subjective insights, intuitions, and hunches fall into this category of knowledge. Furthermore, tacit knowledge is deeply rooted in an individual's action and experience, as well as in the ideals, values, or emotions he or she embraces. (Nonaka and Takeuchi, 1995, p. 8)

The Japanese business organization is a learning organization built on the almost 100 per cent literacy of the labour force. Job training, and particularly on-the-job training, is the mainstay. It makes tacit knowledge a most valuable human asset, nurtured by the flow of work. The concern for product improvement is constant and starts on the shop floor. Suggestion systems, quality control circles and continuous improvement (*kaizen*) are common. Paramount in Japanese eyes is 'best effort' (*gambare*), which usually involves long working hours at a dire cost to private life.[12] Not uncommonly, larger firms entrust some new product development to smaller ones (JSBRI, 2002, p. 104), involving them in high-risk research and short-term R&D (Table 3.10). Intellectual property is better appreciated at the organizational level than at the individual level.

Unilateral, top-down flow of authority is shunned as it interferes with human relations (*ningen kankei*). What prevails is so-called decision making by consensus. However in the Japanese context consensus does not require conceptual agreement; it simply means that where standard procedures have been followed implementation is now in progress. Hence decision making is perceived not as a two-step process (decision plus implementation) but as a one-step process where necessity to come to a decision, imposes implementation. In other words the Japanese style of decision making focuses less on some action that would change reality (action on reality) and more on reaction imposed by the reality (reaction to reality). Neither process is foolproof: neglect of implementation haunts the former, and conformist behaviour

Table 3.10 Trends in the number of patent applications in manufacturing, 1996–2000 (fiscal year)

	1996	1997	1998	1999	2000
No. of employees					
0–50	95	70	84	81	87
51–100	334	345	376	415	463
101–300	1 325	1 360	1 503	1 458	1 939
301 or more	8 648	8 755	9 677	9 757	10 651
SMEs	1 754	1 775	1 963	1 954	2 489
Large enterprises	8 648	8 775	9 677	9 757	10 651
Total enterprises	10 402	10 550	11 640	11 711	13 140

Source: JSBRI (2002, p. 105).

and procrastination haunt the latter. However, decision making by consensus makes it difficult to pinpoint responsibility, especially if some mishap provokes criminal investigation.

The primacy of human resources and the need to increase their capacities by means of assets largely reduce financing to a vicarious role. This basic characteristic of the Japanese economy, long orchestrated by official fiat, has resulted in the conviction that no firm should be abandoned to its fate, for the alleged reason that none stands alone in either economic or social terms. It was only recently that large firms started in earnest to seek equity rather than debt. Smaller firms continue to rely on debt and trade credit; their plight is typical. A recent survey details the sources of funding for new businesses. With personal real estate – traditional collateral in Japan – and savings, additional funds are sought from personal contacts and financial institutions (Table 3.11).

During the economic crisis in the 1990s the annual number of bankruptcies of companies capitalized at less than 100 million yen increased from 14 000 to 19 000, more than half of which were due to the slump in sales and one third of which were in the construction industry (JSBRI, 2002, supplementary Table 3.11). Notwithstanding the restrictive bankruptcy system,[13] this was less than 2 per cent of the more than one million smaller companies. The recent increase in bankruptcies may also reflect the decrease in the number of suspensions of business transactions with banks: from about 40 000 in 1985 to 13 500 in 2002 (Statistics Bureau, 2003, p. 214).[14] Most feared by the smaller firm was the possibility that a chain reaction of failures would engulf it.

Table 3.11 Sources of funding when starting a small or medium-sized business, December 2001 (per cent)

Own capital	80.9
Funding from personal contacts	
Loan or investment by parents, siblings and relatives	27.9
Loan or investment by parent company or former employer	20.4
Investment by individuals and corporations supportive of business	15.6
Loan or investment by friends and acquaintances	14.1
Investment by customers or suppliers	2.7
Institutional finance	
Loan from private financial institution	27.9
Loan from government-affiliated financial institution	13.7
Local government funding programme	5.6
Loan and investment by venture capital or business venture foundation	0.7
Other	2.4

Note: Total exceeds 100 due to multiple answers.
Source: JSBRI (2002, p. 55).

Even more significant is the exit rate, particularly in the case of unincorporated firms. Some entrepreneurs realize at an early stage that they have failed, and close their operations in order to save their resources. Almost one in three newly established firms exits in its first year of existence for lack of business experience and/or appropriate size (JSBRI, 2002). In many older firms the owner-manager quits for lack of a successor. 'In the 1960s and 1970s, the exit rate was around 3–4%. At the beginning of the 1990s, the rate began to rise, and grew strongly between 1996 and 1999, when it reached 5.9%' (ibid., p. 121).

In Japanese eyes, any firm has a vital collective dimension: it stays alive by participating in a stakeholder network.

Stakeholder network

Each of the stakeholders in a network has a specific role, sometimes interchangeable, to participate and benefit in collective survival. Remarkable is the extent to which each and every relationship remains personal and embedded in the current circumstances (Ballon and Honda, 2000). The network is a network of people who can be conveniently sketched in pairs, each with a specific relational format and whose stake (benefit and contribution) varies according to the function in question (Figure 3.1).

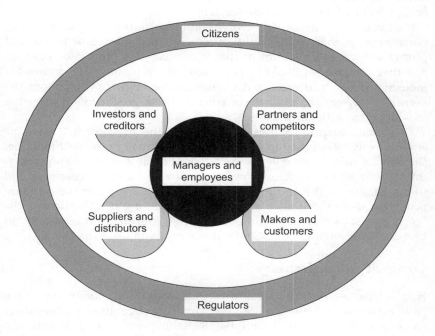

Figure 3.1 Japanese stakeholder network

First, in the historical, social and economic context of Japan's industrialization, one particular set of stakeholders – full-time managers and employees in the business organization – is at the heart of the network. Because of relational employment they represent core of the firm. They are more than employed by the firm, they *are* the firm (as is the in firms union where unions exist). Through them, the network radiates in countless relationships that irrigate the market.

Second, investors and creditors provide relational financing. The shareholder is only one of the stakeholders. In the case of larger firms the shareholders are largely institutions, which themselves are coalitions of stakeholder interests. In smaller firms the owner-manager is the key investor. Both large and small firms depend on individual and institutional creditors to stay in business.[15]

Third, partners and competitors participate in relational transactions. Competition is fierce, but cooperation in the form of associations and industrial groupings flourishes. Large firms have many relational contracts with suppliers and distributors. They raise them to the rank of partners while encouraging them to compete. Smaller firms participate actively in industrial agglomerations.

Fourth, makers and customers are bound by relational trading determining the uptake of the product or service, based on quality, cost and delivery. Consumption is the ultimate test of the product, the finicky user or consumer being a hallmark of the Japanese market.

Finally, at the national level citizens and regulators participate in a relational strategy that professes the overall interdependence of public and private sectors. An environment that is conducive to production-oriented activities – the wherewithal of Japan's survival – is promoted by an explicit industrial policy. Citizens are the common denominator throughout the network; they are the ultimate beneficiaries of a production system that provides them with affluence.

The social intensity of this network, and the need for a compatible environment make it highly vulnerable. Vested interests are mushrooming, shareholder value is being neglected, financial disclosure lacks transparency, the accommodation of idiosyncrasies and procrastination is common, and so on. Because of the people involved, all the weaknesses of the common people are at work, but their strengths are as well. In general solidarity – the 'We Japanese' syndrome – flourishes, while inexorably buffeted by an ever-changing environment. Continuity depends on relentless change.

Continuity through change

For the Japanese, organizational survival depends on the ability of the core participants to react effectively to ever-changing circumstances. Executives and employees in large firms and the owner-managers of and coworkers in small firms are facing a challenge they share with all stakeholders: to survive the current situation. Survival is then perceived less as an action to be decided but more as a reaction dictated by circumstantial necessity. Reacting to necessity is not limited to expected results; it concentrates on the process of survival affected by current risks. Continuity is maintained through change. Such change takes place in the environment (society and the economy) and in the firm in a circular fashion, not necessarily simultaneously but not independently: change that affects the environment affects the firm and *vice versa*. It is as much at work at the macro level as at the micro level.

At the macroeconomic level, direct foreign investment, both inward and outward, is a major manifestation of change imposed by globalization. For a long time targeted industries have been helped to adopt new technology and refine it in order to increase exports of progressively more advanced manufactured products. But today, for example, most Japanese car makers have opted to transfer some management control (at least 33.4 per cent of their equity) to foreign competitors; only two, Toyota and Honda, are still Japanese-run. In the finance industry, several troubled Japanese companies have been restructured after foreign takeover. Meanwhile investment in overseas production grows steadily, regardless of concern about the hollowing out of domestic industries. SMEs are more and more involved in this trend. One significant consequence has been a new attitude towards SMEs, as manifested by an increase in subsidies to small firms that invest in Asia (Solis, 2003):

> The old view, developed in the 1960s, was that small firms were less productive than large ones, and the policy objective was to improve their productivity through modernization and pursuit of economies of scale through mergers. The new view was that small firms were a source of dynamism, flexibility, mobility, and creativity, and therefore the [Ministry of Economy, Trade, and Industry] should develop a more positive stance towards them. (Elder, 2003, p. 177)

The traditional primacy of production is being challenged by the expansion of non-manufacturing industries. In 2002 almost 60 per cent of employees worked in the service and wholesale/retail/restaurant industries, more than one third on a non-regular basis (*Japan Labor Bulletin*, 2002a). Non-core operations are being outsourced. Services are multiplying, propelled by the needs of the ageing population. Daily necessities are being imported on a massive scale. Information technology is in everybody's hands (Cabinet Office, 2002).

At the microeconomic level, product innovation continues to be sought through process innovation and new perspectives are being opened. One example is robotics. Based on the wide dispersion of numerical control equipment, robots were rapidly introduced in the production process. But this was only the start, and today Japan is in the vanguard of the development of human-like robots.[16] Another example concerns industrial pollution: in response to sheer necessity created by population density, Japanese firms are at the forefront of pollution control:

> [D]ealing with global environmental issues requires step-by-step interactions between government and business... [T]he management of global environmental issues must shift from mere adherence to the regulations to the prevention of pollution, and further to the implementation of environmental strategies... It is most important for firms to make voluntary choices in their response to global environmental issues and to implement those choices. (Horiuchi and Nakamura, 2000, p. 380)[17]

It is not, however, products and operations that guarantee organizational survival; they must all be improved, if not replaced, and the faster the better. Continuity is the preserve of the human element in society and in the firm. Currently, large firms adopt two slogans. One is restructuring, with the firm reducing the number of middle-aged and senior white-collar regular employees. The other is the shift of employee evaluation and remuneration from emphasizing skill and seniority to focusing on individual performance. However the degree to which these practices are actually taking place is open to question (Morishima, 2000, 2003; Debroux, 2003). For example, in the case of the former the introduction of job sharing is still more a debate than a reality (Akira, 2002). As for SMEs, apart from being the beneficiaries of government financing and training schemes, they are largely being left to their own devices, within the context of interdependence.

For the Japanese, generations back and today, survival – their continuity as Japanese – is obviously not a choice but a challenge to be faced day by day. Active in large and small firms, of necessity they are adapting to changing circumstances, some contrived by themselves but most arising unbidden. Continuity at the practical level is not a state, it is a process to be maintained.

The specific dimensions of the Japanese approach to business, such as domestic competition, the regulatory system, organizational style, and employment and financing practices, are all components of a changing reality to which Japan's role in the world adds a ceaseless urge. 'Catching-up' industrialization and its sequels are vested in the Japanese as they go about their daily business. The challenge is not continuity *and* change, nor is it continuity *or* change; in Japanese eyes, the challenge is continuity *through* change. And changing continuity is a process essentially performed as a reaction to necessity.

Notes

1. This chapter focuses narrowly on domestic circumstances and stresses their local subjectivity. International implications and comparisons, notwithstanding their relevance, are purposely avoided (see for example Yamamura and Streeck, 2003; Dobson and Hook, 2003).

2. Usually public corporations cannot establish their own subsidiary companies, but their employee associations can. For example the Japan Highway Corporation had 63 quasisubsidiaries, which allowed it to contract work that was not subject to public tender (OECD, 2000). Public works in particular exhibit many deficiencies: jurisdictional overlapping, collusive bidding, preposterous maintenance costs and poor expenditure discipline because of local electoral considerations (OECD, 2003).

3. These three occupations are open after competition of a two-year programme at the (national) Legal Training and Research Institute. About 20 000 candidates apply each year, but less than 5 per cent pass. In addition there are approximately 100 000 other legal professionals, such as tax attorneys patent attorneys and judicial scriveners.

4. '[Rates of litigation] are low because disputants find it relatively easy to agree about the expected litigated outcome. They can agree, moreover, because judges provide relatively clear information about what will happen in court. Rather than spend their money suing, disputants settle out of court by the expected litigated outcome' (Ramseyer, 2000, p. 198).

5. Between 1949, when the Japanese Institute of Certified Public Accountants was established, and 2000 there were 250 000 applicants for the intermediate examination (junior CPA) and less that 10 per cent passed; for the final examination (senior CPA) 50 000 applied and about 30 per cent passed (Ballon and Matsuzaki, 2000).

6. Japanese law recognizes the *zeirishi* as specialists in tax matters but separate from lawyers and certified public accountants, who also are authorized to handle such matters. To qualify, tax agents must pass an examination supervised by a committee appointed by the Ministry of Finance.

7. The Antimonopoly Law was substantially revised in 1996. In 2003 the Fair Trade Commission, originally an external organ of the Ministry of Public Affairs, Post and Telecommunications, became an external organ of the Cabinet Office.

8. 'The estimated unionization rate in 2002 was a record low 20.2 percent, resulting in the biggest year-on-year decrease in the number of union members, 412 000' (*Japan Labor Bulletin*, 2003, p. 4). More than half of the drop was in firms with 1000 or more employees.

9. Interestingly, even today, 90 per cent of the Japanese employed in enterprises run by women are female. Such enterprises tend to be in relatively labour-intensive industries.

10. In order to restore proper *ningen kankei* after some mishap, apologies are expected from all involved; and perhaps even symbolic acceptance of responsibility, for example the resignation of the president whose company was involved in the mishap.

11. See the longitudinal survey of 36 careers in Ohtsu and Imanari (2002).

12. In 2001 the average regular employee took only 8.8 days of paid holidays, or 48.4 per cent of the available 18.1 days (*Japan Labor Bulletin*, 2002b).

13. 'The Japanese bankruptcy system consists of two liquidation procedures, liquidation (*Hasan*) and special liquidation (*Tokubetsu Seisan*), and three reorganization procedures, Corporate Restructuring (*Kaisha Kosei*), Private [Civil] Rehabilitation (*Minji Saisei*) and Corporate Reorganisation (*Kaisha Seiri*). Special Liquidation and Corporate Reorganisation are based on the commercial code, while the rest are based on their own special laws' (OECD, 2000, p. 103). A major breakthrough was the enactment in 2000 of the Civil Rehabilitation Law (JSBRI, 2002). Since 1952, detailed statistics on bankruptcy have been available from private organizations, but they report only cases of enterprises with total liabilities of at least 10 million yen.

14. 'The Japanese clearing system is characterized by a mandatory bank transaction suspension rule, under which banks must suspend their transactions with obligatory payers who dishonour bills or checks. The bank transaction rule was already in existence as early as 1887. Under the present system, all financial institutions participating in a particular clearing house shall halt all current account and lending transactions for two years with a person dishonouring bills or checks twice during a six-month period' (Federation of Bankers Associations, 1994, pp. 15–16).
15. 'Small portions of value-added are paid to shareholders – declaring low profit rates, treating dividends as fixed payments rather than residuals to be maximized, and supporting high rates of internal reinvestment' (Jackson, 2003, p. 266).
16. More than technology may be at stake. Asakura (2003, p. 18) makes an intriguing suggestion: 'There may be a religious basis for Japan's pre-eminence in the field of robotics. In a culture dominated by the belief that only God can create a human being, making a humanoid robot can pose problems. . . . In Japan, however, where the native religion sees *kami* (divine spirits) in all the myriad manifestations of nature, it follows naturally that a robot would have a spirit as well.'
17. ISO 14001 certification has become a standard feature of Japanese industry. 'The stated objective of ISO 14001 is continuously to monitor and improve firms' environmental management processes' (Horiuchi and Nakamura, 2000, p. 375).

References

Akira, W. (2002) 'Work-sharing in Japan', *Japan Labor Bulletin*, 41 (6), pp. 7–13.

Amyx, J. and P. Drysdale (eds) (2003) *Japanese Governance: Beyond Japan Inc.* (London: RoutledgeCurzon).

Aoki, M. (2001) *Toward a Comparative Institutional Analysis* (Cambridge, Mass.: MIT Press).

Aoki, M. and G. R. Saxonhouse (eds) (2000) *Finance, Governance, and Competitiveness in Japan* (Oxford: Oxford University Press).

Asakura, R. (2003) 'The Androids Are Coming', *Japan Echo*, 30 (4), pp. 13–18.

Ballon, R. J. and K. Honda (2000) *Stakeholding: The Japanese Bottom Line* (Tokyo: The Japan Times).

Ballon, R. J. and M. Matsuzaki (2000) *Japanese Business and Financial Disclosure* (Tokyo: Nikkei).

Cabinet Office (2002) *Annual Report on the Japanese Economy and Public Finance 2001–2002: No Gains Without Reforms II* (Tokyo: Printing Bureau).

Callen, T. and J. D. Ostry (eds) (2003) *Japan's Lost Decade: Policies for Economic Revival* (Washington, DC: International Monetary Fund).

Cargill, T. F. and N. Yoshino (2003) *Postal Savings and Fiscal Investment in Japan: The PSS and the FILP* (Oxford: Oxford University Press).

Colignon, R. A. and C. Usui (2003) *Amakudari: The Hidden Fabric of Japan's Economy* (Ithaca, NY: Cornell University Press).

Debroux, P. (2003) *Human Resource Management in Japan: Changes and Uncertainties. A New Human Resource Management Fitting to the Global Economy* (Aldershot: Ashgate).

DiMaggio, P. (ed.) (2001) *The Twenty-First Century Firm: Changing Economic Organization in International Perspective* (Princeton, NJ: Princeton University Press).

Dobson, H. and G. D. Hook (eds) (2003) *Japan and Britain in the Contemporary World: Responses to Common Issues* (London: RoutledgeCurzon).

Dore, R. (2000) *Stock Market Capitalism: Welfare Capitalism. Japan and Germany versus the Anglo-Saxons* (Oxford: Oxford University Press).

Elder, M. (2003) 'METI and Industrial Policy in Japan', in U. Schaede and W. Grimes (eds), *Japan's Managed Globalization: Adapting to the Twenty-first Century* (Armonk, NY: Sharpe), pp. 159–90.

Federation of Bankers Associations (1994) *Payment Systems in Japan* (Tokyo: Federation of Bankers Association).

Flath, D. (2000) 'Japan's Business Groups', in M. Nakamura (ed.), *The Japanese Business and Economic System: History and Prospects for the 21st Century* (New York: Palgrave), pp. 281–324.

Freeman, L. A. (2000) *Closing the Shop: Information Cartels and Japan's Mass Media* (Princeton, NJ: Princeton University Press).

Fruin, W. M. (1992) *The Japanese Enterprise System: Competitive Strategies and Co-operative Structures* (Oxford: Clarendon Press).

Haley, J. O. (1991) *Authority without Power: Law and the Japanese Paradox* (New York: Oxford University Press).

Horiuchi, K. and M. Nakamura (2000) 'Environmental Issues and Japanese Firms', in M. Nakamura (ed.), *The Japanese Business and Economic System: History and Prospects for the 21st Century* (New York: Palgrave), pp. 364–84.

Jackson, G. (2003) 'Corporate Governance in Germany and Japan: Liberalization Pressures and Responses during the 1990s', in K. Yamamura and W. Streeck (eds), *The End of Diversity? Prospects for German and Japanese Capitalism* (Ithaca, NY: Cornell University Press), pp. 261–305.

Japan Fair Trade Commission (JFTC) (1995) *Report on Economic Concentration* (Tokyo: Japan Fair Trade Commission).

Japan Fair Trade Commission (JFTC) (1996) *Annual Report on Competition Policy in Japan (January–December 1995)* (Tokyo: Japan Fair Trade Commission).

Japan Fair Trade Commission (JFTC) (2001) *State of Corporate Groups in Japan: The 7th Survey Report* (Tokyo: Japan Fair Trade Commission).

Japan Labor Bulletin (2002a) 'Number of Firms and Regular Employees Down; Number of Part-Time and Temporary Workers Up', *Japan Labor Bulletin*, 41 (10), p. 3.

Japan Labor Bulletin (2002b) 'Only Half of Granted Holidays Actually Taken', *Japan Labor Bulletin* 42 (1), p. 2.

Japan Labor Bulletin (2003) 'Unionization Rate Drops to Record Low 20.2 Percent', *Japan Labor Bulletin*, 42 (3), p. 4.

Japan Small Business Research Institute (JSBRI) (2002) *White Paper on Small and Medium Enterprises in Japan. The Age of the Local Entrepreneur – Birth, Growth and Revitalization of the National Economy* (Tokyo: JSBRI).

Japan Small Business Research Institute (JSBRI) (2003) *White Paper on Small and Medium Enterprises in Japan. The Road to Reorganization and the Creation of an Entrepreneurial Society* (Tokyo: JSBRI).

Jürgens, U. (2003) 'Transformation and Interaction: Japanese, U.S., and German Production Models in the 1990s', in K. Yamamura and W. Streeck (eds), *The End of Diversity? Prospects for German and Japanese Capitalism* (Ithaca, NY: Cornell University Press), pp. 212–39.

Katzenstein, P. J. (2003) 'Regional States: Japan and Asia, Germany in Europe', in K. Yamamura and W. Streeck (eds), *The End of Diversity? Prospects for German and Japanese Capitalism* (Ithaca, NY: Cornell University Press), pp. 89–114.

Kono, T. and S. Clegg (2001) *Trends in Japanese Management: Continuing Strengths, Current Problems and Changing Priorities* (New York: Palgrave).

Morikawa, H. (2001) *A History of Top Management in Japan: Managerial Enterprises and Family Enterprises* (Oxford: Oxford University Press).

Morishima, M. (2000) 'A Break with Tradition: Negotiating New Psychological Contracts in Japan', in D. M. Rousseau and R. Schalk (eds), *Psychological Contracts in Employment: Cross-National Perspectives* (Thousand Oaks, CA: Sage) pp. 141–57.

Morishima, M. (2003) 'Changes in White-Collar Employment from the Employee's Perspective', *Japan Labour Bulletin*, 42 (9), pp. 8–19.

Muramatsu, M., F. Iqbal and I. Kume (eds) (2001) *Local Government Development in Post-war Japan* (Oxford: Oxford University Press).

Nakamura, M. (ed.) (2000) *The Japanese Business and Economic System: History and Prospects for the 21ˢᵗ Century* (New York: Palgrave).

National Tax Administration (1991) *Hôjin Kigyô no Jittai Heisei 3-Nenbun* (Actual Situation of Juridical Entity Enterprises, Annual 1990) (Tokyo: National Tax Administration).

National Tax Administration (2002) *Hôjin Kigyô no Jittai Heisei 12-Nenbun* (Actual Situation of Juridical Entity Enterprises, Annual 2000) (Tokyo: National Tax Administration).

Noble, G. W. (2003) 'Reform and Continuity in Japan's *Shingikai* Deliberation Councils', in J. Amyx and P. Drysdale (eds), *Japanese Governance: Beyond Japan Inc.* (London: RoutledgeCurzon), pp. 113–33.

Nonaka, I. and H. Takeuchi (1995) *The Knowledge-Creating Company: How Japanese Companies Create the Dynamics of Innovation* (Oxford: Oxford University Press).

Oda, H. (1992) *Japanese Law* (London: Butterworths).

Odaka, K. and M. Sawai (eds) (1999) *Small Firms, Large Concerns: The Development of Small Business in Comparative Perspective* (Oxford: Oxford University Press).

OECD (2000) *OECD Economic Surveys 1999–2000: Japan* (Paris: OECD).

OECD (2003) *OECD Economic Surveys 2001–2002: Japan* (Paris: OECD).

OECD (2004) *OECD Economic Surveys 2003–2004: Japan* (Paris: OECD).

Ohtsu, M. and T. Imanari (2002) *Inside Japanese Business: A Narrative History, 1960–2000* (Armonk, NY: Sharpe).

Patrick, H. (ed.) (1976) *Japanese Industrialization and Its Social Consequences* (Berkeley, CA: University of California Press).

Patrick, H. (2003) 'Comment', in R. M. Stern (ed.), *Japan's Economic Recovery: Commercial Policy, Monetary Policy, and Corporate Governance* (Cheltenham: Edward Elgar), pp. 329–34.

Porter, M. E., H. Takeuchi and M. Sakakibara (2000) *Can Japan Compete?* (Cambridge, Mass.: Perseus).

Ramseyer, J. M. (1986) 'Lawyers, Foreign Lawyers, and Lawyers' Substitutes: The Market for Regulation in Japan', *Harvard International Law Journal*, 27.

Ramseyer, J. M. (2000) 'Rational Litigant Redux: A Response to Professor Hamada', in M. Aoki and G. R. Saxonhouse (eds), *Finance, Governance, and Competitiveness in Japan* (Oxford: Oxford University Press), pp. 195–8.

Ramseyer, J. M. and M. Nakazato (1998) *Japanese Law: An Economic Approach* (Chicago, Ill.: University of Chicago Press).

Rousseau, D. M. and R. Schalk (eds) (2000) *Psychological Contracts in Employment: Cross-National Perspectives* (Thousand Oaks, CA: Sage).

Schaede, U. (2000) *Co-operative Capitalism: Self-Regulation, Trade Associations, and the Antimonopoly Law in Japan* (Oxford: Oxford University Press).

Schaede, U. and W. Grimes (eds) (2003) *Japan's Managed Globalization: Adapting to the Twenty-first Century* (Armonk, NY: Sharpe).

Shiba, T. and M. Shimotani (eds) (1997) *Beyond the Firm: Business Groups in International and Historical Perspective* (Oxford: Oxford University Press).

Shimotani, M. (1997) 'The History and Structure of Business Groups in Japan', in T. Shiba and M. Shimotani (eds), *Beyond the Firm: Business Groups in International and Historical Perspective* (Oxford: Oxford University Press), pp. 5–28.

Small and Medium Enterprises Agency (SMEA) (1997) *White Paper on Small and Medium Enterprises* (Tokyo: Small and Medium Enterprises Agency).

Solis, M. (2003) 'Adjustment Through Globalization: The Role of State FDI Finance', in U. Schaede and W. Grimes (eds), *Japan's Managed Globalization: Adapting to the Twenty-first Century* (Armonk, NY: Sharpe), pp. 101–23.

Statistics Bureau (2003) *Japan Statistical Yearbook 2004* (Tokyo: Statistics Bureau).

Stern, R. M. (ed.) (2003) *Japan's Economic Recovery: Commercial Policy, Monetary Policy, and Corporate Governance* (Cheltenham: Edward Elgar).

Takeuchi, J. (1999) 'Historical Features of Japanese Small and Medium Enterprises: A Comparative Economic Approach', in K. Odaka and M. Sawai (eds), *Small Firms, Large Concerns: The Development of Small Business in Comparative Perspective* (Oxford: Oxford University Press), pp. 197–216.

Taylor, V. (2003) 'Re-regulating Japanese Transactions: The Competition Law Dimension', in J. Amyx and P. Drysdale (eds), *Japanese Governance: Beyond Japan Inc.* (London: RoutledgeCurzon), pp. 134–55.

Traphagan, J. W. and J. Knight (eds) (2003) *Demographic Change and the Family in Japan's Aging Society* (Albany, NY: State University of New York Press).

Upham, F. K. (1987) *Law and Social Change in Postwar Japan* (Cambridge, Mass.: Harvard University Press).

Visser 'T Hooft, W. M. (2002) *Japanese Contract and Anti-Trust Law: A Sociological and Comparative Study* (London: RoutledgeCurzon).

Westney, D. E. (2001) 'Japanese Enterprise Faces the Twenty-First Century', in P. DiMaggio (ed.), *The Twenty-First Century Firm: Changing Economic Organization in International Perspective* (Princeton, NJ: Princeton University Press), pp. 104–43.

Whittaker, D. H. (1997) *Small Firms in the Japanese Economy* (Cambridge: Cambridge University Press).

Yamamura, K. and W. Streeck (eds) (2003) *The End of Diversity? Prospects for German and Japanese Capitalism* (Ithaca, NY: Cornell University Press).

Yanagida, Y., D. H. Foote, E. S. Johnson Jr, J. M. Ramseyer and H. T. Scogin Jr (1994) *Law and Investment in Japan: Cases and Materials* (Cambridge, Mass.: Harvard University Press).

Yashiro, N. (2003) 'Demographic Changes and Their Implications for Japanese Household Savings', in R. M. Stern (ed.), *Japan's Economic Recovery: Commercial Policy, Monetary Policy, and Corporate Governance* (Cheltenham: Edward Elgar), pp. 375–95.

4
The Long Road to Globalization: In Search of a New Balance between Continuity and Change in Japanese MNCs

Schon L. Beechler

It was a Japanese company, Sony, that coined the phrase 'think global and act local' over 25 years ago when it joined the growing number of Japanese multinational corporations (MNCs) that were advancing overseas during the 1970s. While Japanese FDI has increased dramatically since that time and much thought, time and money has been poured into the globalization efforts of Japanese firms, it is questionable how many of them have really accomplished that objective.

In 2002, when meeting with a group of top Japanese international human resource executives to discuss the globalization of Japanese firms, I was struck that we were having nearly the same conversation as I had had when interviewing similar managers in a research study in 1987. Very little had changed regarding the challenges of 'going global.' This experience was repeated recently when I met with a Japanese senior line manager at a major MNC in Tokyo. The following quotation from that interview sums up the situation quite succinctly: 'We've had international operations in this company for over 100 years and we have operations in over a hundred countries. However, we are still not globalized. I need to figure out how to do that in the next five to ten years or we will be dead.'

This chapter first looks at the evolution of Japanese MNCs over the past quarter-century and analyzes the trends in their globalization. Then it details the barriers to globalization and offers a series of recommendations, balancing the need for continuity and change that Japanese MNCs should consider if they want to achieve the long-elusive goal of globalization.

Globalization has changed the boundaries, competitive landscape and organizational structure and strategy of firms operating in the world market (Porter, 1986; Bartlett and Ghoshal, 1989, 2000; Prahalad and Hamel, 1994). Whether large or small, all companies face the problem of how to compete in a world of global competition.

The way in which multinational firms handle the complex requirements stemming from global competition has become a major topic in the field of international and strategic management (Prahalad, 1991; Kim and Mauborgne, 1996). Based on the pioneering work on international strategy by Doz (1986) and Bartlett and Ghoshal (1989, 1998), it is now accepted that the winners will be those firms that can simultaneously integrate their global operations and respond to local conditions, thus balancing the complementary and contradictory imperatives of organizational integration and differentiation (Lawrence and Lorsch 1967; Evans *et al.*, 2002). The organizational capability to achieve this balance is essential to implementing globally competitive strategies, but this capability is not easily developed or sustained by MNCs (Bartlett and Ghoshal, 1989; Pucik *et al.*, 1992; Evans, 1993; Evans *et al.*, 2002).

Although Japanese companies made rapid progress during the 1980s and 1990s, most observers agree that they have had a particularly difficult time making the transition to 'global' and that they still lag far behind their Western counterparts in terms of sophisticated international management (Kobayashi, 1982, 1985; Trevor, 1983; Tachiki, 1991; Campbell and Holden, 1993; Pucik, 1999). Anecdotal evidence and research findings point to the fact that, while there are some exceptions, Japanese MNCs find it difficult to think and act globally.

Globalization of Japanese firms

Foreign direct investment

The word 'global' means different things to different people. One of the earliest conceptualizations focused on the geographic scope and scale of operations of a firm as a measure of globalization. Foreign direct investment (FDI) figures show that Japanese firms began to go global in the late 1970s, and that from 1979 the world witnessed the arrival of a global economic superpower, with Japanese outward FDI between 1979 and 1989 totalling US$67.5 billion (OECD, 1991).

During the late 1970s and early 1980s FDI was driven primarily by the search for cheap labour in the highly competitive electronics and automotive industries. In fact many argue that the competitive advantage of Japanese corporations comes from their operational efficiency and ability to transfer that competitive advantage overseas (Nakamura, 2000; Itagaki, 2002). For example a number of studies of Japanese car manufacturers in North America have found that Japanese transplants outperform their American counterparts in terms of labour productivity and product quality. Similar results have been obtained by Itagaki (2002), who found strong performance in operational efficiency by Japanese electronics and car plants in East Asia.

The initial rush of Japanese firms overseas was followed in the mid 1980s and early 1990s by investments in developed, higher-wage countries in response to local content and trade barrier restrictions on foreign-manufactured goods.

During the 1980s the United States became the major destination of Japanese manufacturing investment abroad, and in the latter part of the decade Western Europe began to experience rapid increases in Japanese FDI. Expansion in FDI was driven by falling tariff barriers, convergence of per capita GNP among a growing number of highly industrialized countries and rising consumption levels in the developing countries, as well as technological changes that lowered the cost of cross-border transportation and communication (Bartlett, 1986).

In the third stage of Japanese FDI, beginning in the mid 1990s, Japanese firms set up overseas headquarters to take advantage of local incentives – in countries such as Singapore. They also established R&D facilities to tap into scientific and technological innovations, plus design centres to understand and meet the demands of non-Japanese consumers, and shifted from import-substitution production to production for the global market (Kono and Clegg, 2001).

While outward FDI from Japan slowed with the economic recession of the late 1990s, it subsequently increased and in the first half of fiscal year 2003 FDI rose 24.5 per cent above the 2002 level to $21 266 million (JETRO, 2004). Most of this increase occurred in the manufacturing sector, where FDI rose by 43.9 per cent in the first half of 2003. Non-manufacturing FDI also rose by 11.9 per cent, but in the financial sector it fell by 26.1 per cent (ibid.), reflecting the turmoil in the Japanese financial industry.

Structures and processes

FDI is not the only measure of globalization. In addition to the size and location of operations around the world, 'being global' can also relate to a way of doing business, a complex set of processes and structures that enable organizations to respond locally and integrate globally.

This approach was captured well by the Harvard Multinational Enterprise Project, which was initiated in 1965 by Ray Vernon, who investigated the question of how to organize effectively for international growth. Drawing on a database of 182 American multinationals, the researchers found that during the early stage of expanding abroad, when foreign sales were of limited volume and scope, an export department tacked onto the domestic sales division was sufficient to handle overseas business. As sales grew the export department became an international division within a divisional structure (which was replacing the functional organization to become the predominant organizational form), and when this international division reached a certain size it triggered a transformation of the company into a multinational structure. Firms selling a wide range of products abroad generally chose a structure with world-wide product divisions, while those with few products but operating in many countries typically organized themselves around geographic area divisions (Stopford and Wells, 1972).

The difficult question was how to organize when the firm had many different products that were sold in many different geographic markets. To deal with this complexity a number of American firms implemented matrix organizations that involved both product and geographic reporting lines, as advocated by the Harvard researchers. However in practice, companies found matrix structures difficult to manage (Evans *et al.*, 2002).

Yoshihara's (1979) subsequent study allowed for explicit comparison between the Harvard study's American MNCs and Japanese firms. Yoshihara found that of the 500 largest Japanese industrial firms in 1975, only 33 qualified as MNCs and 48 were 'export-centred', a new category devised by Yoshihara to explain a pattern found in the Japanese companies in his sample (Westney, 1999). Japanese MNCs also followed a different FDI pattern from their American counterparts. Japanese manufacturing operations were concentrated in developing countries, especially in Asia, and much of the FDI in manufacturing was made by small and medium-sized firms, rather than being dominated by large MNCs, as was the case with American FDI. In addition, other researchers have found that Japanese firms tended to invest in sales and service subsidiaries in the developed countries of North America and Western Europe, with finished products being exported from Japan (Westney, 1999).

In their research on American MNCs, Stopford and Wells (1972) found that firms with a high degree of product diversification and extensive international activities tended to adopt a matrix structure, and many analysts came to view the matrix as the most advanced form of organization for MNCs. However no Japanese firm had adopted a matrix structure by the late 1970s and Yoshihara found only one with a global product division structure; in all the rest of the firms in his study international activities were still being administered by the international division (Yoshihara, quoted in Westney, 1999).

Today Japanese MNCs tend to use one of three structures to manage and control their overseas operations. One is a functional structure, where the production department controls the MNC's production plants around the world, the marketing department controls local sales offices and so on. This type of structure is common in MNCs that produce cars, tyres and textiles (Kono and Clegg, 2001). In the second type of structure the product division controls the company's overseas production and sales companies, as well as production and sales in Japan. Diversified companies such as Kobe Steel, Teijin and Komatsu use this approach. The third and most common structure is the matrix, where the international department controls area divisions, which in turn control production and sales. Product divisions at the head office also control production and sales activities abroad (ibid.).

However for Japanese MNCs and those from other countries it has become increasingly clear that the challenges of global management essentially relate not to structure or strategy but to management philosophy and approach. The matrix, as Bartlett and Ghoshal (1990), the two leading strategy scholars, have noted, is not a structure but a 'frame of mind', nurtured by careful human resource management.

Global mindset

Conceptualizing globalization as a frame of mind, rather than relying only on measures of FDI or organizational structures and processes, is a current trend that harks back to the pioneering work of Perlmutter and Heenan (Perlmutter, 1969; Perlmutter and Heenan, 1979).

Perlmutter distinguished three primary attitudes or states of mind towards managing a multinational enterprise, which he labelled ethnocentric (home-country orientation), polycentric (host-country orientation) and geocentric (world orientation). These orientations, Perlmutter proposed, influence and shape diverse aspects of the MNC, including structural design, strategy, resource allocation and management processes. An ethnocentric orientation is expressed in terms of headquarters and a sense of national superiority: 'We, the home nationals of X company, are superior to, more trustworthy and more reliable than any foreigner in headquarters or subsidiaries' (Perlmutter, 1969, p. 11). A polycentric orientation takes the form of a respectful disengagement from other cultures: 'Let the Romans do it their way. We really don't understand what is going on there, but we have to have confidence in them. As long as they earn a profit, we want to remain in the background' (ibid., p. 13).

Managers with a global mindset, or those with a geocentric orientation in Perlmutter's terms, have a universalistic attitude and downplay the significance of nationality and cultural differences: 'Within legal and political limits, they seek the best men, regardless of nationality, to solve the company's problems anywhere in the world' (ibid.)

If we view globalization as a multidimensional construct comprising geographic scale and scope, structures, processes and mindset, then Japanese MNCs are global in terms of their international investment strategies and structures but many of their processes and mindsets are still far from global. Whether this is because they did not begin to internationalize until the 1970s, much later than their European and American counterparts, or because of inherent, unique characteristics, there are a number of other factors that continue to present formidable barriers to the globalization of Japanese MNCs. It is to these barriers that we now turn.

Barriers to globalization

While strategy and structure are important organizational levers of globalization and are required for international success, on their own they are not enough. A key factor in international success is MNCs' ability to develop and manage a human organization and to replace the relatively inflexible structural solutions often adopted in the past (Kanter, 1991; Ashkenas *et al.*, 1995; Bartlett and Ghoshal, 1998). A number of aspects of Japanese management have proven pivotal to the success of Japanese MNCs overseas. For example, because of their focus on high-quality products, Japanese manufacturers invested heavily in production equipment and in training local employees. They also paid careful attention to staffing and socialization, participative decision making and egalitarianism.

However other aspects of Japanese management have proved to be an Achilles heel for firms operating abroad (Bartlett and Yoshihara, 1988; Kono and Clegg, 2001). For example most Japanese MNCs have had problems with HQ-dominated control systems and with decision making being dominated by Japanese nationals, be they stationed at the HQ or at a local affiliate (Trevor 1983; Bartlett and Yoshihara, 1988; Harzing, 1999; Pucik, 1999; Kono and Clegg, 2001). Japanese MNCs are also characterized by Japanese-centric staffing policies and practices and the presence of a 'rice paper ceiling' (Bartlett and Yoshihara, 1988; Boyacigiller, 1990a, 1990b; Kopp, 1994, 1999; Pucik, 1999; Kono and Clegg, 2001).

National origin of management

One of the most ubiquitous features of Japanese MNCs is the relatively low percentage of non-Japanese nationals at the executive level. Despite repeated calls from both Japanese and foreigners, almost all positions at the HQ and on boards of directors continue to be filled by Japanese nationals.

Japanese dominance of the top positions influences companies' strategies, structures and processes, and it has short-term and long-term implications for their success. While a Japanese-dominated top management team can help to ensure the smooth flow of information throughout the global network, as well as enhance the control of operations by employees who share a common culture, language, values and history with the company, it can hinder the establishment of the mindset needed to pursue a global strategy effectively (Levy, 2003) and manage a global company in today's competitive environment. Executives in the majority of Japanese MNCs have had little or no experience outside Japan and many cannot communicate in any language other than Japanese.

In overseas operations as well, staffing policies tend to be Japanese-centric. Indeed, almost since Japanese companies first ventured overseas, academics, government officials and writers around the world have criticized them for the large number of Japanese expatriates they employ in their overseas affiliates (Yoshino, 1976). Studies of the overseas subsidiaries of Japanese firms have consistently shown that Japanese firms employ a larger number of expatriates than do their Western counterparts. For example Sim (1977) examined a matched sample of 20 Japanese, American and British subsidiaries in Malaysia and found that in Japanese subsidiaries expatriates dominated technical and production positions, and to a lesser extent financial and administrative positions. In contrast, in the British and American subsidiaries expatriates generally held only the chief executive and marketing director positions. The average number of expatriates in the Japanese firms was 5.5 per firm, compared with 2.57 and 2.86 in the British and American firms respectively.

A few years later Negandhi and his colleagues reached similar conclusions from two studies of Southeast Asian and Latin American subsidiaries. They found that in Japanese firms expatriates held almost all the senior management positions (Negandhi *et al.*, 1985) and that expatriate managers were more numerous in Japanese firms than in Western ones (Negandhi and Baliga, 1981b). In one-half of the firms included in their 1981 study, Japanese nationals completely dominated strategic functions such as finance, corporate planning, marketing and, to a lesser degree, production planning.

In the UK, Takamiya and Thurley (1985) found that just over 25 per cent of the personnel in Japanese enterprises were expatriates, although the ratio of expatriates to locals varied between and within sectors. They concluded that power and authority were not being shifted from Japanese expatriates to local managers.

Studies in the United States also revealed an expatriate-intensive staffing pattern. For example Johnson (1977), in a study of 22 US subsidiaries of Japanese firms, found that a Japanese expatriate typically held the top position, two held middle management positions (generally accounting and industrial engineering) and a few worked as technicians. Robinson's (1985) study of 45 Japanese firms in the United States found an average of 40.5 Japanese expatriates in each subsidiary, while Pucik *et al.* (1989) found an average of 26 expatriates per affiliate.

This expatriate-intensive staffing policy was criticized by many as a conscious ploy to keep authority and power in Japanese hands and out of the reach of local employees. However other writers argued that compared with Western firms, Japanese firms were still relatively new to the international scene and lacked experience. These authors rightly noted that when American and European MNCs first went overseas they too employed a large number of expatriates (see for example Franko, 1973). It was argued that as Japanese companies gained greater experience of abroad operating they would gradually reduce the number of expatriates and 'localize' their overseas operations.

However little changed during the 1990s. In a longitudinal study of US affiliates of Japanese MNCs in the period 1974–90, Beechler and Iaquinto (1994) found that the proportion of expatriates to total subsidiary employees did not decrease over time. Similarly a survey of several hundred Japanese MNCs in the early 1990s found that 78 per cent of chief executives or presidents of overseas operations were Japanese expatriates and that department head positions were often held by Japanese nationals (Yoshihara, 1995). Comparing European, US and Japanese MNCs in Indonesia, Shiraki (1995) reported that while 63.6 per cent of the European and US MNCs had put local university graduates in top management positions, only 25 per cent of Japanese firms had done so (cited in Kopp, 1999).

Kopp (ibid.), in a comparative study of 81 European, US and Japanese overseas firms, found that 74 per cent of top management positions in Japanese firms, 48 per cent in European firms and 31 per cent in US firms were staffed by home country nationals. At the managerial level, US MNCs filled 88 per cent of positions with local nationals, European firms 82 per cent and Japanese firms 48 per cent. The Japanese MNCs were also most likely to receive complaints from local employees about the lack of career advancement opportunities – 21 per cent reported complaints versus 4 per cent of the European and 8 per cent of the US firms (ibid., p. 110).

It does not appear likely that this pattern will change in the near future. In a study of 100 Japanese firms in Indonesia, Nakamura (2000) found that neither the duration of the overseas operation nor company size had a significant bearing on the localization of directorships and many firms had no policy to localize top management. Indeed 45 per cent of the firms surveyed did not intend to localize top management, particularly in the case of companies where stock ownership was concentrated in Japanese hands.

Centralization of decision making

The second major barrier to globalization is Japanese firms' approach to decision making and control. When Japanese firms first ventured overseas, researchers characterized parent-company control in Japanese MNCs as 'loose', in contrast with 'close' in US firms. In addition Japanese firms were described as 'disjointed, with a local market orientation', while US firms were more globally integrated (Westney, 1999, p. 15). However this pattern changed during the mid 1980s as Japanese MNCs increasingly adopted a global strategy that functioned through tight parent-company control of decision making.

Focused research on decision making in the overseas affiliates of Japanese MNCs began with studies by Negandhi and his colleagues, who conducted a number of large-scale comparative studies during the 1970s and 1980s on management practices in US, European and Japanese MNCs (see for example Negandhi and Baliga, 1979, 1981; Negandhi *et al.*, 1985; Negandhi *et al.*, 1985). They found that compared with their US and European counterparts, Japanese firms exerted tighter control over their Southeast Asian and South American subsidiaries by placing expatriate managers in almost all senior management positions, by organizing visits from strategic personnel from headquarters, by requiring that regular reports be sent to headquarters, and by ensuring frequent communication between headquarters and the local subsidiaries (Negandhi and Baliga, 1981a, 1981b; Negandhi *et al.*, 1985).

These findings were supported by other researchers. For example in a study of 32 Japanese subsidiaries in the Philippines by the Japan Overseas Enterprises Association (Nihon Zaigai Kigyo Kyokai, 1987) and one conducted by Ichimura and Yoshihara (1985) in eight Asian countries, the researchers found a high degree of centralization and low levels of trust and training for local employees.

In the United States, Yoshida (1987) found that in 10 of the 15 Japanese subsidiaries in his sample there was joint management by corporate headquarters and the subsidiaries. In cases where there was subsidiary autonomy, Japanese personnel were usually in charge and had operating responsibility. Yoshida also found that the larger firms were generally more centralized than the smaller ones. In a later study Kriger and Solomon (1992) found in their comparative study of 31 affiliates of 5 Japanese and 11 American MNCs that Japanese companies delegated more decision-making authority to the boards of their affiliates than did US MNCs. However they did not examine whether it was expatriates or locals who were actually making the decisions.

Findings from empirical studies in Europe parallel those conducted in the United States and Asia. For example Takamiya and Thurley (1985) found that in five Japanese firms operating in the UK in 1976, decision making was concentrated in the hands of Japanese expatriates, although satisfaction was highest in those firms where British managers were involved in taking personnel management decisions. Meanwhile Trevor (1983) identified the presence of many Japanese expatriates, tight control by headquarters and constant communication by telex and telephone between UK subsidiaries and headquarters.

Dunning (1986) examined the staffing and decision-making structures of US and Japanese manufacturing affiliates in the United Kingdom, and found that Japanese operations in the 1980s were comparable to US operations in the 1950s. Overall, however, the Japanese exercised much closer control over the general managerial philosophy and style of the subsidiary than their US counterparts had in the 1950s. He also found that Japanese influence and control over decision making was greater than that exerted by Americans.

Kobayashi (1985) sampled 89 Japanese MNCs, all with overseas investments of more than one billion yen and with at least five management centres abroad, and compared them with nine large multinationals from the United States, West Germany, the United Kingdom and France. Contrary to the studies reviewed above, Kobayashi found that the headquarters of the US and European firms were more involved in management, planning and decision making in their overseas subunits than were their Japanese counterparts.

With regard to where decisions were taken and by whom, Beechler *et al.* (1995) found that in Japanese affiliates in the United States and Europe, 45 per cent of decisions were made by Japanese, 20 per cent were made by locals and 35 per cent were made jointly by locals and Japanese. In terms of location, 22 per cent of decisions were made in Japan, 29 per cent were made in both Japan and the most country, and 48 per cent were made in the host country. The researchers also asked executives where they thought that affiliate decisions should be made. Forty-nine per cent believed that most decisions should be made jointly, 21 per cent said that decisions should be made by Japanese alone and 30 per cent thought they should be made by host-country nationals alone. While host-country executives, not surprisingly, would have liked more decisions to be delegated to local managers, they did not advocate dramatic localization or decentralization of decision making. Joint consultation with the Japanese parent firm and shared decision making between Japanese expatriates and local managers was clearly the preferred form of decision making.

Global orientation and mindset

The importance of having a global mindset has been recognized in the international business literature since the seminal work of Perlmutter (1969) and Perlmutter and Heenan (1979). However little was done to examine the mindset of MNCs until Kobrin (1994) reintroduced the idea of geocentric mindset and its importance in international management. In a study of 68 Fortune 500 firms, Kobrin asked respondents for their judgements, attitudes and expectations of policies and managerial mindsets in their firms. He examined how aspects of a geocentric managerial mindset are reflected in international human resource management policy; or more specifically, the impact of nationality on the selection and career advancement of managers.

A large part of Kobrin's geocentrism scale focuses on the perceived opportunities available to all nationals in MNCs. The opportunity for local nationals to advance has often been seen as problematic, and indeed, as noted earlier, there has been much discussion of the impact of the 'rice paper ceiling' in Japanese firms (Boyacigiller, 1990a, 1990b; Kopp, 1999; Kono and Clegg, 2001).

In the only empirical study of global mindsets in Japanese MNCs, Beechler *et al.* (2004a) analyzed the responses of 521 randomly selected Japanese and non-Japanese employees in 10 organizational units of two highly diversified, high-technology MNCs headquartered in Japan. This research, which was part of a larger study of MNCs from the United States, Europe, South America and Australasia, focused on the global orientation of the top management team, boundary-spanning structures and processes, the geocentric human resource system and the influence of these factors on individual employees' commitment to the MNC. They predicted that a geocentric mindset, operationalized as the perceived opportunities available to employees during their organizational careers (following Kobrin, 1994), would positively influence their degree of commitment.

Beechler *et al.* also looked at global orientation, defined as a characteristic of MNC top management that encompasses an orientation towards the external environment (especially global markets), the ability to view the world from a broad perspective and to integrate geographically distant operations and diverse trends and opportunities in the global environment, the ability of key decision makers in the organization to interact with employees and other key stakeholders from many countries, and to manage culturally diverse interorganizational relationships with customers, suppliers and regulators.

In organizations where managers have a global perspective, employees are more likely to perceive a shared mission that transcends national and subunit boundaries. A global orientation, by acting as a unifying mechanism at the top of the organization, helps to focus employees on a set of common goals and thereby increase their commitment to the firm (Beechler *et al.*, 2004a).

Boundary-spanning structures and processes must also exist if a global orientation is to influence the actual decisions made in MNCs. These structures and processes include global teams, global job responsibilities and global communication networks. Boundary-spanning structures and processes enable multinational firms to cut across functional, geographic and external boundaries and to move ideas, information, decisions, talent and resources to where they are needed most (Ashkenas *et al.*, 1995).

Such structures and processes allow employees to engage with various constituencies both inside (top management, affiliate managers, peers in other functional areas, peers in other affiliates) and outside the organization (customers, unions, suppliers). Because organizational commitment depends on the extent to which individuals internalize or adopt characteristics or perspectives of the organization (O'Reilly and Chatman, 1986), the heightened interaction across boundaries should enhance employers' commitment by broadening their perspective of the total organization.

Indeed Beechler *et al.* (2004a) have found that greater geocentrism does increase employees' commitment to their organization, as does their perception that the top management team is globally oriented and promotes boundary spanning. The more that employees' perceive that their firm is open to promoting employees regardless of their nationality, that the top management team is globally oriented and that cross-border boundary-spanning mechanism exist, the greater their commitment.

We shall return to these research results and their implications in the following section, where we make a number of recommendations for the future.

Recommendations for a new balance between continuity and change

The barriers to globalization in Japanese MNCs are of interest not just because they are different from those in the West (although many writers have focused on this) but also because of their impact on the performance and ultimate success of Japanese firms. There is considerable evidence that Japanese firms' inability to globalize is damaging them in a number of ways.

For example Japanese FDI is often less profitable than US investments, a little less than half in some cases (Itagaki, 2002). Moreover the profitability of some Japanese investments in the United States is less than that of European investments, particularly those made by British and Dutch firms (ibid.)

Part of the reason for this is the interdependence between the production systems and organizational features of Japanese firms, such as long-term commitment, job flexibility, participatory management, a stable personnel management system and harmonious labour relations (ibid.; Kono and Clegg, 2001), which are difficult to duplicate outside Japan. However, because the Japanese have had so much success at home with these deeply intertwined systems they are understandably reluctant to change them and lack alternative models from which to draw.

The impact of this resistance to change is reflected in evidence that in both the United States and Europe the degree of international experience of an MNC is not a predictor of its success. Neither the age of the affiliate nor the extent of the parent company's experience operating abroad have an impact on the affiliate's performance (Beechler *et al.*, 1995, 2004b).

The prevailing management practices and the mindset of Japanese decision makers continue to erect formidable barriers to globalization and overseas success. For example the failure to globalize has led to high turnover rates among the most highly qualified staff (see for example Pucik *et al.*, 1989; Beechler *et al.*, 1995). Outside Japan, Japanese MNCs are not attracting 'the best and the brightest'.

As discussed earlier, two critical barriers that are limiting local talent in Japanese MNCs are the preponderance of Japanese nationals in key positions and the exclusion of local nationals from decision making. If some writers are correct in saying that social capital will determine the success or failure of global firms in the future (see for example Nahapiet and Ghoshal, 1998; Westney, 1999; Kostova and Roth, 2003), these practices will continue to undermine Japanese MNCs' ability to compete. As Westney (1999) observes, the Japanese decision-making processes – which involve intense, informal, horizontal communications among middle-level managers – must be stretched across borders and require the participation of managers outside Japan who are not only fluent in the Japanese language but also fully understand the norms and key assumptions of the company's communication and decision-making network. However, 'for most Japanese companies, the key actors in this network have continued to be Japanese expatriate managers in the offshore subsidiaries, rather than the "geocentric" mix of home country, local, and third-country managers that is the ideal of the transnational model' (ibid., p. 23).

Pucik (1999, p. 186), writing about human resource management practices in Japanese firms, puts the matter bluntly: 'The fundamental obstacle to effective globalization is simple: the continuous expatriate orientation of JMNCs [Japanese MNCs]. The HRM practices will not likely become global as long as the top management infrastructure of Japanese firms world-wide is Japanese'. Interestingly, over 25 years ago Yoshino (1976, p. 178) stressed that 'In order to undertake major expansion internationally, the Japanese must bring about basic changes in their management system – changes that will not be easy to achieve. And in the process, they may well sacrifice those elements that have made their system so effective internally.'

The path to globalization is clear: to achieve the high levels of integration and local responsiveness that are needed for successful international operations, Japanese MNCs must leverage the human side of their organizations and make full use of the talent available to them world-wide.

Management localization, therefore, is not the solution, despite claims to that effect and consequent attempts by a number of Japanese MNCs to decentralize decision making. Key advantages that Japanese MNCs have over local firms is their long-term vision, strict adherence to quality, *kaizen*, and respect for people (Kono and Clegg, 2001). Moreover past experience has shown that localization efforts can fail. During the 1980s the aggressive localization strategies of many US multinationals created fragmented groups of 'pygmy kingdoms' rather than a well co-ordinated global network of interdependent units (Beechler *et al.*, 1995). A number of Japanese MNCs suffered disastrous consequences when they delegated the making of important decisions to (often unqualified) local managers (personal interviews conducted by the author in 2001; see also Kono and Clegg, 2001). The poor business results that followed reinforced the original perception that Japanese control over subsidiary operations was essential to success and prompted the return of decision making to trusted Japanese.

At the same time, the high proportion of Japanese expatriates in overseas subsidiaries not only increases operating costs but also robs local personnel of motivation, making it difficult to recruit talented personnel and retain valuable employees (Itagaki, 2002). Similarly, employing only a small number of non-Japanese nationals in Japanese headquarters deprives top management of diverse perspectives and talents, which MNCs from other countries can exploit to their own competitive advantage.

Where, by whom and how affiliate decisions are made are crucial aspects of managing the tension between global integration and local responsiveness (Bartlett and Ghoshal, 1989). Joint decision making by Japanese and non-Japanese is essential if Japanese MNCs are to become more global. However case must be taken to delegate decision making to the right people. This will require effective selection, training and reward systems to be put in place globally. Expatriates are used extensively in Japanese MNCs because local managers tend to lack the necessary capabilities (knowledge of the Japanese language and global operations, interpersonal relationship skills) that would allow them to perform effectively in this capacity, nor do Japanese firms seem to provide many opportunities for them to develop these capabilities. Hence the primary task confronting Japanese MNCs is to increase the supply of managers with global skills by providing opportunities for local and Japanese employees to develop the necessary capabilities that will enable them to perform effectively in global integration roles (Beechler *et al.*, 2004b).

The focus should be placed on selecting the best person for the job, regardless of nationality. In the short term a geocentric staffing policy would enhance MNC effectiveness by selecting and promoting the best talent available. It would also have a broader, longer-term impact in that a geocentric staffing policy can help to reduce employee dissatisfaction and turnover, thereby reducing costs and increasing firm-specific human assets (ibid.) Japanese firms would also become more attractive to potential job candidates if individuals perceived that anyone could eventually become president.

Japanese expatriates will continue to play an essential integrating role across the MNC. Merely cutting back on Japanese expatriates and promoting local managers, even competent ones, would only be a second-best solution. Japanese MNCs must simultaneously be locally responsive and globally integrated, taking advantage of resources distributed around the globe, both Japanese and non-Japanese. A number of practices currently work against this objective. In Japan employees regularly rotate from position to position. Likewise expatriates rotate in and out of local operations every two to five years and very often the knowledge and experience they have accumulated is not passed on to the incoming staff. In addition, because most Japanese assume that local employees are less competent than Japanese employees, local employees have to prove their worth to each incoming expatriate (Kopp, 1999).

Therefore the Japanese must become more effective in recruiting, motivating, retaining and working with non-Japanese employees, and direct experience is needed to accomplish this. Building international relationships on a person-to-person basis is the only way to break down the barriers to effective communication and trust. Japanese firms are well-known for involving employees in many aspects of the business, and this serves to develop strong cultural norms that bind individuals to the organization. Extending this practice to the international context with Japanese and non-Japanese employees at all levels would be an effective means of enhancing the global human capability of the firm.

While all of these recommendations could help Japanese MNCs to progress further down the path of globalization, there is one final stumbling block to overcome. Defying Western logic, and based on long-held values, many Japanese firms are less concerned with performance and competitiveness than they are with preserving certain human relationships. As witnessed during the recent protracted recession in Japan, even when times are tough Japanese firms usually do everything possible to protect their core (*seishain*) employees. Mutual, long-term obligations between the firm and *seishain* workers have been preserved by the extensive use of non-*seishain* workers and subcontractors to protect the jobs and livelihoods of the *seishain*. The way in which Japanese firms tend to treat non-*seishain* workers (lack of job security, lack of access to decision making and upper-level positions, lack of training and development, and so on) is consistent with how Japanese MNCs treat non-Japanese employees abroad. In fact there is clear evidence that the Japanese have exported their two-tier management system, with rigid categories of core and peripheral employees with very different prospects of job security and advancement (Kopp, 1999). As this practice reflects a deeply held value in Japanese society at large, and if the resistance to change exhibited during the economic strains of the past decade is any indication of what is to come, there is little chance that this value will change significantly in the near future.

However the Japanese economy is continuing to show signs of recovery, and if the economic fortunes of Japanese MNCs improve it is possible there will be opportunities for professional growth and promotion for *seishain* and non-*seishain* alike, be they Japanese or non-Japanese. A growing economic pie could create an environment in which both *seishain* and non-*seishain* will be crucial to growth and expansion. Of course with the next economic cycle and contraction, Japanese MNCs may once again move to protect their core *seishain* at the expense of non-*seishain*. But if the rules of global competition continue to change and only those firms that have access to key talent and that put the best people in the job regardless of nationality are able to survive, the definition of who is 'we' (*seishain*) and who is 'them' (non-*seishain*) may become more nationality-blind.

Conclusion

Looking at the globalization paths taken by Japanese firms over the past 50 years, one thing is clear: Western writers have consistently overestimated Japanese MNCs' economic imperative and consistently underestimated the impact of cultural values and the importance placed on human relationships. But as some Western writers are now emphasizing, this balance between the human and the economic is perhaps more effective and better, not just for individual companies but also for society as a whole. What path is 'better' rests on the fundamental question of what we value most, and therefore the 'right answer' will be a question of considerable debate for a long time to come. While global competitive pressures will no doubt continue to force Japanese firms to change and adapt, their cultural and societal norms and institutions, as well as their historical legacies, will ensure that Japanese MNCs will continue to carry the unique imprint that makes them 'Japanese', no matter where they go in the world.

References

Ashkenas, R., D. Ulrich, T. Jick and S. Kerr (1995) *The Boundaryless Organization: Breaking the Chains of Organizational Structure* (San Francisco: Jossey-Bass).

Bartlett, C. (1986) 'Building and Managing the Transnational: The New Organizational Challenge', in M. Porter (ed.), *Competition in Global Industries* (Boston, Mass.: Harvard Business School Press), pp. 367–401.

Bartlett, C. and S. Ghoshal (1989) *Managing Across Borders: The Transnational Solution* (Boston, Mass.: Harvard Business School Press).

Bartlett, C. and S. Ghoshal (1990) 'Matrix Management: Not a Structure, a Frame of Mind', *Harvard Business Review*, July–August, pp. 138–45.

Bartlett, C. and S. Ghoshal (2000) *Transnational Management: Text, Cases and Readings in Cross-Border Management* (Boston: Irwin/McGraw-Hill).

Bartlett, C. and H. Yoshihara (1988) 'New Challenges for Japanese Multinationals: Is Organizational Adaptation Their Achilles Heel?', *Human Resource Management* 27, pp. 19–43.

Beechler, S. and T. Iaquinto (1994) 'A Longitudinal Study of Staffing Patterns in US Affiliates of Japanese Multinational Corporations', paper presented at the annual conference of the Association for Japanese Business Studies, January.

Beechler, S., O. Levy, S. Taylor and N. Boyacigiller (2004a) 'Does it Really Matter if Japanese MNCs Think Globally?', and *Advances in International Management*, 17, pp. 265–92.

Beechler, S., V. Pucik, J. Stephan and N. Campbell (2004b) 'The Transnational Challenge: Performance and Expatriate Presence in the Overseas Affiliates of Japanese MNCs', *Advances in International Management*, 17, pp. 215–42.

Beechler, S., J. Stephan, V. Pucik and N. Campbell (1995)'Decision Making Localization and Decentralization in Japanese MNCs: Are There Costs of Leaving Local Managers out of the Loop?', paper presented at the annual conference of the Academy of International Business, November.

Boyacigiller, N. (1990a) 'Staffing in a Foreign Land: A Multi-Level Study of Japanese Multinationals with Operations in the United States', paper presented at the annual conference of the Academy of Management, August.

Boyacigiller, N. (1990b) 'The Role of Expatriates in the Management of Interdependence, Complexity, and Risk in Multinational Corporations', *Journal of International Business Studies*, 21 (3), pp. 357–82.

Campbell, N. and N. Holden (eds) (1993) *Japanese Multinationals: Strategies and Management in the Global Kaisha* (London: Routledge).

Doz, Y. L. (1986) *Strategic Management in Multinational Corporations* (Oxford: Pergamon Press).

Dunning, J. (1986) *Decision-Making Structures in US and Japanese Manufacturing Affiliates in the UK: Some Similarities and Contrasts*, Working Paper 41 (Geneva: International Labour Office).

Evans, P. (1993) 'Dosing the Glue: Applying Human Resource Technology to Build Global Organizations', *Research in Personnel and Human Resource Management*, Supplement 3, pp. 21–54.

Evans, P., V. Pucik and J. Barsoux (2002) *The Global Challenge: Frameworks for International Human Resource Management* (Boston, Mass.: McGraw-Hill).

Goldberg, A. I. (1976) 'The Relevance of Cosmopolitan/Local Orientations to Professional Values and Behavior', *Sociology of Work and Occupation*, 3, pp. 331–56.

Franko, L. (1973) 'Who Manages Multinational Enterprises?', *Columbia Journal of World Business*, 8, pp. 30–42.

Harzing, A. (1999) *Managing the Multinationals: An International Study of Control Mechanisms* (Cheltenham: Edward Elgar).

Ichimura, S. (1981) 'Japanese Firms in Asia', *Japanese Economic Studies*, 10, pp. 31–52.

Ichimura, S. and K. Yoshihara (eds) (1985) 'Japanese Management in Southeast Asia', *Southeast Asian Studies*, 22–23, special issue.

Itagaki, H. (2002) 'Japanese Multinational Enterprises: The Paradox of High Efficiency and Low Profitability', *Asian Business and Management*, 1, pp. 101–24.

JETRO (1992) *Nippon 1992 Facts and Figures* (Tokyo: Japan External Trade Organization).

JETRO (2004) www.jetro.go.jp/ecle/articles/changing/docs/2004_01_fdi.html 15 January.

Johnson, R. (1977) 'Success and Failure of Japanese Subsidiaries in America', *Columbia Journal of World Business*, 12, pp. 30–7.

Kanter, R. M. (1991) 'Transcending Business Boundaries: 12,000 World Managers View Change', *Harvard Business Review*, 69, pp. 151–64.

Kanter, R. M. (1995) *World Class: Thriving Locally in the Global Economy* (New York: Simon and Schuster).

Kim, W. C. and A. Mauborgne (1996) 'Procedural Justice and Managers' In-role and Extra-role Behavior: The Case of the Multinational', *Management Science*, 42, pp. 499–515.

Kobayashi, N. (1982) 'The Present and Future of Japanese Multinational Enterprises: A Comparative Analysis of Japanese and US–European Multinational Management', *International Studies of Management and Organization*, 12, pp. 38–58.

Kobayashi, N. (1985) 'The Patterns of Management Style Developing in Japanese Multinationals in the 1980s', in S. Takamiya and K. Thurley (eds), *Japan's Emerging Multinationals* (Tokyo: University of Tokyo Press), pp. 229–64.

Kobrin, S. J. (1994) 'Is There a Relationship Between a Geocentric Mind-Set and Multinational Strategy?', *Journal of International Business Studies*, 25, pp. 493–511.

Kono, T. and S. Clegg (2001) *Trends in Japanese Management: Continuing Strengths, Current Problems and Changing Priorities* (New York: Palgrave).

Kopp, R. (1994) 'International Human Resource Policies and Practices in Japanese, European, and United States Multinationals', *Human Resource Management*, 33, pp. 581–99.

Kopp, R. (1999) 'The Rice-Paper Ceiling in Japanese Companies: Why it Exists and Persists', in S. Beechler and A. Bird (eds), *Japanese Multinationals Abroad: Individual and Organizational Learning* (New York: Oxford University Press), pp. 107–28.

Kostova, T. and K. Roth (2003) 'Social Capital in Multinational Corporations and a Micro–Macro Model of its Formation', *Academy of Management Review*, 28 (2), pp. 297–329.

Kriger, M. and E. Solomon (1992) 'Strategic Mindsets and Decision-Making Autonomy in US and Japanese MNCs', *Management International Review*, 32 (4), pp. 327–43.

Lawrence, P. R. and J. W. Lorsch (1967) *Organization and Environment* (Cambridge, Mass.: Harvard University Press).

Levy, O. (2003) 'The Influence of Top Management Team Global Mindset on Global Strategic Posture of Firms', unpublished working paper.

Nahapiet, J. and S. Ghoshal (1998) 'Social Capital, Intellectual Capital, and the Organizational Advantage', *Academy of Management Review*, 23, pp. 242–66.

Nakamura, K. (2000) 'Localization of Management in Japanese-Related Firms in Indonesia' (www.jetro.go.jp/bulletin 39–07).

Negandhi, A. and B. Baliga (1979) *Quest for Survival and Growth: A Comparative Study of American, European, and Japanese Multinationals* (New York: Praeger).

Negandhi, A. and B. Baliga (1981a) 'Internal Functioning of American, German and Japanese Multinational Corporations', in L. Otterbeck (ed.), *The Management of Headquarters–Subsidiary Relationships in Multinational Corporations* (New York: St Martin's Press), pp. 107–20.

Negandhi, A. and B. R. Baliga (1981b) *Tables are Turning: German and Japanese Multinational Companies in the United States* (Cambridge, Mass.: Oelgeschlager, Gunn & Hain).

Negandhi, A., G. Eshghi and E. Yuen (1985) 'The Management Practices of Japanese Subsidiaries Overseas', *California Management Review*, 27, pp. 83–105.

Nihon Zaigai Kigyo Kyokai (1987) *Firipin ni okeru nikkei kigyo to sono kankyo: Anketo chosa genchi chosa kekka hokokusho* (Tokyo: Nihon Zaigai Kigyo Kyokai).

O'Reilly, C. A. and J. A. Chatman (1986) 'Organizational Commitment and Psychological Attachment: The Effects of Compliance, Identification, and Internalization on Prosocial Behavior', *Journal of Applied Psychology*, 71, pp. 492–99.

Organization for Economic Cooperation and Development (1991) *OECD Economic Surveys: Japan* (New York: OECD).

Perlmutter, H. (1969) 'The Tortuous Evolution of the Multinational Corporation', *Columbia Journal of World Business*, January–February, pp. 9–18.

Perlmutter, H. and D. Heenan (1979) *Multinational Organization Development* (Reading, Mass.: Addison-Wesley).

Porter, M. (1986) *Competition in Global Industries* (Boston: Harvard Business School Press).

Prahalad, C. K. (1991) 'Globalization: The Intellectual and Managerial Challenges', *Human Resource Management*, 29, pp. 27–37.

Prahalad, C. K. and Y. Doz (1981) 'An Approach to Strategic Control in MNCs', *Sloan Management Review*, 21, pp. 5–13.

Prahalad, C. K. and G. Hamel (1994) 'Strategy as a Field of Study: Why Search for a New Paradigm?', *Strategic Management Journal*, 15, pp. 5–16.

Pucik, V. (1992) 'Globalization and Human Resource Management', in V. Pucik, N. Tichy and C. Barnett (eds), *Globalizing Management: Creating and Leading the Competitive Organization* (New York: John Wiley & Sons), pp. 61–84.

Pucik, V. (1999) 'Where Performance Does not Matter: Human Resource Management in Japanese-Owned US Affiliates', in S. Beechler and A. Bird (eds), *Japanese Multinationals Abroad: Individual and Organizational Learning* (New York: Oxford University Press), pp. 169–88.

Pucik, V., M. Hanada and G. Fifield (1989) *Management Culture and the Effectiveness of Local Executives in Japanese-owned US Corporations* (Ann Arbor, Mich.: University of Michigan and Egon Zehnder).

Pucik, V., N. Tichy and C. Barnett (eds) (1992) *Globalizing Management: Creating and Leading the Competitive Organization* (New York: John Wiley & Sons).

Robinson, R. (1985) *The Japan Syndrome: Is There One?* (Atlanta, GA: CBA).

Shiraki, M. (1995) 'A Comparative Analysis of the Human Resource Development and Management of Multinational Corporations in Indonesia with Reference to Industrialization', mimeograph, Kokushikan University.

Sim, A. B. (1977) 'Decentralized Management of Subsidiaries and Their Performance', *Management International Review*, 2, pp. 45–51.

Stopford, J. and L. Wells Jr (1972) *Managing the Multinational Enterprise: Organization of the Firm and Ownership of the Subsidiaries* (New York: Basic Books).

Tachiki, D. (1991) 'Japanese Management Going Transnational', *Journal for Quality and Participation*, 14, pp. 96–107.

Takamiya, S. and K. Thurley (1985) *Japan's Emerging Multinationals: An International Comparison of Policies and Practices* (Tokyo: University of Tokyo Press).

Trevor, M. (1983) *Japan's Reluctant Multinationals: Japanese Management at Home and Abroad* (New York: St Martin's Press).

Tsurumi, Y. (1968) 'Technology Transfer and Foreign Trade: The Case of Japan 1970–1976', unpublished doctoral dissertation, Harvard Business School.

Tsurumi, Y. (1976) *The Japanese are Coming: A Multinational Interaction of Firms and Politics* (Cambridge, Mass.: Ballinger).

Westney, D. E. (1999) 'Changing Perspectives on the Organization of Japanese Multinational Companies', in S. Beechler and A. Bird (eds), *Japanese Multinationals Abroad: Individual and Organizational Learning* (New York: Oxford University Press), pp. 11–29.

Whitehill, A. (1991) *Japanese Management: Tradition and Transition* (London: Routledge).

Yoshida, M. (1987) *Japanese Direct Manufacturing Investment in the United States* (New York: Praeger).

Yoshihara, H. (1979) *Takokuseki Kigyo Ron* (Tokyo: Hakuto Shobo).

Yoshihara, H. (1995) 'Management Localization and Performance of Overseas Japanese Companies', *Association of Japanese Business Studies Best Papers Proceedings*, Eighth Annual Meeting (Ann Arbor, Mich.: Association of Japanese Business Studies), pp. 145–56.

Yoshino, M. (1976) *Japan's Multinational Enterprises* (Cambridge, Mass.: Harvard University Press).

5
Innovation for Whom?[1]

Ronald Dore

The R&D world in Japan was left flabbergasted in January 2004 by a judgement of the Tokyo District Court. Nichia, a relatively small Shikoku firm, was ordered to pay 20 billion yen (£100 million, only a little less than the firm's total profits over the six years 1995–2001) claimed by its former researcher, Nakamura Shuji, currently a professor at the University of California Santa Barbara – and added for good measure that had he asked for it he would have been entitled to 60.4 billion yen. Nakamura had, while working for Nichia, invented a process for producing blue light-emitting diodes (LEDs). The sum was calculated to be the 'appropriate price' (which the Patent Law requires that employees should be paid) for his intellectual property. Those property rights he had automatically, as was the universal custom, transferred to his employer who claimed and received the ownership of the patent, and should therefore, according to the law, have paid the appropriate price.

The case had been going on for some years and had been fought with considerable bitterness. Nakamura was a graduate of Tokushima University in Shikoku who joined Nichia, a local firm with about 200 employees primarily making fluorescent lighting, in 1979. Blue LED was widely seen as a desirable product, but no-one knew how to make it. In 1988, Nakamura decided it was a challenge to be tackled and the firm sent him for a year to the University of Florida to learn a particular technology and bought him the expensive machine which the technology required. In the autumn of 1990 he produced his breakthrough. The claim to fame was enhanced by the fact that the gallium nitrate route which he succeeded in making work through a long process of trial and error, had until then been considered the least promising. The firm applied immediately for a patent and after some challenges and rewriting of the specifications it was granted in 1997.

The firm had a set of regulations under which employees received rewards for inventions. Nakamura received his due: 20 000 yen (£50) on

97

application for the patent and the same sum when it was granted. Meanwhile further work in which Nakamura took part, and further protective patents, led to the development of a mass production process in which the company invested heavily, succeeding thereby in gaining a dominant share of a rapidly expanding world market. Nakamura's fame and his American connections apparently spread as his sense of alienation from his firm increased, and in 1999 he moved to California. It appears that at one point Nichia brought, or thought of bringing, a suit against him for betrayal of trade secrets, but he countered by suing for the 'appropriate price' of his brainchild.

The 60.4 billion yen calculation was based on the two factors which the law specifies as the basis for arriving at the 'appropriate price': first, the extra profits that the firm receives as a result of exploiting the invention (in this case plus interest from the time it was made, plus an estimate of future profits until the end of the patent monopoly, discounted to present value) and secondly an estimate of the contribution to the discovery by the inventor, which in this case the judge set at 50 per cent, remarking with a somewhat rhetorical flourish that this was very different from an invention in one of the well-heeled research labs of a large firm:

in the impoverished research environment of a tiny company, to have been able by his personal ability and creative imagination to arrive at a world-class invention that the whole world was waiting for, and to do it ahead of competitor firms both at home and abroad, makes this an absolutely unusual instance of employee invention. (http/courtdomino2 .courts.go.jp/chizai.nsf)

The judgement has not, on the whole, had a good press. Numerous R&D managers have expressed their alarm at the precedent set. How can one possibly do rational R&D planning if you always have lurking in the background the possibility of being stung for millions ten years down the line thanks to some disgruntled employee? The Chairman of the Association of Corporate Executives (*Doyukai*) said it could have a ruinous effect on Japan's international competitiveness (*Nihon Keizai Shimbun*, 3 February 2004). The chairman of Honda also thought it a bizarre judgement, but added that material incentives for researchers was not a bad thing, but he couldn't understand what sort of firm would offer a derisory £100 (*Nihon Keizai Shimbun*, 4 February 2004). Members of corporate research departments who thought themselves underappreciated were delighted by the judgement, and in a symposium a Tokyo University professor pointed out that in manufacturing, the lifetime earnings of science and engineering graduates were well below those of arts and social science graduates and it would be a good thing if this helped to redress the balance (http.chizai.nikkeibp.co.jp/chizai/gov/20040223.html).

It was also another ex-researcher, formerly of NTT, who launched the most apparently well-informed attack on the judgement. Nakamura's achievements, he claimed, were not so extraordinary given that most of the elements which he integrated in his process had been validated in previous work, and in any case the patent is shaky and might not hold up if challenged in the courts as it well might be. Far from being in 'an impoverished research environment', his initial budget of 500 million yen plus an exceedingly expensive machine was way beyond the average that researchers in large corporate labs could command. The judge had endorsed as a point in Nakamura's favour his claim that at one stage the company president tried to get him to use his machine to switch to a quite different line of product development, but the fact that he simply refused and kept on with his original work just shows how much privileged freedom he was allowed. And so does the fact that, although the firm asked him not to publish his achievement in a scientific journal, he nevertheless went ahead and did it and suffered no ill-consequences. His formal prize may have been only £100, but he was given extra bonuses and quicker promotion which the firm calculates as giving him an extra 62 million yen (£310 000) in the nine years up to his departure. The profit made by the firm depended not only on Nakamura's invention and subsequent research, but on the bold managerial decision to invest heavily in mass production, and the final production process did not use an essential part of Nakamura's invention anyway (Yamaguchi, 2004).

Pointed comparisons were also drawn between Nakamura's relation to his former company and that of another researcher prominently in the news a few months earlier. Tanaka Koichi, a chemist employed by a medium-sized firm, Shimazu Seisaku, was awarded the Nobel Prize for chemistry for his work on protein analysis. Tanaka and his invention clearly had considerable cash value to Shimazu. Sales jumped 6 per cent in the half-year after his prize, and equally important was the fact that, in the competition to recruit the brightest of the bright among new university graduates, Shimazu has greatly raised its power to attract. But as far as one can tell there has been no attempt to calculate the market value of his contributions – either from his inventions or from the fame which his Nobel Prize has brought to the firm. The satisfactions he has gained from his achievement have not been primarily monetary. Apart from visits to his lab by the Crown Prince and the gift of golden sake cups from the Prime Minister, the firm is rewarding him with a modest cash sum, but primarily by providing him with a grand new laboratory and the newly invented title of Fellow of the Firm.

Factory suggestion schemes

One of the things that struck me when I was looking at factories in Japan and Britain 35 years ago was the different way that employee suggestions were treated. In both countries there were formal schemes. They were explained by managers in Britain as being designed not just to improve productivity but also to increase employees' sense of 'involvement', though, as one manager said; squabbles over the value of a suggestion often did more to damage industrial relations than to improve them.

The system was simple. If you had a suggestion you wrote it out on a prescribed form. Your name was then removed and the suggestion was given an anonymous number and sent to the engineers for evaluation. If it was adopted, the engineers also calculated the bottom-line value of the suggestion – how much it would increase or improve production or cut costs over one full year. The author of the suggestion was then paid half of that annual sum for his contribution. There was also the possibility of appeal open to anyone who thought that his suggestion had been under-valued. It was a system which brought out clearly the limited contractual nature of the employment relation. The original contract is for the perform-ance of certain duties. Anything over and above that should be paid for at its market price. There is no reason for one party to the contract, the employee, to make a gift to the other.

In Hitachi by contrast – and this was well before the days of the Quality Circle movement, when the Deming prize was still being given for engineer-led quality control systems – making suggestions appeared in the work rules as one of the occasions for giving rewards. In contrast to English Electric, I wrote at the time:

> the corporation is a micro-polity. As the traditional Confucian classics used to say, the secret of good government is the judicious use of rewards and punishments ... [and] the mark of *good* government was its more frequent recourse to rewards than to punishments. [So] in the Hitachi rules the section on 'Rewards' comes before the one on 'Punishments'. Suggestions for improvements in working methods come here as just one occasion for reward. Others are saving life in danger, preventing disasters, outstanding results in company training schemes, bringing honour to the company by social and national achievements, general excellence in the performance of duties, and being a model to one's colleagues for devotion to one's work. (Dore, 1973)[2]

The rewards were graded, from letters of commendation, to gifts in kind or in cash to extra holidays. Later, of course, as the Quality Circle movement got going in the 1980s, the grading of suggestions, the *happyokai* show-and-tell meetings at which teams described and boasted about their improvement achievements, and the system of graded awards became more elaborate, but at no point was there an attempt to make the bottom-line link, to make rewards directly proportionate to the calculated value-added of any particular improvement.

Typological dichotomies

How should one characterize the above difference? Various terms have been used to point up a contrast between what used to be considered the typical Japanese firm and the typical Anglo-Saxon firm (Table 5.1).[3]

All of these highlight certain aspects of a complex and integrated set of differences, but the one which perhaps relates most closely to the present discussion is the last. By 'appealing to membership motivation' I mean teamwork in the most complete sense, the use of incentives which assume that employees have a quite intimate sense of 'belonging' to a firm, having for the most part an expectation that they will spend the rest of their lives in it, that they conceive of the firm as a really-existing entity for which they have positive affect, and that consequently recognition for some achievement on behalf of that entity enhances their standing among fellow-employees who are for them an important reference group. In addition to recognition and the prospect of promotion to greater power and organizational standing within the group, money incentives can still be important, but, given career employment, they do not need to be immediate and can take the form of the prospect of accelerated promotion.

Market motivation by contrast implies a much more limited sense of commitment within a relation based on a contract in which both parties have tried to maximize self-interest, the terms of which are set by (and legitimated as 'fair' by) values current in the market. The contract is expected to hold only as long as the market – the market for labour, the market for skills and ideas – does not offer the employee something better, and the exchange of favours not specified in the contract should be subject to the same market principles.

The design of Japanese-type suggestion schemes obviously attributes efficacy to membership motivation, while the British schemes assume the need to appeal to market motivation.

Table 5.1 Characteristics of Japanese and Anglo-Saxon firms

Japanese	*Anglo-Saxon*
Organization-oriented	Market-oriented
Communitarian	Individualistic
The firm as entity	The firm as instrument
Quasi-community firm	Company-law-conforming firm
The firm as an aggregation of people	The firm as a nexus of contracts
Jinponshugiteki (human-capitalist)	*Shihonshugiteki* (money-capitalist)
Enduring relational transactions	Limited contractual transactions
Employee-sovereignty	Shareholder-sovereignty
Appealing to membership motivation	Appealing to market motivation

Law and practice

The handling of patentable discoveries by corporate researchers in Japan has hitherto not been very different from the handling of shop-floor suggestions.

The wide gap between the provisions of Japanese company law which require firms to be run for the benefit of their owners and what has by and large hitherto been the social reality that they are run for the benefit of their employees, has long been recognized. There has been a similar gap over the treatment of intellectual property. The principle that the intellectual property in an invention belongs to the inventor, whether or not his invention is made in the course of employment has been a clear prescription of Japanese patent law since the revision of 1921 reversed a 1909 law which gave rights automatically to the employer.[4] The current 1959 law is more explicit than that of 1921. It says that firms may have their employees cede them the rights to their inventions and thus become the owners of the patents produced by their employees, but that the employees are entitled to receive in return an 'appropriate price'. *Taika* is the word used and the assumption of a market-contractual relation could not be more clear.[5] As noted in the Nakamura case the law further specifies the two parameters to be taken into account for deciding what would be appropriate: the profits that the invention is expected to bring to the firm and the extent to which the firm, the inventor and his colleagues respectively contributed to the invention.

In practice, however, as the Nakamura case also made clear, inventors (apart from being named as such in the patent registration) have been offered not a 'price' but recognition and a reward. The Nichia company rules specify for inventions, first of all the award of a scroll of recognition which presumably researchers could have framed and hang on their lab wall. Secondly and separately there were the token cash rewards recorded earlier when the firm applied for, and when it was granted, a patent – a standard 10 000 yen (£50) irrespective of the prospective profits from exploiting the patent rights. These were referred to as *hōshō*, a word which in the Nichia regulations was written with two characters meaning praise and reward, though in other firms a homonym is used with two characters meaning 'recompense' and 'encouragement'. Either or both may have been variations on the 1921 law's *hōshō* meaning 'supplementary compensation'.

The latter is the more 'modern' alternative. By the end of the 1980s, pure 'recognition and token reward' systems were increasingly seen as being a bit outdated. Most of the big R&D spenders revamped their reward systems at the beginning of the 1990s. They usually have the same standard payments as at Nichia when patents are applied for and again when they are granted – though on a rather less niggardly scale than at Nichia. Beyond that the criteria are often complex and use parameters which allow for a fair degree of discretionary evaluation. An estimate of sales of the product in which the invention is to be incorporated, plus an estimate of the contribution the invention makes to the product or products in question are usually the starting point, but the conversion factors which turn these sums into a ranking of the importance or worthiness of the invention are what determines the generosity of the scheme. Where the firm licenses out the invention so that the income from it is clear, the reward may consist in a fixed, and usually small, percentage share. There can also be special payments for, for example, setting an industry standard, producing a patent which plays a major part in securing a production alliance or a joint venture. It is hard to get an idea of the scale of these payments but a report that Hitachi was currently setting up a high-level committee in the president's office to review the system, offered the estimate that the firm currently pays out some 700 million yen (£3.5 m) annually, which amounts to a little less than 0.2 per cent of its 380 billion yen research budget (Nikkei net, 28 February 2004).

Arrangements such as these seemed to evoke little comment, and to be accepted, more or less, as 'the way things are', until 2002–3. There had been the odd case of disputes being brought to court – a Patent Office Committee counted eight in the last century – most had been settled with minor adjustments of claims for the equivalent of a few thousand pounds. But from the turn of the century the pace became faster and the attitude of judges more favourable to literal interpretations of the law. In particular the Supreme Court gave judgement in a landmark case against Olympus in May 2003. It ruled that company schemes which specified maximum rewards for inventions, and any acceptance of such rules, implicitly or explicitly by employees, had no binding contractual force in the face of the mandatory provision of the Patent Law that the inventor was due an appropriate price, calculated as the law specified. In another case against Ajinomoto, the inventor of a new kind of sweetener who had been given, and accepted, a 10 million yen reward, argued successfully that the reward for bringing extra profits to the company (which he estimated to amount to 28 billion yen) was something quite different from the 'appropriate price' to be paid for his transfer, that is, the sale, to the company of his intellectual property.

Alarm bells were rung sufficiently loudly for an *ad hoc* committee to be formed between the Patent Office and the Ministry of Economy Trade and Industry to draft revision of the law. A bill is presently (April 2004) waiting to pass through parliament (it is expected to do so with little controversy). There was some discussion in the committee of alternative foreign models.[6] The British, French, Russian and Italian systems give employers by law intellectual property rights in employee inventions. The German system, like the Japanese, respects the inventor's prior right and assumes that there is indeed an appropriate price, objectively ascertainable by universally, or at least nationally valid principles, and has special administrative procedures and a department of the Patent Office for enforcing it. The American system asserts the rights of inventors, but leaves it entirely to contractual arrangements between the parties as to the terms on which they cede these rights to employers.

The new Japanese system will be a curious modification of the American. The notion of payment of an appropriate price is retained, but individual firms' rules for determining that price are to be respected (and are no longer over-rideable as in the Supreme Court judgement) provided they are procedurally, rather than substantively reasonable. The text reads:

> If the appropriate price is determined by formulae set out in contracts or company regulations, the process of determination must not be unreasonable, the criteria for reasonableness having regard to the extent to which there was consultation between employer and employee in drawing up the formula, the transparency of disclosure of the formula and the opportunities given to the employee to express opinions regarding the application of the formula.
>
> If there is no such formula, or if on the foregoing grounds the price offered be deemed unreasonable, the price shall be determined in the light of the profits derived from the invention by the employer, the cost to and the contribution of the employer in bringing about the invention, the employer's treatment of the employee, etc.

For reasonably managed firms this should at least eliminate the possibility of outlandish judgements such as that in the Nakamura case. It is probable that there will be some modest increase in the sums awarded given all the publicity focussed on the issue. Students of corporate philosophy will be particularly interested to see if the new negotiated company rules speak of 'price' or, as hitherto, of 'recompense and encouragement'. Perhaps firms will have to abandon the – in origin paternalistic – notion of giving 'rewards' for inventions, but there is no reason why they have to abandon the notion that inventions are a collective effort, nor the notion that there is justice in rewarding effort, as well as the natural talent or strokes of luck that enable some people's efforts to be more fruitful than others'. (But see later for the extent to which that notion is currently under attack.)

The main difference from the American system will indeed be that the contracting is to be collective, not individual. In America a researcher with a good track record may be able to drive a good bargain, but not any run-of-the-mill researcher. Employees are required to sign contracts which not only consign the rights in any invention they make when still employed, but also require them to promise not to take their ideas elsewhere. As a software engineer complained in a chat room (www.slashdot.org):

> I believe that something should really be done about the 'sign your life away or we don't give you a job' phenomenon.
>
> This means that any law aimed at increasing the scope and power of copyrights and patents ends up supporting the corporation against the individual.

Engineers as employees lose their intellectual property by virtue of being employees and more so by signing blanket nondisclosure/noncompetition/IP theft contracts, and are prohibited from using their IP in future projects with different companies. This reduces the value of the engineer when applying for the next job (or asking for a raise).

Another difference from Japan, of course, is that Japanese R&D personnel rarely are looking for the next job, and are involved in company-wide wage systems rather than having individually bargained wages. A recent study of R&D careers in Japan (Fujimoto, 2004) makes clear how much high-flyer researchers are concerned with disciplinary professional reference groups (have profession-membership motivation as much as, or more than company-membership motivation) and switch mid-career to university posts. But for a Hitachi man to get a job with Toshiba is still next to unthinkable.

The urge to discover

So the revision of the patent law should reduce the amount of litigation. How will it affect the incentives to invent – the 'national competitiveness' with which so many commentators were concerned?

Patent laws derive from a tradition formed in the days when nearly all inventions were owned by the individual inventor. Their basic assumption is the not unreasonable one that scientific discoveries and technological applications of science are 10 per cent the result of the Promethean urge, the joy of discovery and so on, and 90 per cent the taking of infinite pains, and that the 90 per cent can best be invoked by the prospect of profit. Hence the establishment of property rights as a source of such profit.

In Britain, in 1920, 77 per cent of patent applications came from individuals; in 1981, 73 per cent from companies (Dore, 1987). Doubtless in Japan today, even if one excludes the small inventor-owner-manager whose inventions are owned by his firm, the proportion of patent applications coming from corporations is probably much higher than that 73 per cent.

For companies it is still the prospect of gain – profits and market-share – that determines the size of R&D investment budgets. But for the individual researcher employed by those corporations, the mixture of motivations for the activity which leads to successful discovery are as complex as the motivations for work in general, with the added feature, not common in most forms of work, that a brilliant idea or a lucky piece of serendipity might make one a hero in the firm, or outside the firm in the community of researchers in the same field, or even, by the winning of prizes, a celebrity in the world outside.

It is questionable whether the prospect of a Nakamura-like jackpot, or even a doubling or tripling of current reward levels would make much difference. The findings of the study mentioned earlier showing up the importance of professional-peer reference groups and the prospects of academic careers are significant. Nakamura himself revealed, at one stage in giving evidence, just how much more important his standing in the world of fellow-researchers in other companies was than matters of ownership and material profit (Tokyo Eiwa Horitsu Jimusho 2002):

> At the time my first concern was to get a paper out. Getting the patent applied for was simply a matter of wanting to get that paper out as soon as ever possible but having to make sure that the company did not suffer from somebody stealing the idea when I published. So I had no interest in seeing what it said in the Gazette about the ownership of the patent. I may have seen the notification, but all I was concerned about was the detail of the specification.

But what is clear is that the publicity surrounding recent court cases over inventors' rights, by raising questions about what had hitherto been accepted as conventional practice, has seriously affected attitudes and hence motivations among researchers. Nakamura again, in a newspaper interview (www.neonline.co.jp) soon after he had brought his court case:

> Everybody was cheering me on. I can't name names, but leading researchers in some front-rank corporations told me 'Keep at it. We can't come out into the open, but we're backing you.' A lot of researchers are dissatisfied, but can't say so. It's a pet thesis of mine that Japan is a communist society. When I went off to America some fellow researchers from other companies who were friends of mine had a party for me and they said there: 'even after you've gone to America, speak out as much as you can on our behalf; let people know how dissatisfied we are'. That's why I'm determined to win this suit – on behalf of Japan's researchers – and I am sure I can.

The advance of market individualism

The extent of such subterranean rumblings against the 'communist' oppression of the Japanese employment system is hard to gauge, but the flurry of court cases over the last few years does suggest that it is real, and it is worth asking: why now?

The anonymous author of a press briefing (Foreign Press Center, 2003) which summarized some of the main court cases of 2003 sums up as follows:

> Given the way patent law makes clear that intellectual property belongs in principle to the inventors, it's pretty outrageous to think that companies

can just take their rights away from them for a reward which companies themselves unilaterally specify. But this has not caused much of a problem in Japan hitherto, because it was traditionally the case that employees had a strong attachment to their firm and the firm rewarded them not so much with the specified cash award as by long-term employment and promotion. And by and large employees were satisfied with that.

These recent patent decisions mark a break with that tradition. The direct causes are, first an increase in employees' sense of their own personal rights, and second, the other side of that medal, a decrease in their sense of identification with their firm. As one analyst commented, this is not unrelated to the weakening of the lifetime employment system. (www.fpcj.jp/j/index.html)

There is, in other words, a change in the dominant consensus concerning the meaning of 'justice' in such matters, but I would argue that this is related not just to changes in lifetime employment but to the whole gamut of changes in the direction of market individualism which have taken place in Japanese corporations over the last decade.

What I mean by market individualism is basically the view that, in a market economy based on (fair) competition, the only valid criterion of social usefulness is what the market will bear. What people are willing to pay for is what they value, what has for them utility. Individual choice is an essential element of freedom, and that applies equally to one-man, one-vote democracy and to the one-consumer, one-pocket market. In the case of democracy it does not matter how much citizens differ in understanding, and in the case of the economy it does not matter how much they actually have in their pocket, or what intellectual or personality resources they have to get money in their pocket. The sovereign market, impersonally, objectively – and fairly – should decide everything.

The chief manifestations of the growing force of the market individualist *Weltanschauung* in Japan over the last ten years, other than the insistence on market criteria in the evaluation of employee inventions as in the Nakamura and other cases, are three.

The first is, indeed, all the talk about the desirability of ending lifetime employment. The underlying assumptions of much of the argument in favour of flexible mobile markets are (a) from an individual's point of view, that skills are individual possessions and individuals are well advised to make their careers by selling their gradually cumulating bundle of skills at the best price and under the most satisfying conditions that, from time to time, the market offers; and (b) from a firm's point of view, that the advantage of being able at any moment to fill organizational slots with the best human resource the market offers, outweighs any value derived from loyalty, commitment, identification with the firm, firm-specific skills or organizational learning.

The second manifestation is the widespread introduction of some kind of performance pay. Quite apart from all the (largely untested) empirical theories about incentive efficiency, at the normative level, the basis for the market individualist view that performance pay is *fair* – conforms with principles of justice – is as follows.

First are arguments about the *unfair*ness of traditional *nenko* (seniority and merit) systems. These are quite generally and quite wrongly described in Japan as 'seniority=merit' systems, with only tiny differentials among seniority peers. Such systems are condemned as 'false egalitarianism' (*akubyodo*) verging on what Professor Nakamura would call the 'communistic' principle of 'from each according to his ability; to each according to his needs', the more direct expression of which came in the family allowances which some firms still paid. And as for any functional justification, seniority was a bad proxy for accumulated wisdom.

Nearly all *nenko* systems, however, were in fact 'seniority plus merit' systems no different from European bureaucratic pay structures for teachers, police, civil servants and so on, yielding interpersonal differentials of 50 per cent or more by the age of 40. The trouble with these, runs the argument, is that the assessment of merit tended to put heavy weight on effort often at the expense of performance. But democratic, market-individualist societies are consumer sovereignty societies and the consumer is not interested in effort. The consumer is interested only in performance: does the widget widge at 100 per cent efficiency or not? Hence it is only fair – since we are all consumers, and pleasing consumers is what the corporation's life depends on – that it is performance that should be rewarded.

The reasoning behind the current passionate advocacy of performance pay is, however, more commonly on empirical grounds, appealing to the unassailable goal of national competitiveness. Nitta recently quoted, and effectively demolished, the dogmatic empirical assertions of the judgement of an Osaka judge in a case involving disputes over wage systems:

> In recent times it has become quite clear that we are moving into a period in which international competitiveness is required of Japanese firms, that nenko-type wage systems that have no direct relation to labour productivity are losing their raison d'être, and that the need for wage systems based on ability and performance which recognize the importance of labour productivity grows steadily greater. (Nitta, 2003)

The logic may be faulty, but the sentiment would hardly be challenged in today's Japan by anyone except scholars like Professor Nitta. Even Canon, the highly successful maker of optical and electronic equipment whose president is well known for endorsing the lifetime employment system has recently got rid of the last vestiges of its family allowance system and increased the part played by performance criteria. As one of its public relations officials explains, 'competition cannot be avoided in international capitalist society. In a competitive society the principle of "equality of outcomes" cannot hold. The basis must be the principle of fairness in competition under just rules.'[7]

This form of the market individualist shift is based on a widespread change in social norms. It is not simply something imposed by managers. Many unions have collaborated willingly in revamping their firm's wage system. Indeed, one left-wing publisher which introduced a more merit-based pay system 30 years ago got only grudging acceptance from the union which then sought to sabotage its operation by constant amendments. After a few years it became once again a straightforward egalitarian seniority system. Now it is the union that is demanding a system of pay differentials, claiming the injustice of giving the same wage to an editor with a flair for best sellers and a plodding producer of safe pedestrian titles.

The third manifestation of market individualism is the increasing centrality of the stock market in the Japanese economy and the increasing extent to which managers accept their share price as the most important, objective valuation of their performance. The consequence of adopting that market criterion is that their efforts are more and more concentrated on keeping up (or telling plausible stories to make analysts believe that they will keep up) their ROE and hence their stock market price – at the expense of traditional objectives like growth, market share, and maximizing the common pot of funds available to promote the welfare of the employee community of which they are a part. A further consequence, of this and of changes in corporate governance, is that top managers more and more see themselves as detached from the employee community of which they once felt themselves to be a part. They see themselves more and more as agents of shareholder principals, whose salary is to be determined not as a share in the employee-community pot, but by a compensation committee which judges their worth in the light of the 'going price' for executive talent in an external labour market – a committee which, in the case of the 30-odd big firms which have chosen the new legal structure, is composed of external directors, supposedly representing the shareholder owners.[8]

The presence of the market-individualist syndrome in all these changes should be obvious. What has caused them? Three factors:

- Cultural influence from the Anglo-Saxon economies; at a rough estimate, 85 per cent from America, 10 per cent from the other Anglo-Saxon economies (numerous delegations went to New Zealand to learn from that paragon of successful Thatcherism) and 5 per cent indirectly via continental Europe. This takes many forms: (a) the penetration of Japanese universities by Anglo-Saxon economic theory (neo-classical methodological individualism, theories of market competition as sole guarantor of efficiency, consumer sovereignty and so on) and jurisprudence (the absolute priority of property rights over other rights; the sanctity and centrality of contract); (b) the training of many Japanese in American business schools, transferring not just skills but business ideologies; (c) pervasive assumptions by the media that – in a decade in which Japan stagnated and America flourished – everything American is better.

- Constraints from the globalization of financial markets – requirements for listing on foreign stock exchanges, and for bond issues which subject Japanese firms to the judgement criteria of American rating agencies, plus a pervasive but as yet unsubstantiated belief that global financial markets will starve Japan of capital unless its corporations are as profitable for shareholders as American firms.
- Growing individualism in Japan as a result partly of the above cultural influence but partly also because of structural change – primarily changes in the family (disappearance of the final vestiges of the collectivist extended family) and the school (much greater individual choice), but also the effects of affluence, greatly widening individuals' scope for choice, not only of consumption but also of earning activity.

How much is it the growth of individualism?

The extent to which the last internal-evolution factor is important is a crucial question. That it plays some part cannot be doubted. A young Japanese lawyer, author of an interesting book on cross-shareholdings, wrote this about Japanese so-called human-capitalism some 15 years ago:

Is it really so good for humans? In the truly modern labour contract a worker sells his work; he doesn't sell his soul... The employee-sovereign Japanese firms require Japanese to spend their whole lives, from birth to retirement, in enforced competition, first to enter the firm, then for advancement in it, and for that they have to sacrifice freedom and individuality, human feeling and creativity, cultural pursuits, playing a useful role in the family or community... spiritual poverty in return for material riches. (Nakajima 1990, p. 265)

There certainly are a number of young Japanese who want a 'truly modern labour contract', and doubtless their number is increasing. But, as in any country, there is a wide range of personality differences in Japan and those who want to live in the context of modern 'dry', and options-kept-open contract relationships are more likely to be found in the free professions, law and other business services. But, be it noted, lawyers and judges have a considerable influence on the media and the social norms in general. The splash created by the Nakamura case judge is a case in point, and so is the Osaka judge cited earlier for his beliefs about competition and pay. Moreover, the influence of such people is likely in future to increase, given the vast expansion of legal training with the new graduate law schools. (The intake into the Legal Training School is expected within a few years to be six times greater than in 1990.) It is not only a matter of numbers. These law schools are said to be siphoning off some of the top talent from the top universities' law and government departments which used to aim for the Finance Ministry and MITI.

Let us call the sort of reasoned individualism of the lawyer quoted above, 'principled individualism' – the sort of individualism which in the case of an R&D researcher would cause him to insist that what he got from the company for his invention was a 'price' and not a 'reward'. There are fewer signs of such principled individualism among those who still opt for entry into a large company whether from engineering or law and arts faculties. The assumptions of the 'job for life' are still quite strong. Indeed, for all the talk about the end of lifetime employment, the actual figures for job-hopping – except among the growing number of temporary and contract workers whose hopping is usually not a matter of choice – show little growth for regular workers. Take, for example, as one measure of market mobility, the proportion of 30–34-year old male employees who, according to the wage census, have less than one year's service with their current employer. In manufacturing it was 4 per cent in 1985, rose to 5 per cent in 1990, and was back to 3 per cent in 2002. For university graduates taken separately each figure was one percentage point lower. And only in financial services have mid-career newly arrived graduates – where they amounted to 1 per cent of the age group – been welcomed warmly enough to be paid more than the average of their contemporaries.[9]

Certainly Nakamura hardly counts as a 'principled individualist' in the sense defined above. When he finally achieved the goal he had been working to, the assumption that all inventions belonged to the company was so much taken for granted that the legal formalities in Nichia were largely neglected, as became clear in the subsequent trial. When someone in the R&D centre produced something patentable he was supposed to write out the detailed specifications, and send it to the patent department along with 'a request to file a patent application' (*shutsugan iraisho*). It was the latter which constituted the formal consignment of the intellectual property right to the company, but apparently it was often overlooked, and in the case of the Nakamura patent the only record was of one in pencil which he hadn't bothered to put his seal on. It was only ten years later when he claimed (but failed to establish) that he had not transferred and had not intended to transfer his property to the company that this came into question.

Towards a more litigious system

The revisions of the law mentioned earlier may damp down court litigation, but, whether the individualism involved is principled or opportunistic, are unlikely to stem an increase in the disgruntlements of researchers and friction within firms. And this for three reasons.

The general growth of market individualism works in two ways: first and obviously to encourage the personal assertion of property rights, but secondly because it changes the nature of, and researchers' perceptions of the nature of, the firm which provides the social context of their work. Hitachi researchers who have happily allowed the firm to profit from their brains on the assumption that it all helped to benefit the collectivity of fellow-employees among whom they worked, may come to take a different view when they read that the President of Hitachi has told analysts' meetings something to the effect that increasing shareholder value is his dominant concern. It is a natural reaction to think: 'If all my work is primarily for the benefit of these anonymous shareholders, then I am going to be very sure I get my just share.'

The third factor, not unrelated to, but not the same as market individualism, is the gradual erosion in Japan of the 'productivist' ethic which sees *monozukuri* 'making things' as morally superior to *kanezukuri* 'making money'. This shift was much discussed at the time of the bubble when some of the brainiest new graduates of engineering departments started going for large salaries into the finance industry.

At that time, the shift was not only much discussed, it was much deplored. There were deliberate attempts to resist it. Ten years later, the shift in ideology continues. More and more newspaper pages are devoted to telling their readers how to invest their savings most profitably; fewer and fewer to the celebration of scientific and technological excellence. And deliberate attempts to reverse the shift in values are not apparent.

Final reflections

Half a century after I first started pontificating about the nature of Japanese society, the question I posed above, 'How far is it the growth of individualism' remains for me the big conundrum. When I first went to Japan in 1950, social scientists were preoccupied with 'modernization' as a process and as a goal, movement towards a society of free autonomous, principled, fearless – but cooperative – individuals. The underlying assumption was the marathon view of history – all societies are headed in the same direction; the processes of industrialization and urbanization had similar effects everywhere; it is just that some societies are always ahead of the others. The last chapter of the first book I wrote (Dore, 1958) drew heavily on Riesman and Talcott Parson's 'pattern variables' revamp of Tönnies to argue that a 1950 Tokyo resident differed from – and in many senses was much more individualistic than – his Tokugawa peasant great-grandfather in much the same way that a modern resident of Chicago differed from his Polish peasant ancestors. But that the more rapid arrival of big state and big organization in the trajectory of Japanese development raised questions about whether the trend towards greater individualism would continue towards the level it had reached in the more 'advanced' societies which had grown more slowly and where big bureaucracy had developed at a later stage.

When I started studying these big industrial organizations themselves in the late 1960s and early 1970s I decided that the trend towards greater individualism would indeed not continue, because, thanks, among other things, to individualism's undeveloped nature and to other late developer advantages, Japan had been able to create organizational forms which were in fact much better adapted to exploiting modern technologies, dealing with all the learning problems and distributional conflicts and so on, than the sort of organizations that the more advanced and more atomistically individualistic societies could produce. And that there was a better chance of those latter societies converging on Japan than vice versa. This would not be a bad thing because the less combative transactional forms of the Japanese system had a lot to be said for them on intrinsic value grounds (Dore, 1973).

It was not too difficult in the 1960s and 1970s to find evidence in Britain – and to a lesser extent in America – of such, what came to be called 'reverse convergence', (as opposed to right and proper convergence on the advanced Anglo-Saxon countries). But the relentless marketism of the Reagan–Thatcher years changed all that. My most recent book (Dore, 2001) still maintained that the Japanese system has virtues (even if not as great as those trumpeted by the most jingoistic Japanese in the late 1980s) but asked why so many Japanese are so bent on destroying it in the name of market individualism. Admiration for a resurgent America, the multiple influences of a hegemonic American culture such as were listed earlier, real constraints stemming from international financial markets, pressures from American financial interests – all these doubtless played their part, but another important factor is the change in class structure, the effect of three generations of relative equality of educational opportunity in producing an increasingly hereditary and politically influential upper middle class with quite substantial financial assets whose accumulation and protection becomes their main concern. Such a milieu seems a likely breeding ground for the sort of individualism manifest in recent disputes over patent rights.

So back, full circle, to the assumptions of the 1950s. Perhaps there is something in old-fashioned theories of social evolution. Perhaps there are good grounds for believing that ever greater individualism (if one defines it loosely enough)[10] is – if not quite the 'sign of God's irresistible will' as de Tocqueville described the supposedly inevitable trend to ever greater equality – at least an irreversible consequence of societies' acquisition of greater technological power and greater affluence.

Notes

1. This chapter is based on a talk given at the symposium on Challenges for Technology and Management in Japan, held at the Institute for Technology, Enterprise and Competitiveness, Doshisha University, in March 2004. The author is indebted to Messrs Hatchoji Takashi and Oka Kensuke of Hitachi Seisakusho for information and stimulating discussions.
2. The difference in punishment is equally suggestive. The elaborate gradation of punishments in the community-like Japanese firm assumed a relationship between employee and the firm that had not existed in the United Kingdom since the erosion of paternalism in the nineteenth century.
3. The term 'Typical American firm' is normally used in discussions of influences on Japan today, but 'Anglo-Saxon' has come to be widely used in the 'varieties of capitalism' literature, partly because it was the term used by Michel Albert (1992) who played a major part in getting that literature started, and partly because it points up the similarities shared by the United States, the United Kingdom, Canada, Australia and New Zealand.
4. In the light of the constant appeal by Japan's reformers for 'global standards', it is interesting to note that Baron Yamamoto Tatsuo, when introducing the 1921 law to the House of Peers, assured the house that the committee working on the bill, having spent two years studying foreign systems and the way in which they were evolving, was satisfied that it 'conformed to the dominant trends in the world' (*Kizokuin gijiroku*, 8 March 1921).
5. The 1921 law used the word *hōshō*, literally 'supplementary compensation' – supplementary, presumably, to normal salary.
6. Patent system subcommittee, intellectual property policy committee, Industrial Structure Council, *Improvement of employee-invention system*, December 2003, p. 8.
7. Private communication.
8. The new company law, which came into force in April 2003, allows firms to adopt an American-style system known as the 'company establishing committees etc.', a major feature of wich is the requirement to have compensation, appointment and audit committees, each with a majority of external directors. The total number of listed companies that had adopted this system in March 2004 was 64, but a large proportion were subsidiaries of Hitachi and Toshiba, which converted *en masse*.
9. *Chingin Kihon Chosa*, various years. The coverage is of all firms with ten or more employees in 1985 and 1990, five or more 2002.
10. I once teased out seven different meanings for the word individualism, see Dore (1990).

References

Albert, M. (1992) *Capitalisme Contre Capitalisme* (Paris: Editions Seuil).

Dore, R. (1958) *City Life in Japan, A Study of a Tokyo Ward* (London: Routledge & Keagan Paul, reprinted in 2000 by Curzon Press).

Dore, R (1973) *British Factory, Japanese Factory: The Origins of National Diversity in Industrial Relations* (London: Allen and Unwin, reprinted in 1990 by the University of California Press).

Dore, R. (1987) *Taking Japan Seriously* (London: Athlone).

Dore, R. (1990) *Will the 21st Century be the Century of Individualism* (Tokyo: Simul Press).

Dore, R. (2001) *Stock Market Capitalism, Welfare Capitalism: Japan and Germany versus the Anglo-Saxons* (Oxford: Oxford University Press).

Fujimoto, M. (2004) 'Kenkyusha, gijutusha no Kyaria Pasu to Shiko' (Scientists and Engineers: Their Career Paths and Orientations), in *MOT Keiei no Jissen* (Practice of Management) (Tokyo: Chuo Keizaisha).

Nakajima, S. (1990) *Kabushiki no mochiai to kigyoho* (Tokyo: Shoji Homu Kenkyukai).

Nitta, M. (2003) 'Nihongata nenkoshisutemu nojitsuzo wo saguru: nenkoshugi kara seikashugi e?' (Looking into the Real Face of the Nenko Wage System. From Nenko to Pay by Results?), *Rodo Chosa*, October.

Tokyo Eiwa Horitsu Jimusho (2002) The plaint relating to the procedures etc. for registering the transfer of property rights relating to the blue LED patent (www.tokyoeiwa.com).

Yamaguchi, E. (2004) 'Nihyakuokuenhanketsu: Nakamura Shuuji wa eiyuu ka' (The 20 billion Judgement. Was Nakamura Shuji such a Hero?), *Bungei Shunju*, April, pp. 169–82.

6
Organizational Learning Mechanisms for Corporate Revitalization
Yoshiya Teramoto and Caroline Benton

Introduction

The Japanese economy has lost over a decade of growth since the bursting of the bubble economy in the early 1990s: from a high of 38 915 yen, in 2003 the Nikkei stock average fell below 8000 yen for the first time in 20 years. The attempts by businesses and the government to revitalize the economy have met with little success, and many have only resulted in cosmetic modifications being made to business and industry. For example introducing performance-related pay without accompanying changes in business philosophy and the paradigms behind human resource practices and employee–employer relationships has given the illusion of progress rather than bringing about fundamental change. The Japanese business model, characterized by a stable long-term relationship between employee and employer, and between businesses and their suppliers, partners and customers, is no longer viable. Companies must rethink the manner in which they do business and develop a new model that can respond to the dynamic global business environment while maintaining traditional strengths such as organizational commitment, loyalty and emphasis on quality. The key to recovery will be this balance of change and continuity.

Signs of change, however, are beginning to emerge. Long-established practices that have promoted growth according to traditional business paradigms and have thwarted transformation and innovation, such as lifetime employment, seniority-based promotion and pay, the main bank system, *keiretsu*,[1] corporate group relationships and reliance on government-led intra-industry cooperation, are starting to crumble thus facilitating a reshaping of the social and economic fabric of the country. Only by changing such practices can businesses rid themselves of the social and economic dictates of the past and make new strategic choices. This chapter discusses how companies and organizations can meet the needs of the global society through a more flexible model of organizational learning.

Why institutions and organizational learning are important

Experimental and institutional economists view economic and social institutions as a set of sense-making factors that form the basis of continuous action that facilitates stability and reduces uncertainty in the economy. Without rules on appropriate actions the economy would fall into chaos and agents would not know how the game should be played.

This chapter focuses on the relationship between institutions and organizational learning. The emergence of new rules and methods of doing business will influence how companies perceive, understand and interact with internal and external environmental entities. That is, new institutions will affect how organizations learn, and Japanese companies will be required to make their organizational learning process more dynamic, flexible and less insular. The process must incorporate agents from all sectors of society if companies are to compete successfully in the boundaryless global market. Not all of the old institutions, however, should be discarded, as many embody the traditional strengths of Japanese business that helped create the world's second largest economy, such as tacit knowledge sharing, strong commitment to relationships and organizations, and intra-industry cooperation.

The next section sets the framework of the analysis and discusses how institutions affect the choices of an organization and its learning process. The subsequent section describes the shifting landscape of institutions and outlines how emerging ones affect organizations and businesses. The final section outlines a new model for organizational learning that takes account of changing institutions.

Traditional Japanese institutions and their effects

Various definitions of an institution have been offered by economists. In this chapter it is defined as a 'self-sustaining system of shared beliefs' about the salient rules in which a game is repeatedly played (Aoki, 2001). In the case of businesses the game is one of economic transactions and the players includes all the different agents in the economy including companies, customers, employees, suppliers, supporters, competitors and regulatory agencies. More simply, economic institutions can be said to be the set of perceptions held by economic agents about how interactions, transactions and so on should be carried out.

One traditional Japanese institution that was of great economic significance in the post War World II period was the long-term mutual holding of stock among corporate group members, which afforded tremendous stability in the economy and provided a rich source of cooperation. The six major corporate groups were Sumitomo, Mitsui, Mitsubishi, Fuyo, Dai-ichi Kangyo and Sanwa, which were anchored by major banks, general trading houses and manufacturers in the heavy industry sector. The banks financed the operations of the groups, while the general trading houses acted as import and export agents.

With the bursting of the economic bubble in the early 1990s and the intensification of global competition, however, this institution began to weaken. The financial sector has experienced a wave of consolidation over the last decade, with all the major domestic banks merging with financial institutions outside their corporate group: Mitsui Bank and Sumitomo Bank (belonging to the Mitsui and Sumitomo groups respectively) merged to form the Sumitomo Mitsui Banking Corporation; Sanwa Bank (of the Sanwa group) merged with Tokai Bank (a major regional bank) and the Toyo Trust and Banking Company to form the UFJ Bank Limited; and the Dai-ichi Kangyo Bank (of the Dai-Ichi Kangyo group) and Fuji Bank (of the Fuyo group) merged with the Industrial Bank of Japan to create the Mizuho Financial Group.

Many other companies have been forced to trade mutually held stocks due to declining market prices and corporate value. According to the Daiwa Institute of Research, a leading think tank, by the end of fiscal year 2002 the percentage of corporations listed on the Tokyo Stock Exchange with mutually held stock fell to 5.2 per cent, one third of the percentage a decade before (Nihon *Keizai Shinbun*, 15 June 2004).

According to our definition of an institution, institutions are self-sustaining. This adds to their influence and makes them robust and difficult to change. Institutions are formed through interactions among agents in the economy and are further reinforced as they are reproduced with the actual choices of economic agents. Aoki (2001, p. 12) proposes that the substance of an institution 'is a compressed representation of the salient, invariant features of an equilibrium path perceived by almost all the agents in the domain as relevant to their own strategic choices. As such, it governs the strategic interactions of the agents in a self-enforcing manner and in turn is reproduced by their actual choices in a continually changing environment.'

That is, agents create and follow the rules of the game, and these rules become further embedded in the fabric of the game as more and more agents abide by them when making choices and taking actions. Thus it becomes more difficult for agents to diverge from an institution and over time most will accept its validity. For example the institution of lifetime employment in major Japanese corporations[2] is reinforced each year as new graduates are hired straight from school with the promise of secure employment until retirement. Employers gear their human resource management practices, including evaluation, promotion and training, to supporting this institution. This feeds the patriarchal relationship between management and employees, who are viewed as long-term assets.

Consequently employees have come to view secure employment as a right and have not prepared themselves for a labour market with high job mobility. It has been extremely hard for Japanese companies to break this institution since the recession: companies that have attempted to restructure their organization have faced harsh criticism by employees and the media alike. There is such a taboo about firing employees that companies have resorted to coercing unwanted employees to resign through bullying and emotional abuse, such as shunning, stripping employees of all responsibilities and verbal taunts.

As indicated by the example above, institutions become ingrained and a state of equilibrium is established in the market in that most choices and actions by companies, partners and individuals converge within acceptable boundaries. Equilibrium is maintained until something endogenous or exogenous to the game occurs to shake up the situation. This catalyst can be a variety of things, including a new technology that makes old paradigms obsolete (for example the internet and e-commerce), changes in the perception and needs of the market, the entry of foreign competitors, or an acute and drastic downturn in the economy that causes an intense struggle for corporate and individual survival.

New institutions emerge when such an occurrence causes the discrepancy between what the players in the market and society aspire for and what has been achieved to reach a crisis point, resulting in widespread dissatisfaction. Japan is at that point now, and it is in the midst of fundamental institutional change in all societal domains. The catalysts for the current state of affairs include the following:

- Economic recession and deflation for over a decade has dealt a hard blow to the financial security of companies and they have been forced to review their business models, including their human resource practices and long-term business relationships that can no longer support business development (such as those with suppliers, *keiretsu* partners and wholesalers).
- Globalization is fuelling multinational alliances and the implementation of global standards in accounting practices, which in turn are prompting calls for disclosure and transparency and creating more demanding stockholders.
- There is declining confidence in the government and corporate management due to the series of high-profile government and corporate scandals that have come to light over the last five years.[3]
- Deregulatory measures are weakening the protection that had been accorded to domestic companies.
- The internet has provided the Japanese public with a wealth of information shifting the balance of power toward individuals who are beginning to demand better business practices, prices and corporate responsibility.
- The spread of advanced information technology has facilitated the global coordination of operations and closer relationships between businesses and their suppliers and customers.

These socioeconomic shocks have led to a growing awareness of the need for fundamental changes to the way in which business and government are conducted. However reaching a new equilibrium is difficult as there is much disagreement about how the future is to be shaped due to lingering interests, long-held values and beliefs, and the holding power of the *status quo*. We suggest that if Japanese companies are to thrive again they must maintain their traditional strengths – such as tacit knowledge sharing, intra-industry and industry–government cooperation to realize a common vision,[4] emphasis on high quality and low cost, employee loyalty borne from a mutual long-term commitment, and enthusiasm for incremental innovation – while overcoming their weaknesses, including lack of leadership, accountability and responsibility, and insular and self-contained business practices that overemphasize long-term business-to-business and employee–employer relationships, which curb the acquisition of new knowledge and flexibility, and thus innovation and growth.

Two other important characteristics of institutions are path dependency and institutional complementarity. Path dependency refers to the influence the historical path of an institution has on its future evolutionary path. It was natural for Japan – which prior to the Meiji Restoration of 1868 was based on a feudal system in which local *daimyos* (feudal barons) were obedient to the ruling *shogunate*, or military governor – to evolve into a country of centralized control in which the 47 prefectural governments look to the national government and ministries for guidance and support. The practice of hiring newly retired ministry officials to top management posts in related industries, a system called *amakudari*[5] (which can be literally translated as dissent from heaven) is also reflective of the reverence given to authority and regulatory agencies. The shape of Japanese institutions in the globally networked knowledge society will be affected by the course the country has taken, and its traditional strengths can be maintained if the future path is chosen wisely.

'Institutional complementarity' refers to the impact that institutions have on each other, and the fact that the existence of some institutions is dependent on the existence of others. The abovementioned institution of *amakudari* would not exist if there was not such strong cooperation between the government and industry. The seniority-based remuneration system for salaried workers in large corporations would not be possible without the promise of lifetime employment. A major characteristic of this system is that salaries increase slowly in the early stages of a career, but this is compensated by accelerated pay rises from mid career and a large lump-sum retirement pension. Young professional employees of large corporations have accepted low wages as they have been assured of long-term employment with increasing benefits. Meanwhile corporations use the system to recruit a large number of new graduates at relatively low cost to fuel corporate expansion.

It can also be said that the dissolution of one institution makes possible the emergence of another. For example the weakening of corporations' ties with the main bank has led to an increase in direct finance from the market, which in turn has contributed to an increase in foreign investment and a consequent demand for the implementation of global business standards.

Organizational learning

This section discusses the impact that traditional Japanese institutions have had on organizational learning in Japanese businesses. Since organizational learning involves interactions with the internal and external environments, the rules by which business operations and transactions are conducted significantly affect the process by which businesses learn. It follows that if these rules are changed, the manner in which organizations learn should change as well. It is also the case that as learning is a feedback process, the results of organizational learning are fed back to the structure and contexts of the institutions in question.

Huber (1991) distinguishes four stages in the process of organizational learning: information/knowledge acquisition; distribution of the newly acquired information/knowledge throughout the organization; internalization or interpretation of new information/ knowledge by organizational members so that it has contextual meaning and value; and organizational memorization of the information/knowledge. We suggest that institutions have a considerable impact on each of these stages of organizational learning.

In Japanese industry – with its insular and inflexible business practices that emphasize long-term and stable relationships between the business and its employees, partners and main banks – knowledge acquisition is adversely affected by the limited range of participants in interactions and transactions. That is, information and knowledge exchange tends to be mostly conducted among same set of organizations and companies, resulting in information and knowledge stagnation and limited diversity. It is inevitable, then, that companies begin to lose their viability in a dynamically changing environment, which requires a steady influx of new agents to bring new ideas, viewpoints and knowledge to enable innovation not only in products and services but also in organizational strategy, structure and processes.

On the other hand these same institutions support the distribution, internalization and memorization of tacit knowledge, which is difficult to codify with words, symbols or diagrams. Such knowledge is shared and maintained in the organization through face-to-face interactions and shared experiences among persons who have developed mutual trust, loyalty and commitment, which are relationship characteristics that Japanese corporations have been nurtured with the institutions of long-term employment and business ties. This ability to share and maintain tacit knowledge has been a major strength of Japanese companies and a significant factor in the success of quality control circles and total quality management activities, which have enabled high-quality, low-cost operations.

The institution of decision making by consensus promotes group and organizational commitment and affects all stages of organizational learning. In Japan there is a saying that 'the nail that sticks up gets hammered down', meaning that divergent behaviour is quickly squashed. This cultural trait is often evident in decision making by consensus where innovative or risk-taking opinions, and ultimately decisions that can lead to new knowledge and competitive advantage, are inhibited. The diversity of interpretation of knowledge and value are thereby limited through pressures of conformity. Decision making by consensus requires lengthy group discussions and full agreement, and this affects organizational learning by reducing the speed at which decisions are made. This is especially damaging in the current business environment, where product life cycles are short, competitive advantage does not last long and there is an endless supply of new competitors and technical substitutes. However decision making by consensus does promote knowledge and information distribution and can enhance the speed of decision implementation, as participation and involvement is widespread from the outset.

Table 6.1 lists the effects that the traditional institutions have on domestic organizations and their learning process. As a result of these institutions,

Table 6.1   Effects of traditional institutions on organizational learning

Institution	*Effect on organizational learning*
Long-term business relationships, including *keiretsu* and corporate group relationships	• Limits the diversity of information and knowledge acquired • Limits the diversity of interpretations of information and knowledge • Supports the sharing of knowledge as mutual trust and commitment develop
Decision making by consensus (group orientation)	• Limits diversity of choice and can inhibit individual risk-taking. • Reduces the speed of decision making and thus of learning • Supports the sharing of knowledge as mutual trust and commitment develop
Seniority-based promotion and pay, and the related institution of lifetime employment	• Limits the diversity of information and knowledge acquired • Limits the diversity of interpretations of information and knowledge • Supports the sharing of knowledge as mutual trust and commitment develop
Job rotation	• Supports the diversity of information knowledge acquired • Supports the diversity of interpretations of information and knowledge • Supports the sharing of knowledge as mutual trust and commitment develop
Quality control circles	• Supports the sharing of tacit knowledge among circle members in the same department, leading to incremental improvement rather than radical innovation. • Limits the diversity of interpretations of information and knowledge as activities are mainly conducted within the department • Focus mainly on quality, cost and delivery issues, while disregarding other business processes and aspects.

organizational learning has been internally focused and suited to linear growth and innovation. In contrast radical or non-linear innovation normally requires a fluid input of human resources and partnerships, greater individual risk taking and knowledge diversity. The next section discusses new institutions that are beginning to have an effect on organizational learning.

The emergence of new institutions

As a result of the socioeconomic changes discussed in the previous section, there is considerable frustration among individuals and businesses with the current state of affairs in Japan. Old proven practices that helped propel the Japanese economic miracle in the latter half of the twentieth century are no longer relevant in the current market environment, which is characterized by intense competition, rapid innovation and change, fragmentation of market needs, and growing sophistication and awareness among consumers and business customers. In response a number of new institutions are emerging.

Flexible employment and recruitment practices

Corporations are moving away from lifetime employment and introducing more flexible and varied employment practices. According to the Ministry of Health, Labour and Welfare, the poor state of the economy, changing values among employees, reduced opportunities for promotion, curbs on salary increases and the aging population are responsible for this trend (Ministry of Health, Labour and Welfare, 2003).

The continuing economic recession has necessitated large-scale corporate restructuring. Despite public outcry and media criticism, Nissan Motors closed three large plants in 2001 and two in 2002, and in 2003 Sony announced its intention to lay off over 20 000 workers. (www.nissan.co.jp; www.sony.co.jp).

Meanwhile the need for new expertise, especially in high technology industries such as software development, has resulted in mid-career recruitment; in the past large domestic corporations preferred to recruit young school graduates and mould them to their own needs, culture and value system.

The changing values of young college graduates is also affecting this institution. Not only can graduates no longer expect to stay with one company for their entire career, but also they are increasingly unwilling to do so. Matsushita Electric, one of the more traditional Japanese companies, implemented a programme in 1999 whereby new recruits could choose to receive their retirement pension in advance in the form of an increase in annual remuneration. In a country where the large lump-sum retirement pension served as an incentive for employees to commit themselves to the company for life, Matsushita expected that only approximately 10 per cent of new recruits would opt for this advance payment. In the event, however, nearly half of them chose to do so. This reflects a growing desire among young graduates for more flexible and mobile careers. The Ministry of Health, Labour and Welfare (2003) confirms that the tenure of workers in their twenties and thirties is shortening, and that a greater percentage of these workers have a negative attitude towards traditional employment practices and are seeking jobs that offer more intrinsic value and the opportunity to spend more time on family and community activities.

Flexible and dynamic alliances and networking with partners

Companies are finding that many of their long-term partnerships are no longer providing the benefits they need and therefore they must develop more organic business relationships that will enable tangible (money, products and facilities) and intangible resources to be obtained as required. As a result, partnerships that cross group, *keiretsu*, country and industry boundaries are being established, and the long-term relationships among manufacturers, wholesalers and suppliers are being restructured.

Large corporations and their partners are expanding their business relationships outside the *keiretsu* and corporate group boundaries. As discussed in the previous section, major domestic banks have merged with institutions outside their old corporate groups and mutual stock holding is decreasing, thus weakening corporate relationships. Moreover manufacturers in the electronic and automotive industries are procuring parts from suppliers that do not belong to their *keiretsu* network. For example Nissan's revival plan, which was announced in October 1999, included selling off the stock of all but four of its 1394 affiliates and parts suppliers. Nissan suppliers such as Fuji Kiko, Tachi-S, Ichikoh Industries and Niles have since left the *keiretsu* relationship and expanded their customer base to include competitor manufacturers. Meanwhile Mazda Motors has commented that although there is a relationship among automotive industry firms in the Hiroshima region, where its business operations are centred, there are no *keiretsu* relationships.

Multicultural networks

Many Japanese companies have found that limiting their partnership relationships to domestic firms is not appropriate in today's global economy, so they are forming additional alliances and networks with foreign companies that can provide not only market access but also the diverse knowledge required for competitive advantage.

One of the most high-profile and successful cases of a multicultural alliance is Nissan's alliance with the French car manufacturer Renault. Under the initial terms of the alliance, which was formed in 1999, the French partner purchased a 36.8 per cent share of Nissan and took over operational control of the latter. Entering into the alliance was an embarrassing and humbling experience for the once proud Japanese company, but it was seen by Nissan's top management as offering the only hope of avoiding the bankruptcy of the company, which was burdened with debt.

Under the leadership of Carlos Ghosn, who was sent from Renault to manage the recovery process, Nissan was able to acquire not only capital but also the new knowledge needed to transform the company's business paradigms and philosophy and institute new rules for doing business, including extensive use of cross-country and cross-functional teams, employee empowerment, and human resource practices based on management by objective and employee commitment to individual and group goals and targets. Within roughly a year and a half of the alliance, the company had not only halted its downward spiral but also surpassed its target income and returned to profitability. It posted the largest return in its history, with net consolidated operating income reaching 290.3 billion yen and net consolidated income 3331.1 billion yen by March 2001. Simultaneously the company reduced its debt to less than one trillion yen for the first time in 15 years.

In another example Seiyu, a major supermarket chain, formed an alliance with US-based Wal-Mart Stores. According to Seiyu's annual report, in December 2002 Wal-Mart 'exercised a share option worth ¥52.0 billion to raise its holding in Seiyu to 37.7 percent. This has increased Seiyu's financial stability, and more importantly, has enabled Seiyu to benefit from the superior services and sophisticated expertise of the world's largest retail company' (www.seiyu.co.jp/business/english/company_e/ar/pdf/2003/p02-03.pdf). As can be seen, Seiyu's purpose for entering the alliance was not restricted access to capital, rather it hoped to use the knowledge of the American retail giant to revitalize the company and increase its competences and competitive advantage. For more than six months the partners conducted surveys and analyzed Seiyu's internal and external environments to enable the incorporation of Wal-Mart's expertise in areas such as store operation, store development, logistics, market analysis and business management in a manner that would meet the needs of Japanese consumers.

From indirect to direct financing

The bursting of the bubble economy in the early 1990s caused share and land prices to plummet, thus erasing the value of corporate assets. As a result, Japanese banks became overburdened with bad loans, their credit ratings fell and they had to reduce lending and call in loans. According to the chairman of the US Federal Reserve, Alan Greenspan, the relatively large preportion of indirect financing by banks to corporations had been a major problem for the Japanese economy (*Trader Web Magazine*, November–December 1999). To compensate for the contracting supply of bank loans, corporations have turned to the financial market for funding and reduced their reliance on banks. This has not only weakened the institution of the main bank but also attracted foreign investors who are keen to take advantage of the decreased stock prices.

Increased use of consultancy and research services

The insular focus of Japanese companies used to manifest itself in reliance on internal research and internal acquisition and analysis of data. In other words the use of outside consultancies and research agencies in Japan was very limited. However with the advancement of information technology and the growing sophistication of and rate of change in the market, companies have recognized they need the services of external researchers and consultants. Hence there has been a burgeoning of IT-related and human-resource-related consultancies that respectively provide advice on software, hardware, computer networks and telecommunication technology, and on more flexible human resource practices, including mid-career recruitment and performance-related pay. Mercer Human Resource Consulting, one of the leading global HR consultancies, plans to increase its staff significantly in Japan in order to meet the growing demand.

New model for organizational learning

As with all aspects of individual and organizational behaviour, institutions affect organizational learning. In this section we present a new model for organizational learning that reflects the growing complexity and diversity of and speed of change in the global market. Huber's (1991) model is tuned more to a static and simple environment; it does not holistically consider existing knowledge but starts with knowledge acquisition. Also it does not involve the integrated participation of external individuals and organizations. We propose a model that considers the dynamic and more sophisticated needs of a networked market environment, and takes a holistic view of knowledge creation that starts with a conscious sharing of existing knowledge and value through the active inclusion of external divisions and organizations. Based on a shared understanding of the existing knowledge and value, knowledge is then combined to create the next generation of knowledge, which is validated by developing and testing a hypothesis. This broader-based involvement and perspective allows for increased flexibility in the organizational learning process. Our model is shown in Figure 6.1.

The first step is the sharing of existing value and knowledge among internal and external individuals, groups and organizations. For fruitful collaboration and organizational learning to occur, it is essential to develop an understanding of currently held knowledge and the value that gives meaning and context to this knowledge. This is achieved through direct contact and communication. As noted by Nonaka and Takeuchi (1996),

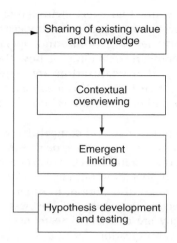

Figure 6.1 Organizational learning

organizations create knowledge through the interaction of tacit and explicit knowledge, the former being defined as the highly personal and hard to formalize knowledge that is embedded in individuals, such as expertise and know-how; and the latter is systematic and formalized knowledge that has been codified in words, numbers and graphs. As tacit knowledge is held within the individual it can only be transferred through shared experience. For example young craftsmen learn their trade by watching master craftsmen, and young recruits to the business world learn how to interact with customers by watching their older colleagues.

Sharing value provides meaning and context to the knowledge that is being shared, and it promotes the trust and commitment required for a successful and fruitful collaboratory relationship. In particular, value sharing is essential in the case of networked, global and interindustry partnerships comprising companies from different backgrounds and with varying goals and value systems, and in the case of mid-career recruits, who also come from varying backgrounds.

In order for Japanese companies such as Matsushita Electric and Mitsubishi Electric to develop and operate plants successfully in mainland China, they must first share their knowledge and value systems with their Chinese partners and employees; without this understanding the partnership is doomed to fail and there will be no synergistic collaboration. Knowledge sharing within a group or organization has traditionally been a strong point of Japanese companies. If this sharing is extended to external organizations and individuals, richer and more complex knowledge becomes possible.

In the second step, contextual overviewing (Teramoto and Nakanishi, 2000), organizations develop a comprehensive understanding of their current business processes and their functional and operational relationships. This involves an in-depth understanding of how the different functions, operations and jobs in the organization are synergistically linked to provide optimal value for customers. It is a contextual and comprehensive analysis of interactions and of how work is done in the company to create the final output.

In an increasingly sophisticated and competitive world, companies must be able to create truly differentiated value, be this in terms of cost, product function, service, quality or brand image. This is only possible if the entire value chain is integrated, including product development, manufacturing, marketing/sales, finance and distribution. In other words it is necessary to have a holistic perspective, in which all business functions undertaken internally and externally are considered seamlessly to provide maximum synergy for maximum value creation.

One of the strengths of Japanese engineering is that throughout application development, product development and production engineering, engineers move along with the technology to the next stage to help with the effective realization of the technology. For example product development engineers assist in the first stages of production engineering to ensure the effective development of the production technology. This allows them to gain comprehensive knowledge of the entire R&D and engineering process.

Canon, a Japanese electronics manufacturer that is noted for its innovativeness, has changed its manufacturing process from one based on conveyor belts and assembly lines to cell production, in which groups of employees undertake the entire production process. This gives employees comprehensive knowledge of the process and promotes the development of leading-edge production technology. According to Canon:

> the shift is in line with our worldwide production system reformation aimed at eliminating labor and space inefficiencies. The beauty of cell production is that it puts the art of creation back where it belongs – in the hands of real people, rather than machines and systems. Spearheading cell production are teams of multitalented individuals, who we call Experts, themselves overseen by Super Experts, who excel in all facets of the production process. Super Experts also provide sound guidance in such areas as parts procurement, machine tool refinements, product inspection and final installation. (www.canon.com/about/production/)

As with the first step, Japanese companies have excelled in linking knowledge within a group or department. If external individuals, departments and organizations are brought into the process, more complex and sophisticated knowledge can be created, and thus even greater value. Manufacturers of computer game hardware such as Nintendo work together with game software producers and manufacturers to provide a rich entertainment experience for gamers.

In the third step, emergent linking, knowledge is combined to create the next generation of knowledge. With the contextual overview gained in the previous step, individuals in companies are able to link different sets of know-how, expertise, skills and technology from different individuals, departments and organizations to create knowledge and value that is more sophisticated and complex than would otherwise be possible. The growing prevalence of cross-functional and interorganizational teams that comprise individuals from different functional areas or companies is due to the effectiveness of bringing together diverse knowledge in the interest of synergy.

This step is increasingly important in a post-industrial knowledge society characterized by customers and competitors whose demands and needs are ever more fragmented and sophisticated. To promote emergent linking of knowledge from diverse individuals, groups and organizations, companies must review their human resource policies and bring them into line with those which support and motivate collaboration among individuals from different departments and organizations. Companies should embrace the more flexible human resource management and recruitment practices that are emerging in order to access the necessary skills and expertise, and to empower front-line staff.

Armed with the knowledge that has been created by linking the tacit and explicit knowledge gained in the previous steps, organizations can now undertake the fourth step: hypothesis development and testing. This involves the formulation and testing of a hypothesis of the new knowledge gained by launching or implementing new products, services and strategies embedded with this new knowledge in the context of the actual environment. In a constantly changing environment it is not possible to know how appropriate new decisions, practices and products or services will be unless they are tested in real market situations and against the competition. It is also necessary to remember that with the growing need for rapid response to market changes, companies cannot spend an inordinate amount of time on debating their choices; speedy refinement of these choices through trial and error is increasingly the key to success.

To maximize the usefulness of feedback from the testing of the hypothesis, this step must be conducted in a methodical and scientific manner. In other words the tests must not be conducted randomly and organizations should refine their process of hypothesis development and testing in the interest of cost and time efficiency. Japanese companies have traditionally been relatively weak in accumulating and analyzing explicit organizational knowledge, and successful adoption of this step in the organizational learning process will strengthen the creation and utilization of explicit knowledge and thus improve their ability to share and create tacit knowledge.

With the advance of information technology, companies are able to test their hypotheses with large amounts of market data. For example the success of market leader Seven-Eleven Japan owes much to its expert gathering and analysis of sales and customer data. Using an advanced point-of-sale system, Seven-Eleven analyzes consumer purchase data from each of its retail outlets on a daily basis to identity discrepancies between the product range offered and local consumer needs. With individual stores ordering fresh comestibles such as lunches and snacks multiple times a day, Seven-Eleven is able to pose hypotheses on sales trends daily.

Katsumi (2002) outlines the secrets of the 'statistical art' of Seven-Eleven. Loosely translated these are: analyzing data from the perspective of the buyer will produce different results; statistical data should not be blindly accepted but should be analyzed thoroughly with context in mind; changing the denominator changes the meaning of the data; statistics cannot be fully understand without considering consumer psychology; only through the development and testing of hypotheses can the most use be made of the data; and do not modify the data to meet your needs.

Thus it is necessary to have a broad perspective of context in order fully to understand the meaning behind the statistical data. In other words, point-of-sale data from one retail outlet must be viewed within the larger perspective of the needs, motivations and demographics of the customer base of that outlet. With regard to 'changing the denominator' data on total sales will show different trends from data on sales by gender or at different times of the day. Hence changing the denominator will give more precise and descriptive readings of consumer needs.

Next, on its own statistical data cannot provide total insight into how best to provide customer value and increase sales. Consumers do not always know precisely what they want and their needs change. Developing and directly testing hypotheses that are fully grounded in statistical data is a feedback process that leads to a deeper understanding and knowledge of consumers' needs and purchasing patterns. For Japanese convenience stores, *obento* (Japanese lunch boxes), sandwiches and desserts are strategic products that bring in customers. Products are added and replaced frequently to spice up the range and entice customers to return regularly. With daily testing and experimenting, Seven-Eleven has been able to continuously innovate its product offering to the customers of each store. This is especially important for convenience stores with very limited shelf space.

All learning, whether individual or organizational, is a feedback process. The knowledge gained and created in the four-step organizational learning model described above affects the existing value and knowledge systems, which become the basis for the next cycle of learning.

Conclusion

Due to numerous socioeconomic shocks, Japan is experiencing sweeping institutional changes in all sectors, leading to a less insular and more open and flexible society. Companies must not shy aware from these changes, but must take advantage of them in order to thrive again in the global market. This can be done by instituting a more flexible and open organizational learning model.

With the arrival of more open, complex and dynamic institutions, companies have access to more diverse and rich sources of knowledge, both individual and organizational. This chapter has presented an organizational learning model that can make use of these knowledge sources by promoting knowledge and value sharing among internal and external partners.

However the traditional strengths of Japanese organizations should not be discarded, rather they should be adapted to changing circumstance. The strong long-term relationship between organizations and their employees and business partners must not be tightly bound indefinitely, but must shift to meet the changing needs of the business environment and allow for new relationships to be formed and old obsolete ones to be terminated. In other words a balance between the cultivation of existing relationships and engaging in new ones must be struck in order to take advantage of new values and knowledge in the external environment.

Incremental improvement activities and the traditional emphasis on quality should also be retained, but balanced with a drive for innovation and value creation to ensure competitive advantage. This can be achieved by means of an organizational learning process that actively involves diverse departments and external organizations and provides an overall perspective of the business process. Only by adopting such a process can organizations satisfy the ever-changing demands of the customer of the twenty-first century.

Notes

1. *Keiretsu* are vertically structured industrial groups consisting of manufacturers and their parts suppliers, wholesalers and retailers.
2. Although it is a widely believed that lifetime employment is standard in Japanese companies, this is only true of larger corporations. Smaller companies have much more fluid labour practices and a much higher employee turnover. Nonetheless, Japanese companies of all sizes tend to have a more patriarched attitude towards their employees than their American and European counterparts. This has fostered loyalty on the part of employees, who are viewed as long-term assets to be nurtured and trained.
3. For a detailed account of the corporate and government scandals see Benton and Teramoto (2002), who also outline how the scandals have fuelled efforts to find a new corporate governance model.
4. For example in the case of third-generation mobile telecommunication technology, the Japanese government and major domestic companies have jointly

established a guiding theme for development efforts, promoting synergistic and accelerated innovation among the major carriers, parts suppliers and contexts developers.

5. *Amakudari*, which literally means descent from heaven, refers to the appointment of high-ranking persons in government agencies and ministries to top management posts in related industries. *Amakudari* executives are expected to use their experience, knowledge and connections in their ministry for the benefit of the corporation that hires them.

References

Aoki, M. (2001) *Toward a Comparative Institutional Analysis* (Cambridge, Mass.: MIT Press).

Benton, C. and Y. Teramoto (2002) 'Revolutionizing Japanese Corporate Governance', in U. C. V. Haley and F.-J. Richter (eds), *Asian Post-crisis Management* (New York: Palgrave), pp. 281–98.

Huber, G. P. (1991) 'Organizational Learning: The Contributing Processes and the Literatures', *Organization Science*, February.

Katsumi, A. (2002) *Suzuki Toshifumi No Toukei Shinrigaku* (Toshifumi Suzuki's Statistical Psychology) (Tokyo: President).

Ministry of Health, Labour and Welfare (2003) *The White Paper on the Labour Economy* (www.mhlw.go.jp/wp/hakusyo/kousei/02/1-4.html – found 15 October 2003).

Nihon Keizai Shinbun (2004) 'Kinyu Kikan No Mochikabuhiritsu' (Percentage of Stock Holdings Among Financial Institutions), 15 June 2004.

Nonaka, I. and H. Takeuchi (1995) *The Knowledge Creating Company* (Oxford: Oxford University Press).

Porter, M., H. Takeuchi and M. Sakakibara (2000) *Can Japan Compete?* (Cambridge, Mass.: Basic Books).

Teramoto Y. and A. Nakanishi (2000) *Chishiki Shakai Kochito To Jinzai Kakushin, Nikkagiren* (Development of a Knowledge Society and Human Resource Innovation) (Tokyo: JUSE Press).

7
Corporate Governance and Law Reform in Japan: From the Lost Decade to the End of History?[1]

Luke Nottage and Leon Wolff

From the lost decade to the end of history?

Much has been made of Japan's 'lost decade'. With economic stagnation, financial crisis and record corporate insolvencies during the 1990s, Japan's once mighty economic machine appears to have lost its way. But its sluggish economic performance stands in contrast to an enormous burst of activity in law reform. On a scale comparable to the massive legal innovations made after Japan reopened itself to the world during the Meiji Restoration from 1868 and the democratization of constitutional and economic law during the Allied Occupation from 1945 to 1952, Japan is embarking on a 'third wave' of legal and regulatory reform. The primary driver of the reform movement is growing desperation to regain economic momentum. A guiding theme is dismantling *ex ante* regulation of businesses by public authorities and introducing more indirect means of *ex post* control by empowering private entities with private or corporate law remedies.[2]

What should be made of these legal developments? An emerging thesis is that Japanese law is in the process of 'Americanization'. According to Keleman and Sibbitt (2002), for example, the Americanization of Japanese law is evident in accelerating economic liberalization, political fragmentation and greater 'legalization' in everyday life in Japan since the lost decade. Similarly Milhaupt (2003) suggests that, despite some 'stickiness' in traditional corporate governance norms, Japanese corporate law is taking on a more visibly American shape. The central claim is that American law represents the global standard in corporate regulation, and that Japan is inexorably inching its way towards adopting this standard.

This thesis of the Americanization of Japanese law recalls Fukuyama's (1992) famous prediction in *The End of History* that US-style political democracy and market-based economic ordering would triumph in the post-communist order. The attraction of Fukuyama's ideas has not been limited to political scientists, economists and business leaders. They have also found resonance in the legal academy. For example Hansmann and Kraakman (2001), law professors at Yale and Harvard respectively, prophesied the 'end of history for corporate law'. They write in support of continued and accelerating convergence on a shareholder-oriented model of corporate governance, involving extensive use of market-based control mechanisms to guide corporate activity and corporate law. Paralleling Fukuyama, Hansmann and Kraakman emphasize the 'failure of alternative models': the 'manager-oriented model' (popular in the United States until the 1960s), the 'labour-oriented model' (entrenched primarily in Germany), the 'state-oriented model' (perceived as dominating post-war France and Japan) and 'stakeholder models' (seen as mere variants on older manager- or labour-oriented models) (ibid., pp. 443–9). They argue that competitive pressures will cause convergence on the shareholder-oriented model and highlight the rise of a shareholder class world-wide. They concede, however, that change has so far occurred more at the level of corporate practices than that of formal legal rules. Other commentators have taken this a step further in the related area of competition law, implying 'the end of antitrust history'.

This triumphalism – that American law represents both the pinnacle of legal achievement and the global standard to which other legal systems should aspire – has attracted much criticism. Some, for example, argue that US antitrust law and practice has a bifurcated tradition, with one strand being closer to the European Union's model of regulation more through administrative agencies rather than private enforcement for the primary benefit of dispersed consumers (Perez, 2002). Others contend that a 'general process of Americanization in legal thinking' – (or 'imperial law') – is 'a dominant layer in worldwide legal systems', but one underpinned by 'a spectacular process of exaggeration, aimed at building consent for the purpose of hegemonic domination' (Mattei, 2003, p. 383) and encountering resistance in continental Europe. Moreover doubts have been expressed about the straightforward Americanization of corporate law. For example, von Nessen (1999, 2003) notes that the wave of reforms to Australian corporate law since the late 1990s, although inspired by some specific US developments and more general concepts, have been filtered through the lens of the British law tradition. Moreover, Australian law reforms have taken account of local circumstances (see Cheffins, 2002). Full-scale Americanization of Japanese law seems equally if not more implausible. Indeed aspects of Japanese private law may be undergoing a new round of 'Europeanization' and idiosyncratic globalization (Nottage, 2004).

This chapter assesses claims of Americanization of Japanese law by critically examining the recent raft of reforms to Japanese corporate governance. At first blush, there is much to suggest Americanization. First, corporate governance has indeed shifted towards a more shareholder-oriented model: the law now provides greater potential for shareholders to monitor opportunistic managers. Second, certain non-shareholders (especially creditors) are endowed with greater arm's-length control mechanisms. However the degree and direction of the transformations vary according to the stakeholder (Nottage, 2001b). For example, direct control by employees, who are still important stakeholders in Japanese companies, is declining only slowly. Furthermore suppliers, consumers, government authorities and even NGOs are still prepared to interact with companies and managers on the basis of trust, rather than insisting on control mechanisms on the assumption that there will always be opportunism or deviance that needs to be guarded against (see also Fukuyama, 1996).

In short, Japanese corporate governance – and indeed Japan's entire system of capitalism – is converging to a degree on the US model, but at a rate that is seemingly related to the resilience of underlying norms and philosophies (see also Sarra and Nakahigashi, 2002). It may be that this is a temporary situation in transition to a more consistent end of history *à la américaine*. But it is more likely that it constitutes a new equilibrium, as seems to have been reached in German corporate law reform (du Plessis, 2004). The picture in Japan is clouded by complexity in economic ordering and greater competition in politics (see Dore, 2000). This rather 'chaotic' outcome, combining change with elements of continuity, may be difficult for economists, political scientists and lawyers to handle, but it should be readily appreciated by practitioners and analysts of business management, where messy practical realities are valued as much as elegant theory.

Realigning stakeholders in Japanese corporate governance

This chapter uses a stakeholder analysis to outline the contours of change and continuity. Although the relationship between managers and shareholders is central to conceptualizing the operation of corporate entities, other stakeholders are also influential, including creditors, employees, suppliers, government authorities and even local residents.[3]

Stakeholder analysis focuses on major problems that are common in all stakeholder relationships. An important problem is incomplete information. If all parties had full information, shareholders and creditors, for instance, would not have to worry about managers wasting their money. Yet in the real world, incomplete information gives rise to the dual problems of 'adverse selection' (hidden information, resulting for example in creditors agreeing to lend money to what turn out to be high-risk firms) and 'moral hazard' (hidden action, for example managers invest loaned funds in excessively high-risk projects). These difficulties are compounded by others, such as (1) the inability to write a stakeholder relationship contract that expressly provides for all possible contingencies, because of the limits on foreseeing future scenarios (Hoshi, 1998); and (2) the inability properly to enforce such a contract. These definitions of adverse selection and moral hazard highlight underlying problems of opportunism and bounded rationality (Williamson, 1996). As will be discussed in the following sections, they can be usefully developed to uncover and structure empirical data on relations involving managers and shareholders, creditors of the firm and employees. The overall picture is one of (1) significant rapprochement of manager and shareholder interests, (2) the elimination of cartel-like regulation of banks and other financial institutions, and (3) less obvious or more gradual pressures reshaping employment relations.

Yet raw opportunism may not be the only force at work. A stakeholder analysis can also reveal robust patterns of cooperative relations among participants. Consider, for example, the automotive industry in postwar Japan, and subsequently in the United States. When an expanding group of participants engage in quite radical information gathering and sharing among one another they are entrenching trust, leading to the emergence of novel forms of corporate governance (Helper *et al.*, 2000). Although the overall trend is towards arm's-length relations in Japan, cooperation is still in evidence. In particular there is evidence of new patterns of cooperation at the state and civil society levels (Schwartz and Pharr, 2003), both of which are increasingly important stakeholders in corporate organizations.

Shareholders becoming primary stakeholders

The separation of ownership from control in public listed companies,[4] leading to the emergence of a distinct managerial class whose interests are no longer necessarily aligned with shareholders, has been an agreed starting point for analyzing corporate governance since it was first highlighted in the United States in 1932 by Berle and Means (see Berle and Means, 1991). Particularly since the US-led occupation of Japan after World War II, successive reforms to Japanese corporate law have often been directed precisely at protecting shareholders' rights (Hayakawa, 1997).

From the perspective of agency theory, two types of constraint are available to shareholders to counter the informational advantage held by managers. The first is 'control oriented'. The shareholders monitor management behaviour, often delegating this to a board of directors whom they elect; and they intervene if necessary, for example by a proxy vote fight, to replace directors and hence managers. However the costs involved in this usually make it more attractive to large shareholders who themselves have good management skills. The second type of constraint, arm's-length control, is more passive. The shareholders do not actively intervene in management, but if they are dissatisfied with managers they may sell shares, which could lower the share price and encourage a hostile takeover. Alternatively, indirect control can be achieved by institutionalizing practices that better align the interests of managers with shareholders, for example the provision of incentives such as profit-related bonuses or stock options

(Hoshi, 1998). The general consensus about companies in postwar Japan is that such arm's-length controls have been particularly weak.

Openly hostile takeovers have certainly been rare.[5] In large part, this is due to the development of extensive cross-shareholdings among firms. The main reason for the emergence of cross-shareholdings remains unclear, although most analyses point to stock market weaknesses soon after World War II, when capital was needed by companies and the threat of takeovers was high. Ironically, cross-shareholding may also have developed because Japanese corporate law, influenced by US law, extended substantive rights to shareholders, yet many of those rights have remained mandatory (Shishido, 2000). Japanese managers may therefore have encouraged the development of cross-shareholding as an alternative way to protect their interests.[6]

Nonetheless some arm's-length control has continued to be exercised through ostensibly friendly takeovers or mergers. These have often occurred in the context of poor performance, reflected in weak share prices; and strong correlations have been found between share price weakness and the resignation of managers (Kaplan and Ramseyer, 1996). Thus while managers are not replaced by those taking over firms, as in hostile bids, they retire 'voluntarily'. Shishido (2000) provides one important causal explanation for this pattern: Japanese firms that perform badly on the share market find it difficult to raise equity finance, and this makes it more difficult to obtain debt finance from banks. Such pressures have grown as Japan has become mired in recession. Conversely, Shishido notes recent evidence that pressures from the Japanese share market are forcing some firms to restructure their labour relations, with compliance being rewarded by higher share prices (ibid., note 112). Moreover aggregate cross-shareholding in publicly traded shares has declined significantly since the stock market collapse and the bursting of the bubble economy in the early 1990s.[7] Further, building on the tradition of indirect control mechanisms and more recent changes to Japan's socioeconomic environment, a few 'norm entrepreneurs' are now openly embarking on hostile takeover activities (Milhaupt, 2001). A growing body of empirical research shows how significant changes could be achieved in Japan by law reforms that legitimized new social norms or reinforced selected existing ones.[8] With takeovers, a quite amenable legal framework has long been in place in terms of formal substantive law provisions, and that may make it easier for social norms to be reformulated and take root. Milhaupt and West (2001) argue that this process is already underway, underpinned by the potential of takeovers to promote efficient diversity in corporate organizations.

More directly aligning the interests of managers and shareholders has had mixed success. Stock option schemes have been progressively liberalized since the mid 1990s, and in 2002 the Tokyo District Court adopted an interpretation that was favourable to the taxpayer. However this has been appealed against by the government, and tax legislation continues to change. Also the stock options involved in this litigation were issued by foreign companies.[9] Nonetheless stock option schemes have steadily gained in popularity, with 800 Japanese companies reportedly having them by 2000 (Ahmadjian, 2003). However, such schemes may be subjected to increasing scrutiny if and when committees for remunerating managers are established (as discussed below) and Japan's share market revives significantly, even though executive remuneration in Japan has remained comparatively low. Problems of excessive remuneration have been exposed in the United States and Australia following spectacular corporate collapses in recent years (Clarke *et al.*, 2003), highlighting the need for transparency and some limits on the size of remuneration packages designed to encourage managers to work in shareholders' interests (Hill and Yablon, 2003). Similar issues arise with bonuses and other forms of remuneration for managers that are tightly tied to performance. Although these have not been common in postwar Japan, performance-linked employment is steadily replacing seniority-based lifetime employment, even in the larger blue-chip companies (Shibata, 2002). Japan's protracted economic stagnation is compounding this shift because shareholders no longer can indirectly control managers by tying their reputation to the company's performance (Tsuru, 1999).

At the same time, control-oriented mechanisms have also been expanding. To be sure, as cross-shareholdings have declined, the potential for cross-shareholders to exercise direct control over managers in the other companies has reduced. However, such control was limited anyway as relatively small blocks of shares were held by rather loosely affiliated groups, perhaps reinforced by a norm against active intervention that made sense during Japan's era of strong economic growth. A much more important direct check on managers has been exercised by the main banks, which often hold an even smaller shareholding in the client firm (statutorily limited to 5 per cent) but are able to monitor its performance by providing a broad array of services, and can intervene if necessary (Milhaupt, 2002). As will be mentioned in the next section, however, the main bank system has come under even greater pressure than cross-shareholdings due to crises in and the deregulation of financial markets, especially since the late 1990s.

At least partially offsetting these two trends, the potential for more control-oriented checks on managers has been increased by the growing importance of institutional investors in Japan, as elsewhere. Japan's pension funds and the like are now finding themselves in dire financial straits, and there is no guarantee even implicit that the government will be inclined or able to bail them out, given its own problem with preparing for a rapidly ageing population (Morgan, 2001). Even more significant, at least to many Japanese managers in recent years, is the growing presence of foreign pension funds, which demand better results and transparency from the firms in which they invest (Ahmadjian, 2003). In the wake of major changes in accounting standards, return on equity has become a pervasive concern even among firms with no or limited foreign investment, as evidenced by the recent popularity of share buy-backs.[10]

Even smaller investors, including a strong proportion from abroad since Japan's stockmarket downturn during the 1990s, can exert direct control through actual or potential derivative actions against managers who fail to act in the best interests of the company and its shareholders. Following a reduction in the filing fee in 1993, the number of derivative lawsuits has grown rapidly. Activist lawyers and groups have emerged, taking advantage of the new institutional realities and promoting another shift in norms governing the 'proper' role for shareholder interests, as illustrated and cemented by a remarkable victory in 2000 against Daiwa Bank executives. While concern on the part of managers about personal liability in such litigation led in 2002 to further law reforms to limit the scope or effects of derivative actions (Black and Cheffins, 2003), the legal and socioeconomic framework for derivative actions is still very different from that which prevailed at the start of Japan's lost decade (West, 2001b).

Some sceptics suggest that the restrictions enacted in 2002 were primarily the consequence of defensive reactions by managers, as indeed were reductions in the size of the traditionally large boards of directors in Japan. Only remaining board members, not the new category of 'executive officers', have been left at risk of derivative actions. However, this shift to smaller boards seems to have begun in the late 1990s (Moerke, 2003), initiated primarily by Sony, a well-managed company with a high proportion of foreign ownership. It also committed itself to including independent directors on the downsized board, emphasizing the board's role as a monitor (especially on behalf of shareholders) of the activities of executive officers and other line managers. Sony's new system can therefore be better explained by pressures such as those described above, particularly the more or less latent demands of investors, plus the realization that other mechanisms to minimize poor managerial performance were being undermined precisely as Japanese companies were being exposed to ever-greater legal and economic risks.

By June 2001, 35.7 per cent of listed companies had already adopted what Puchniak (2003) calls the 'Sony-type company model' and 24.4 per cent of companies were contemplating adopting it. In other words, only 40 per cent of companies were still wedded to the old company model, with a very large board (including many managers with executive responsibilities), complemented by statutory auditors or auditing officers to monitor certain activities of the board. In 2002 the Commercial Code was amended to allow large companies to retain either of these structures, or to adopt either a variant of the Sony model or a reformed version of the old company model, thus boosting the auditor system. As shown in Table 7.1, key differences between the Sony model and the new company model are that

Table 7.1 Japanese corporate governance models after the 2002 reform

	Old company model	Reformed old company model	Sony company model	New company model
Number of outside directors	No requirement for outside directors according to law. No outside directors in practice	One outside director required by law	No outside directors required by law. Two to three outside directors in practice	Two outside directors required by law
Number of directors	Three directors required by law. Twenty to 40 directors in practice	At least 10 directors required by law	Three directors required by law. Ten directors in practice	Three directors required by law
Targets of shareholder class-action law suits	Directors and statutory auditors	Directors and statutory auditors	Directors and statutory auditors. However, many of the decision makers are officers (*shikko yakuin*) who are not subject to derivative actions	Directors and officers (*shikko yaku*). Officers are also subject to derivative actions
Committees	No committees required by law. Managing committee composed of a few senior directors who make all important decisions in practice	Managing committee required by law (three or more members). No outside directors required on managing committee	No committees required by law. Committee system with outside directors in practice	Nominating, remuneration and audit committees required by law (three or more members per committee, the majority being outside directors)
Statutory auditors (*kansayaku*)	Four statutory auditors required by law. At least half of the statutory auditors are required by law to be outsiders	Four statutory auditors required by law. At least half of the statutory auditors are required by law to be outsiders	Four statutory auditors required by law. At least half of the statutory auditors are required by law to be outsiders	Statutory auditors prohibited by law

Source: Puchniak (2003).

the latter requires at least two outside directors, key decisions (for example on remuneration) must be made by committees that include some of them, and officers are open to shareholder derivative suits.

Several criticisms have been directed at this new menu of corporate governance options. The general conclusion is that little real change will result (see for example Rodatz, 2003). First, the requirement that directors (and indeed auditors) be independent is thought not to be strict enough. However that awaits clarification by the courts, and there is a risk that the rules will be further tightened once firms have sunk funds into transforming themselves into reformed old-type companies or especially new-type companies.

Second, it is thought that the reform will not work because companies will not choose to change from being a Sony-type company to a new-type company because this would expose their executive officers to shareholder derivative actions (Kashiwagi, 2003). However the risk of this is limited somewhat by the safeguards enacted in 2002. Anyway, many of those which have already become Sony-type companies are likely to have been better managed or were genuinely desirous of improving their governance and overall performance.

Third, the reform does not force companies to adopt a particular model; in other words, the reform is elective (Nottage, 2003). This criticism tends to be made by US commentators who equate the new-type company model with the US model and view it as the most efficient one. A potential irony here is that at least some Japanese policy makers are probably being consistent with the ideology of market liberalism propounded so vigorously in the United States. Ahmadjian (2003, p. 230) observes that the logic of Japan's Ministry of Economy, Trade and Industry (METI) was that 'the market would eventually decide which form of governance was most effective'. On the other hand she concedes that METI had initially favoured the new-type company model, and that leaving open a choice (to change to a reformed old-type company) 'was a compromise under pressure from Keidanren ... facing its own internal pressures, both from global firms that wanted to reshape their boards to reflect US practices, and from domestic firms which resisted change'.[11] Some pressure on companies to reform their governance structures has also been a hallmark of British Commonwealth governments, which have also drawn to varying degrees on US features when fashioning the options (Puchniak, 2003); and leaving in particular options based on the auditor system may reflect an enduring attraction of German corporate law, which moreover has implemented mostly on an optional basis (du Plessis, 2004). As will be discussed in the final section of this chapter, the element of compromise – and its particular style – leaving in place existing structures and superimposing reformed structures – appears to reflect the 'reformist conservatism' found in other areas of Japanese law and society (Nottage, 2001c).

Thus, it is hardly compelling to argue that Japan's elective corporate governance reform does not go far enough; yet at the same time it does signal a significant step towards American-style corporate governance (Senechal, 2003). More interesting are the comments by Ahmadjian (2003), who argues that this reform nicely illustrates the thesis of 'Japan's managed globalization' based on 'permeable insulation' (Schaede and Grimes, 2003). She predicts the emergence of

> a dual system of governance. Globally oriented firms would increase board independence and introduce auditing, nomination and compensation committees, while more domestically focused firms would maintain the [auditor] system and continue to maintain managerial autonomy and insulation from the demands of shareholders. (Ahmadjian, 2003, p. 231)

To some extent this appears to be happening, judging by reports of firms adopting the new-type company model since this option was laid down in the commercial code in June 2003. However these are still early days, and a final assessment is complicated by what is meant by 'globally oriented firms'. Sony quickly became a new-type company, and indeed went a step further than required by separating out the posts of board chairperson and chief executive officer.[12] The model has also been adopted by large companies – particularly in the consumer electronics sector – with less foreign ownership but exposed to and engaging in highly competitive markets throughout the world. However of the 55 firms that had become new-type companies by August 2003, several are distinctly domestically focused, such as large retailers and smaller banks (Kubori, 2003). It could be that these firms want to become more globally oriented, either by attracting foreign investment or expanding into markets abroad, but that is difficult to prove. Another explanation may be that these firms believe that new-type companies have more efficient corporate governance, which translates into better economic performance, even in domestic markets. They may also think that this is due to the model being 'American', and discount problems in the United States that were exposed by corporate collapses such as that of Enron, or believe in the model's efficiency because they have heard of it or its variants being adopted in British Commonwealth countries and even continental Europe (Hill and Yablon, 2003). But such global considerations may be minimal or non-existent for most of these firms, filtered out in the recommendations by policy makers such as METI and the considerable media reporting on Japan's regular corporate law reforms.

In short the broad adoption of the new-type company model may be better conceptualized as a pragmatic response to abstract or 'indigenized' expectations about governance and its putative links to economic perform- ance.[13] Nonetheless this is occurring in the context of the institutional and normative shifts towards greater control by shareholders over managers outlined above. Many of these involve control-oriented mechanisms that may resonate with non-US traditions in companies. Although seemingly less noted or widely discussed (Kozuka, 2003), arm's-length mechanisms – which are representative of Americanization generally – are continuing to gain strength in this important stakeholder relationship.

Creditors, recession and financial market deregulation

A distinctive feature of postwar corporate governance in Japan has been the greater importance of creditors as stakeholders due to comparatively more use of bank than equity finance. Yet this characteristic has diminished over the last two decades as companies have been able to accumulate earnings and gradual financial market deregulation has enabled them to raise funds more readily through bond issues and so on. More recent reforms of the Commercial Code are aimed at further boosting equity finance by giving investors and managers greater choice over how to capitalize a new venture and meet the ongoing funding needs of the new business – just as share options and buybacks provide more choice over how to design incentive schemes to ensure efficient operation. The logic behind the reforms is consistent with other government initiatives to shake Japan out of its protracted economic malaise. With news still dominated by bankruptcies and rising unemployment, the government hopes the reforms will spark corporate-led economic growth. The reasoning is that more flexible corporate finance tools should allow efficient new businesses to replace failing unproductive industries. More importantly the greater range of financing options should empower expanding businesses to satisfy their ongoing funding needs.

The annual session of the Diet in 2001 enacted a number of changes to allow a Japanese *kabushiki kaisha* (joint stock company, the main focus of this chapter) greater freedom to determine its initial capital structure. The key amendments, which came into effect on 1 October 2001, include the following:

- Abolishing the requirement that the issue price of shares at the time of incorporation must be a minimum of 50 000 yen.
- Removing the prohibition on share splits that cause either the aggregate nominal amount of the issued shares to exceed the stated capital, or the amount of net assets per stock to be less than 50 000 yen. Moreover share splits can now be effected by a board decision without a shareholder vote, even if this requires an amendment to the company's articles of incorporation to increase the number of authorized shares.
- Abolishing par-value shares, thereby eliminating any differences between par-value shares and no-par shares.

- Introducing the voting unit (*tangen-kabu*) system, under which a Japanese company may add to its articles of incorporation the provision that a certain number of its shares will constitute one unit, that is, one voting right.

According to Tanahashi (2002) these amendments have removed significant hurdles for start-up companies. Prior to the amendments, the minimum share price requirement meant that early start-ups, which often lacked significant net assets, could issue only a few shares. Company growth would cause these shares to represent considerable value in the company, making it difficult to raise further funds by granting share options. Furthermore the post-split net asset requirement meant that share splits were not always possible. A possible stop-gap measure of issuing no-par shares at a nominal value pro rata among all shareholders was impractical in post-IPO (initial public offering) companies because it was not realistic to require all shareholders to pay an even nominal consideration for the newly issued shares. Therefore abolishing the minimum share price and the net asset value requirement for share splits and par-value shares, as well as allowing differential voting rights, has given start-up companies greater flexibility when structuring their initial capitalization to allow for future expansion.[14]

In addition, under the Commercial Code amendments that were approved on 21 November 2001 and came into effect on 1 April 2002, companies are able to streamline the means by which they obtain ongoing equity financing, especially when multiple infusions of equity are required over a relatively short period of time. This allows for the smooth financing of companies, particularly in the case of new ventures, which often cannot secure debt funding from banks. Under the former law, companies often needed to secure a special resolution at a properly convened general meeting to access equity finance during periods of high growth. The so-called '4:1 rule' restricted the number of shares a company could issue in a given capital increase to four times the number of shares that the company already had outstanding. This meant that pre-IPO companies that required multiple infusions of equity financing had to convene a general meeting for each new issue to secure a two-thirds vote to amend the number of authorized shares in its articles of incorporation. Adding to this complexity, the Commercial Code granted pre-emptive rights to shareholders for any new issuance of shares. Again a two-thirds shareholder vote was required to issue new shares without honouring such pre-emptive rights.

The new provisions simplify the procedures for growing businesses to acquire equity funding when needed. The 4:1 rule no longer applies to closed companies (that is, companies whose articles of incorporation require director transfers of shares), and shareholders can now authorize the board of a closed company to issue, at its discretion over a one-year period, a specified number of new shares to third parties at favourable prices without honouring pre-emptive rights.

In addition the revised Commercial Code increases the types of share publicly listed companies may issue. These include:

- Preferred shares or non-common shares with no voting rights or limited voting rights.
- Tracking shares, where the dividends are not fixed but linked to the performance of a certain segment or subsidiary of the issuing company.
- Protected shares, where holders can exercise veto rights in respect of certain company actions.
- Mandatory convertible shares, where the shares may be converted into another type of share at the discretion of the issuing company and not the holder.

As these reforms only came into effect in late 2001 and 2002 it is still too early to tell whether the new provisions are having the desired effect. However, as with the steady uptake of stock option and share buyback schemes mentioned earlier, there is some evidence that companies are taking full advantage of their increased financing powers.

Conversely the role of main banks is expected to to decline (Yasui, 1999). The relative importance of equity markets in corporate finance will undoubtedly grow due to the ongoing economic stagnation and severe credit crunch, combined with globalization and broader financial market deregulation. The latter programme, which began at the end of 1996, was a response to the poor return on capital suffered by Japanese financial institutions throughout the postwar period, and especially the rapid loss of global competitiveness in the 1990s. This 'big bang' (or 'long bang'!) is now complete, and the legislative and structural reforms are very wide-ranging.[15]

As mentioned above, as with other stakeholder relationships the relationship between creditors and managers gives rise to the problem of adverse selection (leading to credit being extended too readily to risky firms) and of moral hazard (inadequate monitoring resulting in poor projects by management). Blame for the abrupt decline of the Japanese financial sector during the 1990s lies in part with the Japanese government, particularly the Ministry of Finance (the Bank of Japan having become a more independent policy maker only recently), but the financial institutions were also partly responsible for their own plight, having embarked on a huge spending spree in the late 1980s that led to the massive bad debts reported in recent years. This disaster stemmed from distortions in evaluating and pricing risk, or more specifically, from problems in corporate governance that encouraged financial institutions in Japan to lend to (and invest in) risky firms, and then fail adequately to monitor the managers in those firms (Kanaya and Woo, 2000).

One solution for such tensions between creditors and managers is to give creditors shares in the companies to which they lend, as shareholders can generally overcome agency problems *vis-à-vis* managers. In addition creditors can monitor managers in two main ways. One involves arm's-length control: the creditor still delegates considerable control to the managers but may step in to force bankruptcy, thus creating an incentive for managers to pursue creditors' interests (Hoshi, 1998). Forcing bankruptcy must also be a credible option, but Japanese bankruptcy law has had various problems that only started to be addressed seriously towards the end of the 1990s (Anderson, 2000, 2001; Anderson and Steele, 2003). One consequence has been the enactment of a more functional corporate reorganization regime in 1999. Between April 2000, when the Civil Rehabilitation Law came into effect, and August 2002, 31 reorganizations had been initiated and 16 had been resolved in about six months, compared with an average of two years under the old Corporate Reorganization Law (Xu, 2003). West (2003a) notes that this regime also applied to individuals but was little used by them until amendments were added in 2000 (home mortgage exemptions and so on). He argues that its more ready availability and uptake since then has helped legitimate bankruptcy and reduce its social stigma, even contributing to a decline in debt-related suicides. Although fewer or different stigmas are attached to bankruptcy for companies, it is likely that the 'norm shift' prompted by the law reform will increase the use of corporate insolvency options as arm's-length control mechanisms by creditors over the managers in the firms to which they lend.

Alternatively, or in addition, creditors can adopt a more control-oriented strategy. They can directly monitor the behaviour of managers and intervene if necessary in their appointment or replacement. One way in which Japanese banks have been able to directly monitor their borrowers' managers, or at least in Japan, has been to provide a range of services (such as general business advice or match-making) rather than just loans. However that has been difficult in the case of overseas lending; and it has also encountered difficulties domestically as Japanese companies have become more sophisticated and competition has intensified as a result of accelerating financial market deregulation (Ouandlous and Philippatos, 1999). The latter, combined with the recessionary environment facing Japanese financial institutions in particular, has also made it more difficult to maintain the long-term relationship required to be a firm's main bank (Yasui, 1999). A key aspect of this is that the primary lender holds shares over lengthy periods, and intervenes when the debtor experiences financial distress by seconding bank managers. If banks become strapped for funds, however, they may call in their loans or simply refuse to lend more; an increase in lender liability claims by debtors was noted already in the mid 1990s (Milhaupt, 1996). More recently, cases have been reported in which main banks have not saved companies by providing loans, and in other instances they have not borne a disproportionate burden of the losses that follow liquidation. A related phenomenon is a belated 'flight to quality' in lending, perversely exacerbating the present credit crunch. Finally, there is evidence of banks selling off their shareholdings, reportedly after client firms have offloaded their stocks in the banks and in the shadow of a dangerous decline in the ratio of market value over book value (4:1 in 1986 but only just over 1:1 in 1998 – Fukao, 1999). Unwinding shareholdings prevents financial institutions from remaining or developing into a main bank, and therefore are less able to monitor debtor firms, and it reduces the incentive to send their own managers to debtor firms that are in distress (especially as even the big banks have considerable problems of their own nowadays). Reputation as a main bank can unravel quickly, and is difficult to regain (Tsuru, 1999).

Such breakdowns have become even more likely since foreign financial institutions began to take advantage of deregulation to enter the Japanese market from the late 1990s (Sibbitt, 1998a). These outsiders are unlikely to take over, and certainly not take on, even small shareholdings in debtor firms in such a rapidly changing environment. Even if they do, they may refuse to 'take turns' with other creditor/shareholders to send valuable management resources to help keep debtor firms in business. Their inclination, no doubt often in their short-term interest, may be to enforce their strict legal right to call in their security or force bankruptcy. After all, lending institutions (and associations) in Japan have long made sure that their rights are well protected by contract and commercial practice at the time of lending (Kanda, 1998).

Three other factors are undermining the main bank system (Milhaupt, 2001). The first has arisen from the nationalization and reprivatization of the failed Long-Term Credit Bank. The government sold this bank to a group of foreign investors, including Citigroup, and gave them a 'put option' to return any assets (loans) that declined from the book value (as of 1 March 2000) by 20 per cent or more within three years. But this would be lost if the bank accepted a borrower's request for loan forgiveness. In mid 2000 the reprivatized bank refused to forgive debts owed by Sogo Department Store, thus forcing it into bankruptcy and going against what was traditionally expected of a main bank. More generally, bank actions such as this undercut an implicit guarantee against them given by the Japanese government (Milhaupt and Miller, 1997) in exchange for strong institutions supporting weak ones through the main bank system. Finally, the Asian financial crisis and Japan's long recession are perceived to have caused a significant shift in belief about the benefits of bank-oriented corporate finance and governance.

Employees and the vicissitudes of the labour market

Another famous aspect of Japanese corporate governance is under threat: the importance given to employees (see for example Miwa, 1998). Japanese corporate governance has been notable for the orientation of companies first towards people (that is, employees), then products (technically excellent goods), then profits (for shareholders). This contrasts with the German model, in which products come first, then people, then profits, and the Anglo-American model – first profits, then products, with people coming last. The importance of employees in Japanese companies has undoubtedly been strong, or at least in the case of permanent employees in large corporations (now a steadily declining proportion).[16] Yet this can also be analyzed in terms of agency problems, and how their stakeholding in companies relates to that of other stakeholders. Such an analysis, together with observed tendencies in the labour market and important legislative amendments, points to other pressures on Japanese corporate governance.[17]

Discussions of relations between employees and managers usually centre on the latter as 'principals', who hire the former as 'agents' despite the possibility of adverse selection, and monitor their delegated activities despite moral hazard ('shirking', due again to imperfect information in the relationship). This can be reversed to analyze implications for corporate governance. The question then becomes, how can employees, as principals, constrain managers (agents) from frittering away company funds on themselves? One solution is to give employees shares in the company. However employee share ownership programmes do not play a major role in Japanese corporate governance (Hayakawa, 1997), and they can only constrain managers to the extent that agency problems between shareholders and managers are generally resolved (see the previous section). Otherwise the only realistic alternative is to introduce more control-oriented measures. One example is the two-tier board structure in Germany stock companies, in which a supervisory board is partly elected by the employees, and then it appoints the management board (du Plessis, 2004). Japanese corporate law provides no such formal mechanism for employee supervision of managers, but control arises in practice because most managers in large Japanese companies have been appointed from the ranks of existing employees in the system of lifetime employment, under which promotion is based primarily on seniority. As a consequence of this the external labour market has not developed significantly.

The origins of this employment practice are unclear. As with several supposedly distinctive features of Japanese law (such as limiting the number of practising lawyers – Haley, 1978), the practice of lifetime employment seems to have taken root only quite recently (see Foote, 1996). Gilson and Roe (1999, p. 520) observe that

> from World War I through to the end of World War II, worker mobility in external labour markets eroded labour stability when labour was tight, and employers' willingness to fire even senior workers eroded labour stability when labour markets were not tight. Employers tried but failed to build wage and seniority structures to induce workers to stay during labour shortages. Government intervention reduced but failed to stop turnover.

They argue that lifetime employment arose shortly after World War II (when there was an extreme labour surplus) because of exceptional political events. Rapid unionization and radical worker activism (strikes and plant takeovers) prompted a 'deal' to give a privileged segment of labour (mainly surviving employees) lifetime employment. Thereafter 'Japan's economic problem was to craft associated institutions that could function effectively given the politically imposed lifetime employment', including restrictions on external labour markets (ibid., p. 524). Nowadays Japan faces a very different political and economic environment, with record unemployment (and underemployment), and institutional changes opening up the possibility of growing worker mobility through the expansion of the external labour market. Gilson and Roe identify several significant 'stress points' in the postwar Japanese system (ibid., p. 540). For instance it does not cope well during times of dramatic technological change,[18] and competition among lifetime employees for promotion in the internal labour market does not work effectively when firms are no longer growing.

Rather similarly, Shishido (2000) points out that labour turnover rates in the 1920s and 1930s were almost the same as those in the United States, but the latter jumped in the 1940s and have remained much higher ever since. He argues that the situation in the United States can be linked to the Great Depression, and that if the Japanese recession continues there will be an irreversible decline in lifetime employment as a key aspect of the corporate governance system. More generally, the ongoing recession is creating a zero-sum situation and is heightening the conflict between employees and other stakeholders, notably shareholders. The latter will no longer tolerate employees being treated as *de facto* residual claimants, for instance receiving wage hikes or bonuses when dividends remain constant or decline (see also Ghosn, 2003). In parallel there has been a considerable strengthening of the external labour market and the corporate control (share) market (Shishido, 2000).

Labour law scholars such as Yamakawa (1999), perhaps due to their reliance on historical data, are more impressed by the enduring quality of the postwar model, but note a number of major challenges to this model. One is the broader political and economic environment. The recession plus deregulation have resulted in greater variability in corporate profitability, a key factor as the credit crunch still facing Japanese financial institutions is encouraging companies to turn to the stock and bond markets – often global and more demanding of good corporate and managerial performance. In addition, the service sector is growing in importance, bringing the need for (and the possibility of) more flexible working hours (see Hanami, 1999). Both factors are related to changing demographics in the labour force in general, which is now characterized by larger numbers of mature people, women and part-time workers (Kezuka, 2000). This is also affecting the retention of lifetime employment as a core concept in the Japanese corporate world. However Yamakawa (2001) concludes that it will remain, albeit with some modifications. Data from various surveys support this conclusion, although they also show a move towards performance-related pay.[19] However a problem with most of these surveys is that they question incumbents within firms. To obtain a better picture of the future of Japan's employment and corporate governance systems, more research should be conducted into what young people want nowadays. Certainly they are unhappy with the fact that the current employment practices are strongly biased towards the incumbent, older generation, especially those in lifetime employment (Genda, 2000).

Major changes have been made to labour legislation (Yamakawa, 2001). These should cement or encourage broader transformations in the labour market in Japan, sometimes following changes in norms and/or underlying socioeconomic institutions (as with takeovers – Milhaupt 2001) and sometimes rather prompting them (as with consumer bankruptcy reform – West, 2003a). These changes include, the following:[20]

- In 1998, amendments to the Labour Standards Law allowing longer-term labour contracts, requiring written clarification of working conditions upon hiring and reasons for termination (a growing source of tension), and divorcing overtime payments from hours worked (indicating more emphasis on quality of work).
- In 1997, amendments to the Equal Employment Opportunity Law (Wolff, 2003b) prohibiting discrimination in recruitment, assignment, promotion, dismissal and retirement, compelling employers to engage in mediation if requested by employees, and addressing the problem of sexual harassment (a frequent source of litigation since the early 1990s).
- In 1995, an amendment (taking effect from April 1999) to the Child Care Law extending leave to provide care to elderly family members (Webb, 2002).
- In 1999, enactment of the Fundamental Law for a Gender-Equal Society (which should encourage affirmative action programmes or other broad transformations of women's work – see Miller, 2003).

- In 1999, amendments to the Working Dispatching Law abolishing the positive list system of limiting dispatching to specified (professional) job categories in favour of a negative list system, and putting pressure on companies that use temporary workers to give them first refusal if the company decides to hire employees for the work done by them (potentially creating a new hybrid category of employee).
- Amendments to the Employment Security Law changing to a negative list system for the private placement of non-temporary workers, clearer licensing for businesses that do this, and replacement of a blanket fee maximum chargeable (which hampered attempts to head-hunt and place managers) (West, 2003b).
- Moves to promote pension plans based on defined contributions rather than just defined benefits (which had discouraged voluntary job-switching because complete vesting was unusual).

In addition to the above, and the political and economic changes described at the start of this section, globalization is beginning to have a direct effect on the Japanese labour market. In the boom years of the 1980s, guest workers were brought in for blue-collar work jobs that Japanese were unwilling to touch. Many have stayed on, often illegally. A significant feature since the 1990s has been a gradual increase in the number of foreign white-collar employees and managers, even at the highest executive level. This is most evident in the financial sector, but it is tied to broader patterns of foreign direct investment, especially the growth of mergers and acquisitions involving companies from abroad (Milhaupt and West, 2001). While it is too early to say what independent effect these developments will have on the labour market in Japan, cumulatively they reinforce the changes described above, impacting on the future of corporate governance in Japan.

Conflicting tendencies in industrial production and the state?

The above application of principal–agent theory to analyze three key aspects of Japanese corporate governance suggests that the interests of managers and shareholders have drawn closer together, that severe challenges have emerged for corporate finance centred on main banks, and that pressures reshaping employment relations may consolidate in the longer term. Overall this amounts to convergence towards the arm's-length relations that characterize Anglo-American corporate governance. Further complicating the picture, however, the notion of opportunism underlying principal–agent theory may not be the only force at work. This becomes apparent when we look at other stakeholders in the firm.

Another important set of stakeholders consists of the firm's outside suppliers and customers. Particularly interesting are the cooperative relations that have developed among firms (especially in the automotive industry), notably in postwar Japan but later finding root in the United States. Some recent studies of industrial organization have focused on 'learning by monitoring', which involves (1) benchmarking (exacting surveys of current and likely future products and processes) to uncover new general products, (2) simultaneous engineering (where the subunits responsible for components undertake similar benchmarking, while considering the implications for other subunits, which may lead to redefining the project as a whole), and (3) systems of strict error detection and correction for the new routines, with further extensive information sharing to respond quickly if the consequences could prove disastrous (Helper *et al.*, 2000). The emergence of this paradigm suggests that pervasive information sharing may entrench cooperation, which is seen not just as a means of securing individual benefits but also as an end in itself, underpinned by a vision of 'enlarging the pie' rather than trying to obtain a larger slice at the others' expense. History also shows how dramatic changes in conditions can unravel such collaborative relations (as in the US automotive industry in the 1950s to 1970s), but then build them up again as underlying mechanisms become apparent (as in the 1980s to 1990s) (ibid.)

It is not yet clear what has happened to relations among firms in the Japanese automotive industry, especially since the late 1990s, when the changes to the other aspects of corporate governance described above appeared to take hold. Despite some notable developments, the economic and social logic underpinning cooperative interfirm relations may prove resistant in that industry, which has been demonstrably more successful and still holds reserves to draw on, compared with for instance, Japan's weak financial sector. Although Japan's car manufacturers are now using e-commerce to unwind *keiretsu* or preferential relationships with suppliers for standardized products, they seem to be retaining such relationships for more technologically complex parts.[21] Relative stasis in such an important production chain would present a tension with the trends for change identified above, even if the latter relations (mostly within the firm) are more determinative of corporate governance. But a similar tension arguably existed in the United States during the 1980s and 1990s, when contracting among firms (or at least in some manufacturing and service sectors) came to be based on information sharing and learning by monitoring, while arm's-length control and market-based coordination increasingly characterized corporate governance in its narrower sense (Sabel, 1996).

The (re-)entrenchment of learning by monitoring mechanisms in industry in the United States and their possible retention in Japan may encourage the emergence of novel forms of corporate governance in both countries: 'corporate incubators' for strategic thinking in firms, performance metrics based on baskets of measures that are subject to continuous review and redefinition, and venture capitalism. However these applications are less well established than in industrial production, and are thought to be at risk of being displaced by more straightforward market-based corporate governance mechanisms (Helper *et al.*, 2000).

On the other hand, they may be supported by similar processes of learning by monitoring being played out at other levels, implicating two further stakeholders in corporate organizations. The first consists of individual consumers and their organizations, as opposed to the business customers of firms. The three elements that characterize learning by monitoring – benchmarking by the person requiring the goods, simultaneous engineering by production subunits and careful error detection and reporting – seem at least partially applicable to the relationships that build up between consumers and manufacturers via retailers. A key premise is the existence of proactive and demanding consumers who are prepared to voice their needs and complaints, and this is precisely what has emerged since World War II and particularly since the 1990s.[22] In recent years this has seemed to involve a more cynical and confrontational attitude on the part of consumers. However a new equilibrium may now be close, involving more widespread and balanced information sharing that may bring norms of cooperation based on mutual respect.

The model is more directly applicable to the state as a second, broader stakeholder in corporate organizations. An important parallel trend in advanced industrialized democracies is 'democratic experimentalism' (Dorf and Sabel, 1998), in which: (1) central authorities 'create a framework for experimentation by defining broad problems, setting provisional standards, pooling measurements of local performance, aiding poor performers to correct their problems, and revising standards and overall goals according to results'; and (2) 'local units doing most of the problem-solving but which are accountable to the centre, and to their local constituents, who participate in formulating its plans, and judge it both against those goals and in comparison to the performance of other locales in like circumstances' (Sabel and O'Donnell, 2000, p. 17). Key parameters in experimentation involving the state are transparency and participation by diverse actors to facilitate access to – and effective use of – the information needed to develop effective collaborative relations. Important trends in this direction in Japan include the following:

- Sweeping deregulation programmes, although these have tended to get bogged down in detail and bureaucracy (Katz, 2003).
- Enactment of comprehensive official information disclosure legislation in 1999 (Shultz, 2001).
- Greater engagement with foreigners and foreign models, at some levels (Clark, 2000; Takao, 2003).
- Some legal recognition of previously marginalized ethnic groups (Stewart, 2003).

- Adroit attempts by other minorities to avoid 'bureaucratic capture' while improving their lot (Nakamura, 2001).
- More support for such initiatives through reforms of legislation involving non-profit organizations (Pekkanen, 2000).
- Greater opportunities to build on traditions of local autonomy (Jain, 2000).

These trends are underpinned by major reforms since 2001 in respect of access to justice in Japan, driven by business interests (Kitagawa and Nottage, 2005). Such steps towards a more vibrant civil society (Schwartz and Pharr, 2003) may have been even more faltering than in neighbouring countries such as South Korea (see for example Ginsburg, 2001), yet there has been considerable momentum in Japan over the last decade, pointing to the approach of a more sustained, polyarchic, 'deliberative democracy' (see Cohen and Sabel, 1997). This adds further difficulties to assessing existing and potential changes in Japanese corporate governance, pressuring firms into taking corporate social responsibility more seriously (Iwai and Kobayashi, 2003). But the more political dimensions may prove to be the most crucial, despite having been overlooked by most theorists during Japan's lost decade.[23] The seeming paralysis of Japanese policy makers, then, can be seen in a more positive light. Perhaps it has concealed important elements of 'democratic experimentalism', with the central authorities slowly reorganizing key building blocks after extensive analysis of global trends, but leaving it primarily to socioeconomic subunits (such as major stakeholders in firms, including creditors, employees and their peak associations) to find a new balance and forms of governance that combine efficiency with normative acceptability (see for example West, 2001a). However this more positive assessment depends crucially on whether the Japanese state is and will remain committed to fostering information flows and decentralized participation in decision making among diverse socio-economic groups.

Conclusions

This chapter has outlined a broad conception of corporate governance that incorporates a variety of stakeholders both within and outside the firm, and has considered information flows among some of them. A primary aim has been to assess the extent of change in Japan, and particularly the possibility of a move towards a US model dominated by shareholder interests and arm's-length relationships. Key actors and relationships, and some of the shifts, are depicted in Figure 7.1.

At the core are the stakeholders who have traditionally been of most concern to corporate law on public listed companies. First, shareholders' relationship with managers has grown in practical importance since the

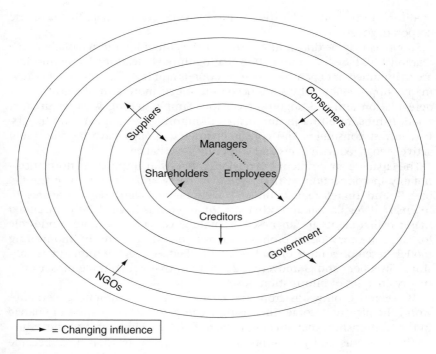

Figure 7.1 Concentric circles of stakeholder influence

1990s, with shareholders being pulled towards the centre of Japan's brave new world of corporate governance. Although the growing power of shareholders has been partly achieved by the exercise of direct controls (such as derivative suits), arm's-length control has also increased. Second, while the stakeholder position of employees has only recently been highlighted in corporate governance discussions of Anglo-American and Australian law and practice, particularly in the aftermath of large corporate insolvencies (Hill and Yablon, 2003), its significance has been apparent in Japan since at least the 1950s, especially in the form of lifetime employment and other *de facto* constraints on managers of large companies. Despite the durability of the latter model, however, distinctions and arm's-length relationships are emerging between employees and managers. The role of employees as independent monitors of managers is therefore declining.[24]

Creditors have also found little formal recognition in corporate law, yet their stakeholder role became strong in postwar Japan through the main bank system. The latter's decline and simultaneous moves towards equity financing, underpinned by financial market deregulation, may even propel creditors further outside the realm of core stakeholders in Japanese corporate governance.

Suppliers may be drawn into or nearer the core if long-term collaborative relationships based on information sharing through 'learning by monitoring' are maintained or expanded. Their position is ambivalent, however, because many supply relationships are becoming much more arm's-length due to deregulation and the ongoing recession. Simply exiting is easier in such relationships, resulting in diminished monitoring by suppliers and buyers. In contrast consumers and consumer interest groups have become more actively engaged with firms and corporate governance.

The Japanese government has obvious interests in corporate performance – notably in connection with economic recovery and restoration of the tax base – and therefore is a direct stakeholder. Government measures to intensify deregulation and other structural reforms have already prompted major realignments in Japanese corporate governance. A more subtle role for the state may be to promote variants of the learning by monitoring model, based on a more optimistic and embedded view of human relationships (Swedberg and Granovetter, 2001) than that which underpins agency theory analyses of information flows.

As we move outwards from the core of Japan's corporate governance world the picture becomes increasingly complicated. The extent of change in the relationships that affect more peripheral stakeholders, and the nature of the concerns and philosophies that drive those relationships, become more difficult to explain or predict. By contrast change is clearer at the core, even allowing for the tendency of comparative lawyers to see more transformations or convergence when comparing law-related phenomena more narrowly (Nottage, 2001a). There is indeed a tendency for convergence towards a shareholder-oriented model of corporate governance, at the expense of employees and main banks.

Yet the current control mechanisms are not just the arm's-length ones that best fit US socioeconomic ideology. Straightforward Americanization is being undermined by the adoption of German (and now EU) traditions and British Commonwealth variants of the US model. Perhaps most importantly, as we progress beyond the main concerns of corporate lawyers, the complex and shifting role of the state reminds us that much will depend on political contingencies. On the one hand Japan's recent elective corporate governance reforms reveal a reformist conservatism that is consistent with other recent law-related reforms, notably legal education (Nottage, 2001c). A sense emerges of a wide-ranging crisis about which something must be done, but the change ends up superimposing a new model on top of the old one (rather than abandoning the latter) with more or less incentives to adopt the new model. The incentives have been more pervasive in legal education reform, but weaker or more disparate for corporate organization, depending on the degree to which firms and their sectors are open to global competitive pressures (Schaede and Grimes, 2003). On the other hand there are likely to be limits to generalizations about Japan's new political environment and policy-making processes (see Grimes and Schaede, 2003). Broader promotion of learning by monitoring within and by Japan's polity may also reinforce the growth of value pluralism (Moehwald, 2000), and it may be possible to track the latter's bedding-down and specific policy-making processes that impact on corporate governance and commercial regulation (Huntington and Harrison, 2000). However ultimately, or in some areas, the interactions may become so complex that they can be better understood by applying chaos theory, which focuses on how small and regular iterations can result in large and often counterintuitive changes (see for example Williams and Arrigo, 2001).

What is already clear from the analyses of changes in corporate governance outlined in this chapter, is that corporate law in Japan is playing an integral part in this process (see also Kanda and Milhaupt, 2003). Indeed the changes to corporate law – and areas of law that affect stakeholders in a broader sense than those focused on by corporate law – seem to have been quite dramatic and effective. This is ironic, given that in the United States corporate practices and expectations changed well before corporate law was transformed, and prominent commentators have claimed that this phenomenon probably also pertains elsewhere (Hansmann and Kraakman, 2001). Other commentators seem to have underestimated the potential for the law to prompt socioeconomic change in Japan (for example Milhaupt, 2003; Aoki, 2003). Yet the law's precise role remains ambivalent: sometimes cementing or following social norms or institutional changes; sometimes prompting considerable transformations.

Notes

1. This chapter builds on Nottage (2001b) and its working paper version (www.iue.it/ PUB/WorkingPapers.shtml). It has been extensively updated and supplemented by further research (Nottage and Wolff 2000–3). In addition to the people acknowledged therein, we acknowledge valuable feedback and information from Phil Jamieson of Nagashima Ohno Tsunematsu and participants in the 2004 Corporate Law Teachers' Association Conference (8–11 February, Australian National University). All the internet references in this chapter were available at the cited URLs in February 2004.
2. However Schaede (2000, 2003) argues that public regulation is giving way to self-regulation by private industrial associations. Less globally competitive industries are tending to adopt self-regulation with greater risk of anticompetitive effects.
3. See also Kester (1996), Ballon and Honda (2000). Tsuru (1999) cautions that such a broad definition of corporate governance risks analytic looseness (see also Cioffi, 2000; cf. Aoki, 2003).
4. There are about 9000 such companies in Japan (Kanda, 1998, contains useful corporate data), including about 6330 with sufficient capital for listing (Yasui, 1999). Closely held companies, in which the shareholders are typically managers or are closely related to managers, offer different avenues for opportunistic behaviour. Despite their aggregate importance in the Japanese economy, these companies' problems

have not generated the same degree of law reform and discussion in recent years (see for example Shishido, 1990). This chapter therefore only mentions them in passing.

5. Nonetheless there have been several major hostile takeover battles since the late 1990s. Tokumoto (2001) discusses four that resulted in court judgments, and criticizes Japanese judges for too readily thwarting takeovers by allowing incumbent directors to issue shares to third parties (ostensibly due to the need to raise capital). Another well-publicized case of 'greenmail' involved a US investor, T. Boone Pickens, between 1989 and 1991 (Reich, 2001).

6. See also Takahashi (1997). Managers in the United States and elsewhere have been able to use other techniques after tailoring their corporate constitutions and so on, for example 'poison pills', whereby debentures and the like must be issued if an investor purchases more than a set percentage of shares, or limiting the voting rights to a minority percentage even if the investor obtains more than that percentage of shares. The liberalization of stock option schemes in Japan may open the way to such stratagems, but this possibility has tended not to be openly discussed (Kozuka, 2003). It probably awaits a more comprehensive move towards proactive commercial lawyering linked to the major reforms now underway in the Japanese legal profession (Kobayashi, 2003).

7. Takahashi (1997). Indeed the pace seems to be accelerating (see for example Shishido, 2000, Table 6, p. 226). As well as banks' immediate need to cash up, this trend may be underpinned by a more forward-looking appreciation that main bank shareholdings have tended to be in firms with less prospect of growth (see Osano and Hori 2002).

8. For example West (1997), Feldman (2001) and Nottage (2004).

9. Watanabe (2004), discusses Microsoft case, which was judged on 26 November 2002. He notes that on the same day the Tokyo District Court ruled on a quite similar case involving Compaq.

10. Amendments to the Commercial Code removed the restrictions on share buy-back schemes as of 1 October 2001. Under the new provisions, share buy-backs are permitted provided the repurchase is authorized beforehand by shareholders at the annual general meeting and the repurchase is funded out of distributable profits. Share buy-backs give shareholders a greater share of company profits. This is because share repurchases transfer wealth from the selling shareholders to the residual shareholders and increases earnings per share. Major Japanese companies (spearheaded by Sony, Matsushita, NTT, Honda and Toyota) are increasingly using this new power to protect the value of shareholders' equity investments. According to a report in the *Japan Times* (20 May 2002), Japanese companies listed on the first section of the Tokyo Stock Exchange announced share buy-back plans involving 4.2 trillion yen's worth of shares, double the total amount repurchased in fiscal year 2001.

11. Nippon Keidanren was formed in 2002 by the amalgamation of two important business organizations: Keidanren (the Japan Federation of Economic Organizations) and Nikkeiren (the Japan Federation of Employers' Associations). The former included larger firms that increasingly pushed for liberalization in Japan as they expanded their operations world-wide (Yoshimatsu, 2000). The current chairman of Nippon Keidanren (and Toyota) has been robust in his criticism of the Koizumi administration for not being decisive and innovative enough when carrying out structural reforms (Okuda, 2003). For changes in METI's stance on economic reform see Elder (2003).

12. 'Revised Commercial Code Introduces US-Style Corporate Governance', *Japan Labor Bulletin*, May 2003, p. 2. Kashiwagi (2003) sees this step as crucial to the

success of new-type companies in terms of fracturing the practice of chairpersons (typically also CEOs) electing their successors, despite nominating committees in new-type companies being formally required to have a majority of outside directors.

13. On pragmatism and 'creolisation' in globalization involving Japan, see Befu (2003). Kubori (2003) highlights another important practicality. By June 2006 even old-type companies must have at least two outside statutory auditors. Because this is as challenging as finding independent directors, he expects that the majority of well-known companies will become new-type companies.

14. More generally on venture business, see Sibbitt (1998b).

15. A comprehensive chronology is available from the Ministry of Finance (www.mof.go.jp/english/big-bang/ebb33.pdf). See also Sibbitt (1998a).

16. Lehmann (1997). This relative ranking accords with survey evidence in Tachibanaki (1999). The proportion of non-regular employees continues to grow (Abe, 2002).

17. See also Fukao (1999). However Haley (2002) asserts that Japan will not change its fundamentally 'communitarian' orientation without a change in what he sees as the most distinctive and central institutional feature of postwar Japan: 'entry level hiring coupled with a central personnel office staffed by senior career manager(s) with full responsibility for the recruitment, training, assignment and promotion of career staff'.

18. Including significant developments in IT in the late 1990s, after an admittedly slow start compared with the United States (Nottage, 1998; Ibusuki and Nottage, 2002; Jain, 2002).

19. See the three surveys (conducted in 1999–2000) summarized in Nottage (2001b). See also Abe (2002).

20. Further details on these and related changes that are affecting Japan's external labour market are set out in Nottage and Wolff (2000–3) and Nottage (2001b). Updated information can be found in the regular publications freely available from the Japan Institute for Labour Policy and Training (www.jil.go.jp/english/index.html), as well as from the recent references cited in the text.

21. Kashiwagi (2001). See also Farrell and Findlay (2004). On the ambivalent changes in the industry see Ghosn (2003).

22. See Maclachlan (2002), Nottage and Trezise (2003) and Nottage (2004).

23. See, however, Fort and Schipani (2000), Ballon and Honda (2000), and Gilson and Roe (1999).

24. Proposed whistle-blowing legislation may offset this tendency, despite problems with the draft legislation submitted to the cabinet ('A Whistle-Blower Bill Has Insufficient Safeguards', *International Herald Tribune*, 24 January 2004). However whistle-blowing may actually reinforce the distinction between employees and managers and it can help other stakeholders (notably shareholders), so law reform and practice in this area constitutes another facet of the new corporate governance regime now evolving in Japan.

References

Abe, M. (2002) 'Corporate Governance Structure and Employment Adjustment in Japan: An Empirical Analysis Using Corporate Finance Data', *Industrial Relations*, 41, pp. 683–702.

Ahmadjian, C. (2003) 'Changing Japanese Corporate Governance', in U. Schaede and W. W. Grimes (eds), *Japan's Managed Globalization: Adapting to the Twenty-First Century* (Armonk, NY: M. E. Sharpe), pp. 215–42.

Anderson, K. (2000) 'The Cross-Border Insolvency Paradigm: A Defense of the Modified Universal Approach Considering the Japanese Experience', *University of Pennsylvania Journal of International Economic Law*, 21 (4), pp. 679–779.

Anderson, K. (2001) 'Small Businesses Reorganizations: An Examination of Japan's Civil Rehabilitation Act Considering U.S. Policy Implications and Foreign Creditors' Practical Interests', *American Bankruptcy Law Journal*, 75 (3), pp. 355–407.

Anderson, K. and S. Steele (2003) 'Insolvency', in V. Taylor (ed.), *Japanese Business Law Guide* (Sydney: CCH Australia) (looseleaf).

Aoki, M. (2003) 'Institutional Complementarities between Organizational Architecture and Corporate Governance', paper presented at the RIETI conference on Corporate Governance from an International Perspective: Diversity or Convergence, Tokyo, 8–9 January (www.rieti.go.jp/en/events/03010801/pdf/Aoki.pdf).

Aronson, B. (2003) 'Reconsidering the Importance of Law in Japanese Corporate Governance: Evidence from the Daiwa Bank Shareholder Derivative Case', *Cornell International Law Journal*, 36, pp. 11–57.

Ballon, R. and K. Honda (2000) *Stakeholding: The Japanese Bottom Line* (Tokyo: The Japan Times).

Befu, H. (2003) 'Globalization Theory from the Bottom Up: Japan's Contribution', *Japanese Studies*, 23, pp. 3–22.

Berle, A. A. and G. C. Means (1991) *The Modern Corporation and Private Property* (New Brunswick, NJ: Transaction).

Black, B. and B. Cheffins (2003) 'Outside Director Liability across Countries', *Stanford Law and Economics Research Paper Series* 266 (http://ssrn.com/abstract=438321).

Callen, T. and J. Ostry (eds) (2003) *Japan's Lost Decade: Policies for Economic Revival* (Washington, DC: International Monetary Fund).

Cheffins, B. (2002) 'Comparative Corporate Governance and the Australian Experience: A Research Agenda', in I. Ramsay (ed.), *Key Developments in Corporate Law and Trusts Law: Essays in Honour of Professor Harold Ford* (Chatswood: LexisNexis Butterworths), pp. 651–64.

Cioffi, J. (2000) 'State of the Art [Review Essay]', *American Journal of Comparative Law*, 48, p. 501.

Clark, G. (2000) 'Why Is Japan Turning to Foreigners for Help?', *Japan Echo*, 27 February, p. 123.

Clarke, F. L., G. W. Dean and K. G. Oliver (2003) *Corporate Collapse: Accounting, Regulatory and Ethical Failure* (Cambridge: Cambridge University Press).

Coffee, J. (1999) 'The Future as History: The Prospects for Global Convergence in Corporate Governance and Its Implications', *Northwestern University Law Review*, 93, p. 641.

Cohen, J. and C. Sabel (1997) 'Directly Deliberative Polyarchy', *European Law Journal*, 5, p. 123.

Dore, R. P. (2000) *Stock Market Capitalism, Welfare Capitalism: Japan and Germany Versus the Anglo-Saxons* (Oxford and New York: Oxford University Press).

Dorf, M. and C. Sabel (1998) 'A Constitution of Democratic Experimentalism', *Columbia Law Review*, 98, p. 267.

Du Plessis, J. J. (2004) 'Reflections on Some Recent Corporate Governance Reforms in Germany: A Transformation of the German *Aktienrecht*?', *Deakin Law Review*, 8 (2), pp. 389–404.

Elder, M. (2003) 'Meti and Industrial Policy in Japan: Change and Continuity', in U. Schaede and W. W. Grimes (eds), *Japan's Managed Globalization: Adapting to the Twenty-First Century* (Armonk, NY: M. E. Sharpe), pp. 159–90.

Farrell, R. and C. Findlay (2004) 'Automobiles: An Industry Study', in P. Drysdale (ed.), *The New Economy in East Asia and the Pacific* (London: RoutledgeCurzon), pp. 257–72.

Feldman, E. A. (2001) 'The Landscape of Japanese Tobacco Policy: Law, Smoking and Social Change', *American Journal of Comparative Law*, 49 (4), pp. 679–706.

Foote, D. H. (1996) 'Judicial Creation of Norms in Japanese Labor Law: Activism in the Service of Stability?, *UCLA Law Review*, 43, pp. 635–709.

Fort, T. L. and C. A. Schipani (2000) 'Corporate Governance in a Global Environment: The Search for the Best of All Worlds', *Vanderbilt Journal of Transnational Law*, 33, p. 829.

Fukao, M. (1999) 'Japanese Financial Instability and Weaknesses in Corporate Governance Structure', paper presented at the OECD conference on Corporate Governance in Asia: A Comparative Perspective, Seoul, 3–5 March.

Fukuyama, F. (1992) *The End of History and the Last Man* (New York and Toronto: Free Press).

Fukuyama, F. (1996) *Trust: The Social Virtues and the Creation of Prosperity* (London: Penguin).

Genda, Y. (2000) 'Youth Employment and Parasite Singles', *Japan Labour Law Bulletin*, 39 (3) (www.jil.go.jp/bulletin/year/2000/vol39–03/05.htm).

Genda, Y. (2003) 'Dangers Facing Businessmen in Their 20s and 30s Who Work for Large Companies', *Japan Labor Bulletin*, 42 (2), pp. 7–11.

Ghosn, C. (2003) 'Japanese-Style Management and Nissan's Revival', *Japan Echo*, 30 (5), pp. 15–18.

Gilson, R. and M. Roe (1999) 'Lifetime Employment: Labor Peace and the Evolution of Japanese Corporate Governance', *Columbia Law Review*, 99, p. 508.

Ginsburg, T. (2001) 'Dismantling the "Developmental State"? Administrative Procedure Reform in Japan and Korea', *American Journal of Comparative Law*, 49 (4), pp. 585–625.

Grimes, W. W. and U. Schaede (2003) 'Japan's Policy Making in a World of Constraints', in U. Schaede and W. W. Grimes (eds), *Japan's Managed Globalization: Adapting to the Twenty-First Century* (Armonk, NY: M. E. Sharpe), pp. 17–46.

Haley, J. (1978) 'The Myth of the Reluctant Litigant', *Journal of Japanese Studies*, 4, p. 359.

Haley, J. (2002) 'Law in Japan 2002: A Turning Point?', *Washington University Working Paper* (http://law.wustl.edu/Academics/Faculty/Workingpapers/TurningPoint.pdf).

Hanami, T. (1999) 'Japan', in R. Blanpain and M. Biagi (eds), *Non-Standard Work and Industrial Relations* (The Hague: Kluwer), p. 109.

Hansmann, H. and R. Kraakman (2001) 'The End of History for Corporate Law', *Georgetown Law Journal*, 89, pp. 439–68.

Hayakawa, M. (1997) 'Shareholders in Japan: Attitudes, Conduct, Legal Rights and Their Enforcement', in H. Baum (ed.), *Japan: Economic Success and Legal System* (Berlin: de Gruyter), p. 251.

Helper, S., J. P. MacDuffie and C. Sabel (2000) 'Pragmatic Collaborations: Advancing Knowledge While Controlling Opportunism', *Industrial and Corporate Change*, 9 (3), p. 443.

Hill, J. and C. Yablon (2003) 'Corporate Governance and Executive Remuneration: Rediscovering Managerial Positional Conflict', *Vanderbilt Law and Economics Research Paper* 03–02 (http://ssrn.com/abstract=375240).

Hoshi, T. (1998) 'Japanese Corporate Governance System', in K. Hopt (ed.), *Comparative Corporate Governance: State of the Art and Emerging Research* (Oxford: Clarendon Press), pp. 847.

Huntington, S. P. and L. E. Harrison (eds) (2000) *Culture Matters: How Values Shape Human Progress* (New York: Basic Books).

Ibusuki, M. and L. Nottage (2002) 'IT and Legal Practice and Education in Japan and Australia', *UTS Law Review*, 4, pp. 31–54.

Iwai, K. and Y. Kobayashi (2003) 'Assessing the State of the Japanese Company', *Japan Echo*, 30 (5), pp. 9–14.

Jain, P. (2000) 'Japan's Local Governance at a Crossroads: The Third Wave of Reform', *ANU Pacific Economic Papers*, 306.

Jain, P. (2002) 'The Catch-up State: E-Government in Japan', *Japanese Studies*, 22, pp. 237–55.

Kanaya, A. and D. Woo (2000) *The Japanese Banking Crisis of the 1990s: Sources and Lessons*, IMF Working Paper WP/00/7, January (www.imf.org/external/pubs/ft/wp/2000/wp0007.pdf).

Kanda, H. (1998) 'Comparative Corporate Governance – Country Report: Japan', in K. Hopt (eds), *Comparative Corporate Governance: State of the Art and Emerging Research* (Oxford: Clarendon Press), p. 921.

Kanda, H. and C. Milhaupt (2003) *Re-Examining Legal Transplants: The Director's Fiduciary Duty in Japanese Corporate Law*, Columbia Law and Economics Working Paper 219 (http://ssrn.com/abstract=391821).

Kaplan, S. and J. M. Ramseyer (1996) 'Those Japanese with Their Disdain for Shareholders – Another Fable for Academy', *Washington University Law Quarterly*, 32, p. 403.

Kashiwagi, N. (2001). 'I Can't Turn You Loose: The Termination of Distributors and Agents in Japan', paper presented at the conference on Change Continuity, and Context: Japanese Law in the Twenty-First Century, Ann Arbor, 6–7 April.

Kashiwagi, N. (2003) 'A View of Recent Trends in Japanese Corporate Governance', paper presented at the 18th Biennial Conference of Lawasia, Session 3, Tokyo, 1–5 September.

Katz, R. (2003) 'Ten Years to Recovery', *Foreign Affairs*, 82 (1), pp. 101–21.

Kelemen, R. D. and E. C. Sibbitt (2002) 'The Americanization of Japanese Law', *University of Pennsylvania Journal of International Economic Law*, 23, p. 269.

Kester, W. C. (1996) 'American and Japanese Corporate Governance: Convergence to Best Practice', in S. Burger and R. Dore (eds), *National Diversity and Global Capitalism* (Ithaca and London: Cornell University Press), p. 107.

Kezuka, K. (2000) 'Legal Problems Concerning Part-Time Work in Japan', *Japan Labor Law Bulletin*, 39 (9) (http://www.jil.go.jp/bulletin/year/2000/vol39-09/06.ht).

Kitagawa, T. and L. Nottage (2005) 'Globalization of Japanese Corporations and the Development of Corporate Legal Departments: Problems and Prospects', in G. Chin and W. Alford (eds), *From 'Litigation Cudgels' to 'Doctors for People's Social Lives'? The Changing Place of Lawyers in East Asia* (Cambridge, Mass.: Harvard University Press).

Kobayashi, I. (2003) 'Relational Contracts in Japan: Reformation of Contract Practice under the Unique Corporate Governance Structure', *Asian Law (Legal Scholarship Network)* (http://ssrn.com/abstract=479921).

Kozuka, S. (2003) 'The Use of Stock Options as Defensive Measures', *Zeitschrift für Japanisches Recht / Journal of Japanese Law*, 8 (15), pp. 135–41.

Kubori, H. (2003) ' "Iinkai to Secchi Kaisha" and Corporate Governance in Japan', paper presented at the 18th Biennial Conference of Lawasia, Session 3, Tokyo, 1–5 September.

Maclachlan, P. (2002) *Consumer Politics in Postwar Japan* (New York: Columbia University Press).

Mattei, U. (2003) 'A Theory of Imperial Law: A Study on US Hegemony and the Latin Resistance', *Indiana Journal of Global Legal Studies*, 10, pp. 383–448.

Milhaupt, C. J. (1996) 'A Relational Theory of Japanese Corporate Governance: Contract, Culture, and the Rule of Law', *Harvard International Law Journal*, 37, pp. 3–64.

Milhaupt, C. J. (2001) 'Creative Norm Destruction: The Evolution of Nonlegal Rules in Japanese Corporate Governance', *University of Pennsylvania Law Review*, 149 (6), pp. 2083–129.

Milhaupt, C. J. (2002) 'On the (Fleeting) Existence of the Main Bank System and Other Japanese Economic Institutions', *Law and Social Inquiry*, 27, p. 425.

Milhaupt, C. J. (2003) *A Lost Decade for Japanese Corporate Governance Reform?: What's Changed, What Hasn't, and Why*, Columbia Law School Centre for Law and Economic Studies Working Paper 234 (New York: Columbia Law School), pp. 1–36.

Milhaupt, C. J. and G. P. Miller (1997) 'Cooperation, Conflict, and Convergence in Japanese Finance: Evidence from the "Jusen" Problem', *Law and Policy in International Business*, 29 (1), pp. 1–78.

Milhaupt, C. and M. West (2001) 'Institutional Change and M&A in Japan: Diversity through Deals', *Columbia Law and Economics Working Paper* 193 (http://papers.ssrn.com/sol3/papers.cfm?abstract_id=290744).

Miller, R. L. (2003) 'The Quiet Revolution: Japanese Women Working around the Law', *Harvard Women's Law Journal*, 26, pp. 163–215.

Miwa, Y. (1998) 'The Economics of Corporate Governance in Japan', in K. J. Hopt (ed.), *Comparative Corporate Governance: State of the Art and Emerging Research* (Oxford: Clarendon Press), pp. 853–88.

Miwa, Y. and J. M. Ramseyer (2002) *The Legislative Dynamic: Evidence from the Deregulation of Financial Services in Japan*, Harvard Law and Economics Discussion Paper 373, (http://ssrn.com/abstract=324601).

Moehwald, U. (2000) 'Trends in Value Change in Contemporary Japan', in J. S. Eades (ed.), *Globalization and Social Change in Contemporary Japan* (Melbourne: Trans Pacific Press), p. 55.

Moerke, A. (2003) 'Rumble in the Boardroom? The Change of Japanese Corporate Governance Schemes', *Zeitschrift für Japanisches Recht/Journal of Japanese Law* 8 (15), pp. 142–60.

Morgan, C. A. (2001) 'Demographic Crisis in Japan: Why Japan Might Open Its Doors to Foreign Home Health-Care Aides', *Pacific Rim Law & Policy Journal*, 10 (3), pp. 749–79.

Nakamura, K. (2001) 'Manipulating the System from Within: Deaf Civil Society Organizations in Japan', paper presented at the conference on Change, Continuity, and Context: Japanese Law in the Twenty-First Century, Ann Arbor, 6–7 April.

Nottage, L. (1998) 'Cyberspace and the Future of Law, Legal Education, and Practice in Japan', *Web Journal of Current Legal Issues* (http://webjcli.ncl.ac.uk/1998/issue5/nottage5.html).

Nottage, L. (2001a) *Convergence, Divergence and the Middle Way in Harmonising or Unifying Private Law*, E.U.I. Working Paper in Law No. 2001/1 (www.iue.it/LAW/res/nottage/EUIWorkingPaper4.pdf).

Nottage, L. (2001b) 'Japanese Corporate Governance at a Crossroads: Variation in 'Varieties of Capitalism', *The North Carolina Journal of International Law & Commercial Regulation*, 27 (2), pp. 255–99.

Nottage, L. (2001c) 'Reformist Conservatism and Failures of Imagination in Japanese Legal Education', *Asian Pacific Law and Policy Journal*, 2, pp. 28–65 (also at www.hawaii.edu/aplpj/2/16.html).

Nottage, L. (2003) 'Japan Inc Goes Global: Elective Corporate Governance Reform', *CCH Asiawatch*, 57, pp. 6–8.

Nottage, L. (2004) *Product Safety and Liability Law in Japan: From Minamata to Mad Cows* (London: RoutledgeCurzon).

Nottage, L. and M. Trezise (2003) 'Mad Cows and Japanese Consumers', *Australian Product Liability Reporter*, 14 (9), p. 125.

Nottage, L. and L. Wolff (2000–3) 'Japan', in *Doing Business in Asia* (Singapore: CCH) (looseleaf).

Okuda, H. (2003) 'A Business Leader on the Offensive', *Japan Echo*, 30 (2), pp. 47–50.

Osano, H. and K. Hori (2002) *Financial Relations between Banks and Firms: New Evidence from Japanese Data*, Kyoto Institute of Economic Research Discussion Paper 546 (http://ssrn.com/abstract=357943).

O'Sullivan, M. (2000) 'Corporate Governance and Globalization', *Annals of the American Academy of Political and Social Science*, 570, p. 153.

Ouandlous, A. and G. Philippatos (1999) *The Effect of Japanese Financial Liberalization on Keiretsu, the Main Bank System, and Japanese Corporate Financing: Evidence for 1972–1992* (Legal Scholarship Network: http://ssrn.com/abstract=250374).

Pekkanen, R. (2000) 'Japan's New Politics: The Case of the NPO Law', *Journal of Japanese Studies*, 26 (1), p. 111.

Perez, A. (2002) 'International Antitrust at the Crossroads: The End of Antitrust History or the Clash of Competition Policy Civilizations?', *Law and Policy in International Business*, 33, pp. 527–54.

Puchniak, D. W. (2003) 'The 2002 Reform of the Management of Large Corporations in Japan: A Race to Somewhere?', *Australian Journal of Asian Law*, 5 (1), pp. 42–76.

Reich, P. (2001) 'T Boone Pickens and Corporate Governance in Japan: A Retrospective View of Three Sides of the Story and Recent Developments', *Law in Japan*, 27, pp. 27–36.

Rodatz, P. (2003) 'Bemerkungen zur Struktur der japanischen Unternehmungsleitung nach den jüngsten gesellschaftrechtlichen Reformen', *Zeitschrift für Japanisches Recht/Journal of Japanese Law*, 8 (15), pp. 161–9.

Sabel, C. (1996) 'Ungoverned Production: An American View of the Novel Universalism of Japanese Production Methods and Their Awkward Fit with Current Forms of Corporate Governance', paper presented to the Institute of Fiscal and Monetary Policy conference on Socio-economic systems for the 21st Century, Tokyo, (www2.law.columbia.edu/sabel/papers/Japan.html) 28/29 February 2000.

Sabel, C. and R. O'Donnell (2000) 'Democratic Experimentalism: What to Do About Wicked Problems after Whitehall (and What Scotland May Just Possibly Already Be Doing)', paper presented to the OECD conference on Devolution and Globalization: Implications for Local Decision-makers, Glasgow, (www2.law.columbia.edu/sabel/papers/glasPO.html) 28/29 February 2000.

Sarra, J. and M. Nakahigashi (2002) 'Balancing Social and Corporate Culture in the Global Economy: The Evolution of Japanese Corporate Culture and Norms', *Law and Policy*, 24, pp. 299–354.

Schaede, U. (2000) *Co-operative Capitalism: Self-Regulation, Trade Association, and the Antimonopoly Law in Japan* (Oxford: Oxford University Press).

Schaede, U. (2003) 'Industry Rules: From Deregulation to Self-Regulation', in U. Schaede and W. W. Grimes (eds), *Japan's Managed Globalization: Adapting to the Twenty-First Century* (Armonk, NY: M. E. Sharpe), pp. 191–214.

Schaede, U. and W. W. Grimes (2003) 'Introduction: The Emergence of Permeable Insulation', in U. Schaede and W. W. Grimes (eds), *Japan's Managed Globalization: Adapting to the Twenty-First Century* (Armonk, NY: M. E. Sharpe), pp. 3–16.

Schultz, D. M. (2001) 'Japan's Information Disclosure Law: Why a Law Full of Loopholes Is Better Than No Law at All', *Law in Japan*, 27, pp. 128–69.

Schwartz, F. J. and S. J. Pharr (eds) (2003) *The State of Civil Society in Japan* (Cambridge and New York: Cambridge University Press).

Senechal, M. (2003) 'Reforming the Japanese Commercial Code: A Step toward an American-Style Executive Officer System in Japan?', *Pacific Rim Law & Policy Journal*, 12, pp. 535–59.

Shibata, H. (2002) 'Wage and Performance Appraisal Systems in Flux: A Japan–United States Comparison', *Industrial Relations*, 41, pp. 629–52.

Shishido, Z. (1990) 'Problems of the Closely Held Corporation: A Comparative Study of the Japanese and American Legal Systems and a Critique of the Japanese Tentative Draft on Close Corporations', *American Journal of Comparative Law*, 38, pp. 337–72.

Shishido, Z. (2000) 'Japanese Corporate Governance: The Hidden Problems of Corporate Law and Their Solutions', *Delaware Journal of Corporate Law*, 25 (2), pp. 189–233.

Shishido, Z. (2001) 'Reform in Japanese Corporate Law and Corporate Governance: Current Changes in Historical Perspective', *American Journal of Comparative Law*, 49 (4), pp. 653–77.

Sibbitt, E. C. (1998a) 'A Brave New World for M&A of Financial Institutions in Japan: Big Bang Financial Deregulation and the New Environment for Corporate Combinations of Financial Institutions', *University of Pennsylvania Journal of International Economic Law*, 19 (4), pp. 965–1027.

Sibbitt, E. C. (1998b) 'Law, Venture Capital, and Entrepreneurism in Japan: A Microeconomic Perspective on the Impact of Law on the Generation and Financing of Venture Businesses', *Connecticut Journal of International Law*, 13 (1), pp. 61–106.

Stewart, A. D. (2003) *'Kayano v. Hokkaido Expropriation Committee* Revisited: Recognition of Ryukyuans as a Cultural Minority under the International Covenant on Civil and Political Rights, an Alternative Paradigm for Okinawan Demilitarization', *Asian Pacific Law and Policy Journal* 4 (2), (www.hawaii.edu/aplpj/pdfs/v4-stewart.pdf).

Swedberg, R. and M. S. Granovetter (eds) (2001) *The Sociology of Economic Life* (Boulder, CO: Westview Press).

Tachibanaki, T. (1999) 'Surviving the Recession without Slashing Payrolls', *Japan Echo*, October, pp. 32–54.

Takahashi, E. (1997) 'Changes in the Japanese Enterprise Groups?', in H. Baum (ed.), *Japan: Economic Success and Legal System* (Berlin: de Gruyter), pp. 210–34.

Takao, Y. (2003) 'Foreigners' Rights in Japan: Beneficiaries to Participants', *Asian Review*, 43, p. 523.

Tanahashi, H. (2002) 'Japan: A Better Environment for Start-Ups and Venture Capital', *International Financial Law Review*, 65, p. 65.

Tokumoto, M. (2001) 'The Role of Japanese Courts in Hostile Take-overs', *Law in Japan*, 27, pp. 1–16.

Tsuru, K. (1999) 'Japanese Corporate Governance in Transition', *paper presented at the EUI conference on The Political Economy of Corporate Governance in Europe and Japan, Florence, 10–11 June*.

Von Nessen, P. (1999) 'The Americanization of Australian Corporate Law', *Syracuse Journal of International Law and Commerce*, 26, pp. 239–66.

Von Nessen, P. (2003) 'Corporate Governance in Australia: Converging with International Developments', *Australian Journal of Corporate Law*, 15, pp. 189–224.

Watanabe, T. (2004) 'Tax Treatment of Stock Options', *Japan Bulletin for International Fiscal Association*, 58 (1), pp. 31–8.

Webb, P. (2002) 'Time to Share the Burden: Long Term Care Insurance and the Japanese Family', *Japanese Studies*, 22, pp. 113–29.

West, M. D. (1997) 'Legal Rules and Social Norms in Japan's Secret World of Sumo', *Journal of Legal Studies*, 26, pp. 165–201.

West, M. D. (2001a) 'The Puzzling Divergence of Corporate Law: Evidence and Explanations from Japan and the United States', *University of Pennsylvania Law Review*, 150 (2), pp. 527–601.

West, M. D. (2001b) 'Why Shareholders Sue: The Evidence from Japan', *Journal of Legal Studies*, 30 (2, pt1), pp. 351–82.

West, M. D. (2003a) *Dying to Get out of Debt: Consumer Insolvency Law and Suicide in Japan*, Michigan Law and Economics Research Paper 03–15 (http://ssrn.com/abstract=479844).

West, M. D. (2003b) *Employment Market Institutions and Japanese Working Hours*, Michigan Law and Economics Research Paper 03–016 (http://ssrn.com/abstract=479882).

Williams, C. and B. Arrigo (2001) *Law, Psychology and Justice: Chaos Theory and the New (Dis)Order* (Albany, NY: State University of New York Press).

Williamson, O. (1996) *The Mechanisms of Governance* (Oxford: Oxford University Press).

Wolff, L. (2003a) 'Beyond Japan Inc: Facilitating Flexibility in Equity Financing', *CCH Asiawatch*, 58, pp. 9–11.

Wolff, L. (2003b) 'Japanese Women and the "New" Administrative State', in J. Amyx and P. Drysdale (eds), *Japanese Governance: Beyond Japan Inc* (Sydney: Routledge), pp. 157–70.

Xu, P. (2003) 'Bankruptcy Resolution in Japan: Corporate Reorganization vs Civil Rehabilitation', paper presented at the RIETI conference on Corporate Governance from an International Perspective: Diversity or Convergence, Tokyo, 8–9 January (www.rieti.go.jp/en/events/03010801/pdf/Xu.pdf).

Yamakawa, R. (1999) 'The Silence of Stockholders: Japanese Labor Law from the Viewpoint of Corporate Governance', *Japan Labor Bulletin*, 38 (11) (www.jil.go.jp/bulletin/year/1999/vol38–11/04.htm).

Yamakawa, R. (2001) 'Labor Law Reform in Japan: A Response to Recent Socio-Economic Changes', *American Journal of Comparative Law*, 49 (4), pp. 627–51.

Yasui, T. (1999), 'Corporate Governance in Japan', paper presented at the OECD conference on Corporate Governance in Asia: A Comparative Perspective, Seoul, 3–5 March.

Yoshimatsu, H. (2000) *Internationalization, Corporate Preferences and Commercial Policy in Japan* (Houndmills and New York: Macmillan and St Martin's Press).

8
A Perfect Financial Storm
James C. Abegglen

The changes in Japan's economy as it has moved from historic high growth to full industrial and demographic maturity are nowhere more striking than in the sourcing, structure and management of corporate finance. These changes, taking place from the mid 1990s, were driven by an extraordinary combination of low and erratic growth rates of the economy, long-continued deflationary price drops, massive declines in asset values, and sharp changes in accountancy rules – in finance, a perfect storm. Companies have weathered the storm by a focus on reducing debt with bank borrowings very much lessened and other sources of finance more widely used. Careless and unmanaged proliferation of subsidiaries and affiliates has been corrected. Holding company structures allow establishing financial structures for separate businesses. Pension obligations are fully recognized. All this at considerable cost; all made necessary by a brutally difficult economic environment and changed regulations; all now largely accomplished as a new era begins.

Japan's companies, in all sectors, have been on a severe diet for a number of years. Low demand levels and continued price deflation have forced reductions in labour costs, in numbers of competitors, in overstated asset values, in excessive diversifications and over-grown capacity. By 2003, the results of the diet were becoming evident as the economy was regaining its balance. Japan's companies, across the economy, were becoming lean and vigorous, recovering confidence and profitability.

Some of the changes in financial management in the difficult years were driven by the economic situation, and are not likely to be permanent as growth resumes and balance sheet pressures are reduced. Cross-shareholdings between banks and clients, now very much diminished, are likely to be renewed to some degree. Indirect financing through bank borrowings is likely to increase again with renewed capital expenditure. The institution of the main bank will have a lessened role, but the main bank in a more limited role is to continue. The emerging Japanese pattern is a complex one, with a great deal of change, but largely within the broad and familiar patterns of the past.

Financing historic high growth

Financing of corporations in Japan from the mid 1950s was driven by – and was driver of – the very rapid growth of the economy. To appreciate the impact on finance, the magnitude of the growth achievement needs be kept clearly in mind. In the 45-year period from 1955 to 2000, the economy grew in yen terms by a factor of about 65 and in US dollar terms by a factor of about 210. This massive shift from real poverty to significant wealth resulted from very high levels of investment. Gross domestic investment as a percentage of GDP averaged 32 per cent from 1960 to 2000, half as much again as in the cases of the United States and Germany during the same period.

These overall figures were the sum of countless corporate decisions regarding financial management, decisions shaped by the compulsion to grow assets and sales to hold and to improve competitive position. Under conditions of very rapid growth, a failure to match competitors' growth rates would mean in a short time a brutal loss of market share and thus of cost position and long-term profitability. Markets during these long periods of high growth not uncommonly doubled each year for several years. Failure to double manufacturing capacity by indulging for a single year in a focus on profitability would mean the instant halving of market share, with a commensurate disadvantage accruing in production costs. The name of the game became market share/growth.

However, in a capital-short economy, this growth could not be funded by sale of new shares. Nor could it be funded through high prices/profits since the high prices would block market share growth. The solution was, inevitably, high levels of debt borrowed from commercial banks. Not only was bank debt more available than direct debt or new equity, but it was also low-cost since the central bank was prepared to provide money supply through the banks to meet growth requirements. Debt is always less expensive than equity in any case, since interest is a tax-deductible expense while dividend payments for equity are high and are only after-tax.

No surprise then that the growth was debt-financed in Japan (as it is in all fast-growing economies like Korea and China in their turn). Debt-equity ratios reached a high in post-oil shock 1975 of nearly 6:1 in all businesses and about 5:1 in manufacturing. At this kind of debt level, US commentators were prone to see Japanese companies as having an unfair advantage, as these levels of debt were not available from US banks.[1] Asset growth reached a maximum in 1991, when it was at an index of 161 with 1975 as 100. Capital investment similarly peaked in the 1990–92 period, having climbed steeply through the bubble period of the mid to late 1980s.

Partly because of the high debt levels, returns on equity were rather good, generally in the 8–9 per cent range through the 1970s and 1980s. Dividend policy was fairly consistent over time, with the dividend payout ratio around

35 per cent. It might be noted here that despite all the mythology about Japanese managements' indifference toward shareholders, dividends have been paid at a quite consistent level whatever the profitability might be – which can mean a more than 100 per cent payout rate in a loss year:

> The shareholders in Japanese companies have done well in the long run. The return on the NRI 350 index (Nomura Research Institute stock market index of 350 Japanese stocks) since the early 1970s is about the same as the return on Standard & Poor's 500 during that period. (From the first quarter of 1971 until the third quarter of 1995 the annual growth rate of the NRI 350 was 12.16 per cent. Over the same period, the annual growth rather of the S&P 500 was 12.17 per cent.) (Allen and Gale, 2001, p. 16)

Shares in the company held by whoever now has them represent a capital investment. That investment is entitled to a return, and that return is provided when at all possible. But there is no further obligation to, nor right held by the shareholder. The main stakeholders in the company are the employees. The US and UK have somehow developed a curious view that the shareholder has total and entire ownership of all the assets of the company. This is not the Japanese view of the matter.

Recent changes in law have made possible share buy-backs and stock option programs. Both changes are aimed presumably at supporting and increasing share prices. Neither program has achieved any significant role in Japan's financial management. Share options have been announced by small start-up companies in most cases, and are not part of the compensation of management in most large companies. Employee share ownership programs have a long history in Japan, but these are in no sense stock option programs. Share buybacks do occur but in amounts very far below what is termed 'share buyback ability', available surplus cash totals. Cash surpluses like Toyota's $20 billion, Takeda's $10 billion, Fuji Film's $10 billion are reserved for presumed future business needs – and are not used to support share price by reducing significantly shares outstanding or by increasing dividends greatly. Share price remains a marginal goal, and is not the measure of corporate performance in Japan.

The role of the shareholder has been, not surprisingly, a lesser one since the great majority of corporate funds have been sourced from banks rather than through issues of equity. The bank provided most of the money; the bank could, if it chose, have the louder voice in affairs. This flow of funds through banks, indirect financing rather than financing directly through bonds and other capital market instruments, led to the phenomenon of the 'main bank':

> There is no single agreed definition of the term 'main bank', but in cases where a number of banks have made loans to a particular firm, it generally refers to the bank that has a particularly long and continuous record of

business relations with the firm and has advanced the largest loans. In some cases a comprehensive range of business dealings, including share-holdings and directorships in the firm, and handling its pensions and financial settlements, are considered the characteristics of a main bank. Currently many firms in Japan have this sort of special relationship (though not always of the same type) with their 'main bank', and the arrangement is said to serve a variety of beneficial functions with regard to monitoring the firm, spreading associated risks, and so on ... The main bank system is regarded as a fundamental component of the so-called Japan-style capitalism. (Teranishi, 1999, p. 63)

As part of the financial structuring of Japanese companies, cross-shareholdings between the corporation and its main bank became a key part of the share ownership structure. These often had long histories, as the companies in the historic groupings – Sumitomo, Mitsui, Mitsubishi – used the group's bank as main bank with the bank holding shares in the company and the company shareholder in the bank. These mutual shareholdings, or 'cross-holdings', came to as much as a third of total group company shares in the case of Sumitomo group companies at the 1987 peak of cross-holdings. Thus not only the debt portion but the equity portion of the company as well was dominated, indeed largely controlled, by the main bank. And thus the risks associated with the very high debt levels incurred to fund rapid growth were greatly tempered by the deep relationships between lender and borrower, with the Bank of Japan providing the essential assurance that there would be no bank failures.

This in general was the dominant pattern of corporate financing through the period to the early 1990s: a focus on growth and market share driving massive capital investments, these funded by bank borrowings to a very high level, the bank borrowings largely from 'main banks' with mutual shareholdings. High debt helped in the achievement of very good returns on equity and all this provided attractive returns to shareholders, even with modest levels of dividend payouts. The system was based on high growth – and required high rates of growth to continue as a viable approach to financing.

The grand climax – and denouement

Rapid economic growth had as its corollary rapid growth in exports. Japan has never been a large exporter; exports are generally around 10 per cent of GNP, well below the average for most major economies. Exports are around 22 per cent of GNP for France and Italy and 30 per cent for Germany, although only around 7 per cent in the US case. However, while exports as a proportion of total output changed little, exports did increase as total output increased. The growth was not 'export-led'; rather, exports in any given product followed after high growth and lowered costs in domestic demand and output.

The United States was for long the dominant export market. When the US economy went through a difficult period in the early 1980s, in the usual US fashion, the cause was argued to be foreign plotting. Japan was held to be a major cause of industry problems, much as China has been made villain in more recent years. However, in 1984 Japan's exports to the US increased considerably, in that year by 16 per cent. The yen had for several years been weakening against the dollar – from a 201 rate in 1978 to 252 in 1984, and reasonably enough the low yen value was seen as cause of the export increase.

Not surprising then that at a meeting of finance ministers of the major economies in 1985 there emerged the 'Plaza Accord,' an agreement to adjust exchange rates, and in particular to move the yen up substantially – and so in fact the JPY did move, from 252 to 122 to the US dollar in only three years, doubling its exchange value. To meet US demands, and as well to deal with the deflationary potential of so rapid and drastic an exchange rate shift, Japan's money supply was increased explosively, by 10 per cent annually to 1991. Along with this, naturally enough, went a drastic drop in the discount rate of the Bank of Japan to a low in 1988 of 2.5 per cent, half the earlier rate levels.

All of this triggered Japan's nearly fatal 'bubble', the extraordinary increase in the values of real estate and corporate shares in the 1985–1991 period. The causes are not unlike those that led to the US 'bubble' of the late 1990s, with the Federal Reserve greatly expanding money supply, holding interest rates at a moderate level. In both cases, asset values took off, while consumer price levels increased rather little, a case of asset inflation rather than the usual price inflation.

The magnitude of the 'bubble' was astonishing. Land prices in Japan tripled in only six years from 1985 to their peak in 1991. Share prices nearly tripled in four years from 1984 to a peak in 1988. Nominal GDP growth reached eight per cent in 1990. Total national wealth doubled from 1984/5 to a 1990 peak. One hazardous myth born in this period was the conviction that in land-short Japan land prices would rise forever. Golf club memberships soared in value and became major financial instruments as investments.

The price:earnings ratios of shares went over 60 as prices far outstripped earnings, even while earnings were doing well. As asset values rose, corporations were able to increase borrowings with equal rapidity as banks lent with these increasingly valuable assets as collateral. This was the case through the period of high growth, and the pace even accelerated from the mid-1980s as the 'bubble' grew. Then, quite suddenly, financial policies changed drastically as fears over asset inflation took command. The increase in money supply, 10 per cent annually to 1991, dropped to 0.1 per cent in 1992.

Money supply was simply turned off. The central bank discount rate, 2.5 per cent in 1988, went to 6.0 per cent in 1990. No surprise then that share prices plunged, losing over the next decade more than three-quarters of their value on average. Urban land prices dropped even more drastically, to a mere 15 per cent of their earlier level. The resulting situation is summarized by Richard Koo of Nomura Research Institute as follows:

> During the 1970s and 1980s, Japanese companies took out massive loans with which to expand their businesses...The value of the assets, which should be at least as large as the size of their debts, has collapsed. As a result, the balance sheet, or the financial health of the companies, has deteriorated drastically. The sheer magnitude of the decline in assets prices suggests that perhaps there are hundreds of thousands of businesses in Japan whose liabilities exceed their assets, or whose financial condition is close to it. For these companies, the excess liabilities mean that they are actually bankrupt. (Koo 2003, p. 4)

This is the crisis situation that Japanese companies found themselves in as the bubble burst and asset values plunged. Financial managers could hardly have imagined so severe a set of problems. The like has in fact not been seen in the world since the experience of the United States in the Great Depression of the 1930s. That period of US deflation ended only with the outbreak of World War II and the massive government expenditures that resulted. Japan's government did not have so dramatic a remedy for deflation and lack of growth ready to hand.

A long-continuing deflation was in fact the critical outcome. There is a certain fashion ,to blame the deflation on government policy failures in terms of money supply, interest rates and fiscal policy. No doubt perfect moves in each of these aspects could have mitigated the problem. But policies – clever or clumsy – were not the cause, nor the remedy. Deflation was the consequence of long-sustained massive capital investment, continuing far longer than basic demand warranted. The extent of investment can be gained by noting that through the entire period from 1960–2000, gross domestic investment as a percentage of GDP was half as much again greater in Japan through the entire period than was the case for the United States or Germany. With high demand growth, so high a level of investment made excellent economic sense. As demand growth slackened and as the economy matured, overcapacity became all too commonly the rule.

With money supply down, interest rates up, and share and land prices dropping sharply, demand inevitably began weakening. Especially given over-capacity in any case, production needed to be cut back and costs reduced. This in turn further reduced demand as wages began to fall and job security lessened. And this in turn made for further cuts in capacity and capacity utilization – and so on down the vicious deflation cycle. GDP real growth went from 5.5 per cent in 1990 to 0.4 per cent only two years later, with negative real growth in 1997 and 1998. Demand plunged; growth stopped; companies were in crisis. The magnitude and abruptness of change can be gauged from the Bank of Japan's report that real business fixed investment averaged a very high 8.4 per cent from 1981–1990, and averaged precisely 0.0 per cent from 1991–2002.

Stated asset values of Japan's companies peaked in 1991, after a rapid run up in values from the mid 1980s, and began to decline in 1992. A decade later, in 2002, corporate asset values had declined by nearly 60 per cent from the 1991 peak. Banks had been lending aggressively against the ever-higher asset positions of companies that served as attractive collateral for loans. And quite abruptly the backing for those bank loans began to disappear rather rapidly. Shareholder equity, at 100 in 1991, was only 40 by 2002. That is, the average Japanese company lost well over half of its value in a decade (although for larger companies the decline was to 70 – small and medium-sized enterprises took the major beating, although no one came through with great damage).

Koo of Nomura describes this cycle in financial, rather than in industrial capacity terms:

> A balance sheet recession typically emerges after the bursting of a nation-wide asset price bubble that leaves a large number of private sector balance sheets in need of serious repair. In order to repair their balance sheets, the affected companies are forced to move away from their usual profit maximization to debt minimization...When everyone moves in that direction at the same time, aggregate demand shrinks and worsens both the economy and assets prices. This, in turn, forces the companies to pay down debt even faster, resulting in a vicious cycle. (Koo 2003, p. 269)

And pay down debt they have. Even against the sharp drop in equity values, the ratio of debt to equity, the usual measure of a company's financial strength or lack of it, went from 3:1 in 1990 to under 1:1 in 2002 – and continues to decline. 'In 1997, corporate debt in Japan and America was nearly equal at US$ 900 billion each. By 2002, however, total American corporate debt had risen to more than double that of Japan' (*The Economist*, September 2003, p. 101). And Japan's companies continue to reduce borrowings – causing considerable grief for Japan's troubled banks. There is a certain irony in all this since throughout the 1980s, as Japan grew mightily and the US stagnated, it was customary in the US to view with self-righteous alarm the very high levels of Japanese corporate debt – 'You cannot have that much leverage and still be a company', said one US investment banker (ibid.), looking at average debt to equity ratios of 6 to 1 and even higher. There has been a nice reversal of circumstances and views from that decade through the next one.

Indeed, a good number of Japan's leading companies now have no debt. This is true not only of top manufacturers like Canon, Takeda Chemical, Murata and Rohm, but of the top retailer, Seven-Eleven Japan, as well. This reduction of leverage – and especially its total absence – makes devotees of the return on equity number unhappy as that measure of profit is depressed when leverage is low. One group of ROE devotees, the staff of Goldman Sachs, state, 'In a low interest rate environment like Japan's where the cost of equity is well above the cost of debt, companies that can afford to do so should in fact be raising financial leverage rather than reducing it – i.e. indeed, the exact opposite of what most firms have been doing over the past several years' (Goldman Sachs, 2003, p. 9). Not only is this a quite extraordinary reversal of earlier US conventional wisdom, but it is also a statement seemingly oblivious to the crucial factors that have driven debt reduction by Japan's companies. So long as deflation continues, there will be a drive to reduce debt levels.

Inflation pays off debt; deflation magnifies it

Recognition of the need to repair balance sheets and regain financial stability did not come early nor yet easily. Neither government nor business fully realized the changed nature of the economic environment and the shift from growth to maturity that the ending of the bubble signalled. The initial downturn was generally seen as simply another cyclic change, a temporary condition to be remedied in the usual fashion with reduced interest rates and increased government expenditures. When that failed to work in the first year or two of downturn, the conclusion was to try again, with more. And when that too failed to deal with the increased problems, there was finally a realization that this was and is a new era, needing new measures, a structural crisis requiring structuring change. On the level of government policy, the Hashimoto government's move in 1996 to the financial system 'big bang' was a clear indicator of the conclusion that real changes were required. For companies too the mid 1990s was the time when restructuring plans began to be put in place.

Weathering the perfect financial storm

As Japan's companies began facing up to the greatly changed environment, a series of accounting changes hammered the problems home with a vengeance. Through what has been called the 'Accounting Big Bang', new accounting rules were put in place beginning in 1999, implemented in stages over the next several years and bringing Japanese accounting practices into line with international standards in several key respects. A first major change in rules was the requirement that companies report on a consolidated basis, corporate results to include all firms in which the parent has control – not simply majority share ownership but effective or substantial influence on subsidiaries and affiliates.

The impact of this change has been substantial. For a long time, it was the practice in Japan for companies to report only the results of the parent company itself – consolidated corporate returns were not required nor yet even customary except for those rather few companies subject to the US Security Exchange Commission rules for reporting. Businesses doing badly could be spun off as subsidiaries, with losses not reflected in the parent's reported results. And indeed very promising businesses also could be spun off to free them from the parent's bureaucratic tendencies and to allow promising young executives a field to practice in.

Around the mid 1980s, the numbers of subsidiaries of Japanese companies generally increased rather suddenly to very large numbers indeed. Even in 2003 both Hitachi and Sony reported more than 1000 subsidiaries, Mitsubishi Shoji nearly 600, Sumitomo Trading more than 500, Toshiba and Matsushita Electric more than 300. And so on and on. It would seem a remarkable achievement for the management of Sony and Hitachi simply to remember the names of all those subsidiaries, much less keep track of or discipline performance. And these numbers include only subsidiaries, and do not include the considerable numbers of affiliates accounted for by the equity method.

Now, many of these subsidiaries no doubt serve marketing purposes in foreign jurisdictions and separate corporate status is useful and for some companies, subsidiaries served as locations for relocating personnel deemed redundant in parent operations. But in any event, whatever their purpose, the sudden requirement of consolidating balance sheets of so vast a number of odds and ends of businesses placed enormous pressure on what were already precariously balanced corporate results.

As an example of magnitude of the problem subsidiaries can present, a news report on the subsidiaries of Mitsui & Co. in the English edition of the *Asahi Shimbun* of 15–16 September 2003 provides an interesting and no doubt representative example:

> Mitsui & Co. said Friday it will cut the number of its consolidated subsidiaries and affiliated firms by nearly 30 percent by the end of March 2005 to reduce negative effects on group earnings from poor-performing units. The trading house selected about 190 of the 702 consolidated units in Japan for liquidation, sale or merger with other firms... Mitsui's consolidated units booked losses totalling 71.1 billion yen in the year ended March 31, and the company hopes to reduce the losses to around 10 billion yen by the end of March 2005.

There is a real question of management competence when problems of this magnitude are allowed to fester unattended for a long period. In any case, the change in the accounting rules to require consolidated reporting is in turn requiring that management move to bring order to these sprawling complexes of subsidiaries, used all too often in the past as a device to move business mistakes from the front steps to the rear alley. Economic performance can only be improved as a result of cleaning up these odd bits and pieces. And, in fairness, a great many leading companies have had little or no resort to the subsidiary device – Fanuc 17 subsidiaries, Takeda Chemical 54, Rohm 48, Hoya 52, Murata, 52. No surprise – these are among Japan's most profitable companies, clearly more tightly managed than many.

The second major change in accounting rules was market value accounting, or 'mark-to-market'. Investment portfolios and real estate holdings, previously valued at either acquisition cost or the lower of acquisition cost and market value have now to be stated at current market value. In a growth environment, with rising share prices and increasing land prices, this accounting requirement would make for very positive balance sheet results, the number getting steadily better. In Japan's economic environment of 2001 when the new rule came into full effect, the impact was disastrous in most cases. Share prices and land prices were dropping as GDP growth went negative. Assets acquired at peak prices in the 1980s reached new lows in market value in 2001 – and those low values had to be reflected on company balance sheets.

Closely related to the change in asset value accounting was the change in accounting for pension obligations. Like market value accounting, this was introduced in fiscal 2000. The new rule required that pension obligations be fully accounted for and valued at current market value. It became an extremely punishing accounting requirement in the context of falling interest rates and steeply declining share prices.

An appreciation of the impact of these changes in accounting rules in the context of declining share prices can be gained by looking at the case of NEC. A US$ 40 billion sales company founded in 1899, NEC has been Japan's leader in telecommunications equipment for more than a century. But with the telecom and semiconductor markets collapsing at home and abroad, with NEC involved in a government procurement scandal, and with some mistaken diversifications dragging down results, NEC struggled for several years in a massive effort to reconstruct. In the midst of this effort, the accounting rule changes made problems distinctly more difficult. In fiscal year 2003:

NEC incurred a loss of Y132.2 billion ($1,120 million) from the minimum pension liability adjustment due to a falling investment returns on pension plan assets reflecting slumping stock prices and a reduction in the discount rate for calculating benefit obligations, and losses from marketable securities of Y45.2 billion ($383 million), reflecting the realization of the unrealized gains due to the sale of marketable securities and an increase in unrealized losses on marketable securities due to worsening market conditions. (NEC, 2003, p. 33)

Despite heroic restructuring efforts, the shareholder equity ratio fell to only 8.7 per cent. NEC's is an extreme case in some ways, but not unique by any means, as more rigorous accounting standards were introduced at an especially difficult time for companies already struggling with distressed balance sheets and already near enough to bankruptcy.

Certainly Japanese accounting standards needed to be brought into general conformity with international practice. Certainly increased transparency regarding corporate affairs and results is highly desirable. Equally certainly, these changes in accounting practice came at an especially difficult time for Japan's companies. The impact on financial management was very great indeed. Companies had been already making frantic efforts to avoid balance sheet bankruptcy as asset values fell and debt levels were still high, though falling. Consolidated returns, mark-to-market pricing of assets and acknowledgement of pension liabilities very much compounded the problem and did so in the 2001 period when the economy was in especially bad shape. One might reasonably wonder how companies managed to get through all this alive.

It is something of a tribute to Japanese financial management that companies did in fact weather this almost perfect storm. Increased cash flow became the name of the game – not increased sales, and certainly not increased profits. Instead, to deal with the mountain of debt, made even more towering by accounting changes, the focus was on maximizing cash flow to reduce debt. A first measure was handed to the companies by the central bank, as nominal interest rates dropped by 70 per cent over a 10-year period to a historic low. Personnel costs were cut, most easily by taking out overtime and slashing bonus payments, then by early retirement and much reduced recruiting, along with seconding staff to subsidiaries with less generous benefit terms. Another factor in personnel cost reduction was the closing of plants abroad, in Europe and the United States.

Cash flows were also much increased by quite drastic cuts in capital expenditure. For example, capital expenditure at Toray, Japan's leading synthetic fibre producer, peaked in 1997 at more than 140 billion yen and then dropped rapidly to only a little over 50 billion yen in 2002. Cash flow was not down but capital expenditure was way down, by nearly two-thirds. (Note that the Accounting Big Bang required that there be cash flow statement disclosures, so cash flow data is now ready to hand.) The reductions in capital expenditure showed up in reduced bank borrowings but also showed up in ageing plant and equipment. By mid 2003, nearly half of Japan's manufacturing companies were operating at full capacity. No surprise that capital expenditures finally began to rise, rather sharply, as 2003 played out, a significant factor in the economy's recovery. The long, painful, deflation-ridden era of massive over capacity moved toward an end finally. But the reductions in capital expenditure and increases in free cash flow served their purpose in improving the balance sheet. Along with all this went of course efforts to speed inventory turns and to shorten the times of trade receivables, also contributing to increased free cash flow available to reduce debt – and in time, and as appropriate, to increase capital investment.

The lifting of the ban on establishing holding companies of late 1997, allowed such combinations as JFE Holdings, a combining of Kawasaki Steel and NKK, with attendant rationalization of facilities and reduction of personnel. With holding company structures and a subsequent revision of the Commercial Code facilitating spin-offs of businesses, it became possible to separate out pieces of the company as separate corporations. Thus Hitachi set up Hitachi Display and NEC separated out NEC Electronics, realizing cost improvements and equity income as well when the spin-offs went public.

All of these, and other measures, took cash flow levels up in order to deal with the balance sheet and accounting crises. By 2003, free cash flows were at their highest since reporting began in 1999, with the beginnings by that time of increased dividends, increased share buybacks, and increased capital expenditure. Some companies began further repairs on balance sheets by issuing new equity in substantial amounts in 2002/3 – Fujitsu 250 billion yen, Mitsubishi Shoji 150 billion yen, Nikon 56 billion yen. Sony sold 250 billion yen's worth and Casio Computer 20 billion yen's worth of convertibles. Other, rather less secure companies, not surprisingly many in the deeply troubled construction industry, chose to issue preferred shares, e.g., Haseko with 142.8 billion yen's worth. With major balance sheet repairs well underway, the crisis was nearing an end; the storm had been weathered.

End of the main bank system?

There has been a considerable trend to place the blame for the bubble and its aftermath on the banks of Japan, and to attribute slow economic growth to the failure of the banking system to deal with enormous amounts of non-performing loans. There is a curious arrogance in much of this commentary. The banks during the bubble were doing as they always had, and were expected to do – making loans against client asset collateral. As the value of collateral rose, so did the amounts of the loans. Were there unusually large numbers of errors in credit evaluation? Only if one argues that the banks should have realized what no one else seem to realize – that this was a bubble with a spectacular life and ghastly aftermath. The banks simply acted as did nearly everyone else, including Japan's government agencies.

It seems only fair to Japan's financial institutions to note that despite the horrific effects of the bursting of Japan's bubble, sheer theft by collusions of banks and clients was not the kind of problem that was revealed by the bursting of the US bubble:

> Investment banks...all too often trafficked in distorted or inaccurate information, and participated in schemes that helped others distort the

information they provided and enriched others at shareholders' expense. The offences of Enron and WorldCom – and of Citigroup and Merrill Lynch – put most acts of political crookedness to shame...The scale of theft achieved by the ransacking of Enron, WorldCom, and other corporations in the nineties was in the billions of dollars. (Stiglitz, 2003, pp. 167–8)

Japan has its scandals. None are of these magnitudes nor yet involving theft from shareholders by bank and management conspiracy.

The Japan bank problem was non-performing loans. With the unpredicted and in some ways unpredictable deflation, and with client companies in very deep financial trouble, non-performing loans not only were very large indeed, but became larger with each reckoning as deflation continued to drive down the value of collateral and companies' capacity to pay on the loans continued to diminish. Of course, the loans could be called, immediately, as many outside commentators proposed. And then of course there would be mass bankruptcy, mass unemployment and widespread economic chaos – surely too high a price to pay for financial tidiness. Better a period of working through the problems, even if that period is a long one and exacts an economic price of its own.

The banks were not the basic cause, but only a part of and participant in the causes of the terrible storm. And the banks are not the entire remedy, only part of the process of remedying the ill effects of the bubble. Indeed, a case can be made that the banks of Japan are more sinned against than sinners. The fact is that for several years now Japan's corporations have steadily reduced their bank borrowings, and that process continues. Japan's banks were built on the business of lending to companies. They were not built on consumer finance, home mortgage loans, or the like. And the business of company loans has dried up – except of course possible loans to those companies so troubled that no bank chooses to lend to them. Outstanding bank loans in Japan declined steadily for a number of years. Will there be some revival of corporate borrowing? Certainly. However, make no mistake, the role of the banks in Japanese financial management has changed. There will be no return to the pattern of the past with banks virtually the entire source of funding. Management will exercise options in sources and types of funds.

As noted, a special characteristic of Japanese financial management has long been the 'main bank system'. Much discussed, it is variously described as a residual and partial restructuring of pre-war holding company relations, as a result of the way credit was allocated during World War II, and as a result of capital shortages through the early post-war period. Whatever the causes, the main features of the system include a long-term relationship between bank and client, substantial mutual shareholdings between bank and client, and the bank as the instrument for corporate control as the client might become financially at hazard.

Of these special features of the main bank system, the one that has most changed over recent years – and one that has been basic to the system – is that of mutual share ownership, or cross-shareholdings. Aoki (1995, p.64) describes the development of mutual shareholding as a post-World War II phenomenon:

> The event that first triggered mutual shareholding was a take-over attempt in 1952 by an individual investor against Yowa Fudosan (predecessor of Mitsubishi Estate), which owned and managed Mitsubishi real estate of the former Mitsubishi zaibatsu in Tokyo's Marunouchi District . . . Eleven major former Mitsubishi firms joined together and devised a way to increase holdings of Yowa Fudosan stock among the group . . . The primary direct incentive for mutual shareholding under managerial leadership was the need for a defence strategy against hostile takeover. When stock acquisition by non-Japanese nationals was liberalized in the mid-1960s, the mutual shareholding rate rose even more rapidly.

Survey data confirms this view of the role of cross-shareholdings:

> Firms were asked to specify the single most important benefit of cross shareholding. The result of this (1993) survey shows that three kinds of benefits, namely 'preventing hostile takeover' (36.2 percent), 'providing the stability of firm's transactional relationships' (27.0 percent), and 'long-term stability of share price' (22.8 percent), stand out as the most important functions of cross shareholding. (Okabe, 2002, pp. 37–8)

Cross-shareholdings were as high as 18.4 per cent of the value of all shares traded in 1987. The total value of cross-shareholdings remained at the 16–17 per cent level until the mid-1990s. Then as corporate efforts to deal with weak balance sheets intensified, the cross shareholding percent dropped rapidly to 7.4 per cent and seemed likely to continue to decline even further.

As part of the massive effort to reduce debt that has been noted, both banks and companies sold off shares. With bank share prices dropping most sharply, bank shares became a main target for selling share investments by Japan's companies. Banks too have needed to raise cash and have been selling off their investment portfolios as have the companies, although to a much lesser degree, presumably in hopes of retaining companies as clients. Strengthening share prices will slow disinvestments, but a rebuilding of cross holdings to the earlier levels seems unlikely, still another factor that will diminish the power of banks over their clients.

What about cross holdings as a defence against hostile takeovers? It seems quite possible that in fact cross holdings have not really been needed as a defence, whatever the general view. Even with the sharp decline in cross holdings there have not yet been any hostile takeovers. There have been agreed-on takeover bids, both by domestic and foreign interests. These have to date involved companies in some trouble, with the takeover an agreed-on rescue operation. There have been some well-publicized efforts at hostile takeover. So far, all have failed. It is not clear that cross holdings have played a critical role in limiting take-overs, hostile or friendly. The fact that relatively few Japanese shares are traded for most companies, with 'stable' shareholdings a considerable and non-traded proportion, may be the actual defence against hostile bids, since obtaining a majority of shares through open market operations is not possible.

In fact, Japanese companies and businesses are for sale only when in deep trouble, with sale of the company an alternative to bankruptcy. The company is a social organization above all, not a simply economic apparatus, and like any other community is not for sale or purchase under anything like normal conditions, to either foreign or Japanese interests. Thus the very considerable entry of foreign corporations into the economy has been mainly through establishing new, wholly owned operations – Intel, Nokia, Microsoft, Dell and the like, or through purchase of bankrupted or near-bankrupted companies – Yamaichi, Nissan, and Long Term Credit Bank as examples. Thus in insurance, AIG and American Family are very successful insurers established by and wholly owned by foreign interests, while AXA, Manulife, and ING among others are bought out Japanese failures, with nearly 20 per cent of Japan's life insurance industry now in foreign hands.

The risks of buying into failures are real. Shinsei, once the Long Term Credit Bank, has been a case of successful foreign buy-in but owes its success to the $38 billion spent by the government of Japan to deal with the bank's bad debts. Daimler is looking to put several billion dollars more into a Mitsubishi Auto disaster, while Merrill Lynch dropped hundreds of millions into an unsuccessful Yamaichi takeover and GE finally sold out its failed acquisition of Toho Insurance to AIG. Foreign involvement in finance in Japan has a mixed record of success and failure, but in any case cannot be seen as a critical or central factor in Japanese corporate finance.

Much has been made about the main bank role as providing a corporate control mechanism, as a delegated monitor. It is said that the main bank system is important in times of financial distress, but of little significance when the client is doing well. But surely banks everywhere will, when they find that a firm to which they have lent very large sums is in danger of non-payment, make every effort to intervene to protect the bank's vital interests. Furthermore, as noted by Allen and Gale (2001, pp. 8–9), it is suggested 'that close relationships with banks – the Hausbank in Germany and the main bank in Japan – provide a substitute for control by the market. Although there has been a lot of theoretical support for these ideas, the empirical evidence is weak.'

The real change in bank and financial management is the shift away from bank borrowings described above, along with a related move to direct debt. As an example, Sumitomo Chemical's debt since 1996 has changed little in total. However, the majority of debt is now direct, as corporate short- and long-term bonds, with bank borrowings sharply down. Equity has nearly doubled. Sumitomo Electric is rather similar. While total debt is up for Sumiden, bank borrowings are about flat while debt in the form of bonds has nearly doubled. Perhaps more important, for both of these companies, equity has nearly doubled since the mid-1980s. All this change to more independent financing is despite the fact that both companies consider themselves part of the Sumitomo group still, and as such are close to and much involved with the strong Sumitomo Bank (now Sumitomo Mitsui Banking Corporation).

There are other indicators of this shift to more complex financing than simple bank borrowings. The increasing use of new equity issues and preferred share issues was noted. Bank borrowings were a third of total assets in the early 1980s, and are now about a fifth of total assets. The Bank of Japan reports that bonds and commercial paper (much of course still in bank management) has increased in proportion in six years by 10 per cent to over 40 per cent of total financing. And we have seen how drastically total debt to equity ratios have shifted. All this means of course that the central role Japan's banks once had in all aspects of corporate finance is very much diminished while a range of other financing channels is available and is being utilized.

Some caution is in order before deciding to write off the main bank as a major factor in Japanese financial management. Nihon Keizai Shimbun in September 2003 surveyed the corporations that make up the Nikkei 500 Stock Average. 343 companies responded and nearly all – 96 per cent – cite one or several specific banks as their 'main banks.' Only 14 respondents stated that they had no main bank or banks, including Toyota and Sony, telecom and power utilities and non-bank financial institutions. About a fifth of the companies had increased their ratio of main bank borrowings as they were reducing overall interest-bearing debts while maintaining their main bank involvements. There seems a kind of bimodal development since about the same proportion of the total sample, one-fifth, reported a reduction in main bank borrowings (*Nikkei Financial Daily*, 3 September 2003).

In any case, it is clearly much too early to refer to the main bank phenomenon in the past tense. Okabe (2002) notes:

> It is true that banks did sell off shares of such firms that had a low dependency on bank loans, or firms with poor financial performance, for instance, firms in construction and real-estate industries. But they retained or increased the shareholding of client business firms, large and small, with which they expected to maintain or increase transactional ties in the future.

We might assume too from the persistence of main bank relations by the vast majority of companies, that these companies will repurchase main bank shares as their balance sheets fully recover, in order to confirm what they clearly see to be a useful, even necessary, financial relationship. The full majesty of the main bank's earlier position with its clients will not be regained. But the main bank institution will, in modified and lesser degree, continue.

In Japan's economy, as in the wider society, relationships remain highly valuable, to be maintained and reinforced. The great changes that have taken place in the financial sector are in the structure of the corporate balance sheet, in the holders of shares in the marketplace, and in the formal rules governing transparency of financial position of the company. In those aspects that involve social values and behaviours – compensation levels and systems for example – the changes are few and gradual. In finance as in so much else, the Japanese system adapts to new conditions, changing in a great many ways, while holding firmly to the underlying cultural values that give Japanese society its great strength and capacity to endure.

Note

1. For a detailed discussion of these matters see Chapter 7 of Abegglen and Stalk (1985).

References

Abegglen, J. C. and G. Stalk Jr (1985) *Kaisha, The Japanese Corporation* (New York: Basic Books).

Allen, F. and D. Gale (2001) *Comparing Financial Systems* (Cambridge, Mass.: MIT Press).

Aoki, M. (1995) *Information, Corporate Governance, and Institutional Diversity* (Oxford: Oxford University Press).

Goldman Sachs (2003) *Goldman Sachs Global Strategy Research* (Tokyo: Goldman Sachs).

Koo, R. C. (2003) *Balance Sheet Recession* (Singapore: John Wiley & Sons).

NEC (2003) *Annual Report 2003* (Tokyo: NEC).

Okabe, M. (2002) *Cross Shareholdings in Japan* (Cheltenham: Edward Elgar).

Stiglitz, J. E. (2003) *The Roaring Nineties* (New York: W. W. Norton).

Teranishi, J. (1999) 'The Main Bank System', in T. Okazaki and M. Okuno-Fujiwara (eds), *The Japanese Economic System and its Historical Origins* (Oxford: Oxford University Press).

9
Japanese Human Resource Management: From Being a Miracle to Needing One?

Markus Pudelko

Introduction

One major characteristic of the Japanese business model is the importance attached to human resources, and accordingly to human resource management (HRM). An indication of the weight given to the latter is the prominent position occupied by the HR department (Rehfeld, 1995). The head of HR is often, after the president, the second most important manager in a Japanese company (Thurow, 1993). It is therefore not surprising that HRM has been identified by many authors as one of the main factors in the astonishing achievements of Japanese companies in the world markets (Inohara, 1990), particularly during the heydays Japanese success story in the 1980s and early 1990s. During that time Japanese HRM practices were widely studied in the West to discover what might be learned from them (see for example Dore, 1973, 1987, 2000, 2002; Vogel, 1979; Ouchi, 1981; Pascale and Athos, 1981; Kenney and Florida, 1988, 1993). Huczynski (1986) described the fascination with Japanese HRM in the West as a major management fad, and books suggesting what Western managers could adopt from Japanese practices joined the best-seller lists and gained almost cult status. Vogel's *Japan as Number One* (1979), Ouchi's *Theory Z* (1981) and Pascale and Athos's *The Art of Japanese Management* (1981) are but three examples.

Yet only a decade later, and most certainly also because of the crisis of the Japanese economy, the Japanese management model is increasingly viewed as uncompetitive and outmoded. Paradoxically, the same HRM practices that only recently were so admired are now perceived as being at the root of the malaise. As a result more and more authors are calling for major changes and an increased orientation towards Western management principles (Frenkel, 1994; Smith, 1997; Yoshimura and Anderson, 1997; Crawford, 1998; Ornatowski, 1998; Dalton and Benson, 2002). Others, however, while acknowledging the need for some change, insist that the main principles of Japanese HRM are still valid (Dore, 2000; Kono and Clegg, 2001). In this book Ballon (Chapter 3) and Methé (Chapter 2) speak in this context about 'continuity through change'. Sano (1993), Morishima (1995a) and Matanle (2003) take a more conciliatory approach, describing a partial convergence towards Western HRM practices.

In view of this controversial debate on continuity versus change, this chapter examines whether and to what degree the Japanese HRM model is subject to change or even extinction in response to the crisis of the Japanese business and management model. In other words, and in reference to the title of McLeod and Garnaut's book on the East Asian crisis (1998), the question is: does Japanese HRM need a miracle to regain its competitiveness or are Japanese companies finding the right balance between maintaining traditional strengths and adopting new approaches?

This chapter is structured as follows. Four HRM functions essential to the setting up of any HRM model will be looked at: the recruitment and dismissal of personnel, training and development, employee appraisal and promotion as well as remuneration. For each of these functions, first the key concepts and the internal logic of the traditional Japanese HRM practices will be outlined. Subsequently their shortcomings and the direction of possible change will be described. In the case of the latter, reference will be made to a large-scale empirical study conducted by the present author. The concluding section summarizes the key findings and provides suggestions for improving the competitiveness of Japanese HRM.

Recruitment and dismissal of personnel

A fact that is often overlooked when discussing the so-called 'Japanese HRM model' is that at no point in time did it apply to more than about a third of the Japanese workforce. In the dual structure of the Japanese employment system, 'Japanese HRM' only pertains to the core workforce of large companies, described by Ballon (1992, p. 33) as the 'employee aristocracy'. For all other employees – that is, workers in small and medium-sized companies and the marginal workforce of large companies (in particular women, part-timers, temporary workers and formally retired personnel who stay on) – key elements of the Japanese HRM model have never applied (Holland, 1992). What is more, it is only the employment of the marginal workforce, particularly temporary workers, that has given the overall labour system the necessary degree of flexibility to implement the Japanese HRM model for the core workforce. During economic downturns the marginal workforce has thus acted as a buffer to shield the core workforce from major adverse effects. This fact should always be remembered when referring to the 'traditional Japanese HRM model'.

It is argued here that despite this qualification, the entire employment sector in Japan (and beyond, the entire education system) continues to focus on producing a highly motivated and skilled core workforce for large companies. Small and medium-sized companies have to adjust their HRM practices to the environment dictated by large companies. The white-collar employee of large Japanese firms, the 'salaryman', is in the words of Matanle (2003, p. 9) 'the principle normative embodiment of Japan's success and, as such, he is a cultural icon and ideological model'.

This clear distinction between the core workforce of large companies and all other employees holds particularly true for one of the key elements of the traditional HRM model – the so-called lifetime employment. According to this concept, once school or university graduates join the core workforce of a large company they will remain with that company for their entire working life. Ouchi (1981) regards lifetime employment as the most important characteristic of a Japanese organization; Inohara (1990) describes it as the most essential distinction between Japanese and non-Japanese companies; and as recently as 2003 Matanle (p. 8) considers that 'the lifelong employment system in large corporations is the defining characteristic of the Japanese management system and can be regarded as the core institution of the Japanese firm'. Indeed, as will be demonstrated, lifetime employment affects the entire spectrum of HRM, including training and development, employee appraisal, and promotion and remuneration.

Recruitment under the lifetime employment principle signifies adherence to a family-like relationship in which loyalty, commitment and motivation are traded for material and non-material care and support. This special relationship can be illustrated by two Japanese terms that are so specific to the Japanese context that no words in the English language fully carry the same meaning. *Ie* literally translates as 'household' or 'family'. Its meaning, however, can be extended to any social relationship, including the one with and within the employing company. Because of its extended meaning, *ie* is frequently connected with the concepts of 'paternalism', 'groupism' or 'familiarism'. This sentiment of belonging is also expressed by the term *kaisha*, which is usually translated as 'firm' but has more the connotation of 'my' or 'our' firm (Durlabhji, 1993). The Japanese company may thus be perceived as the 'fictive kin group' (Nakane, 1970) and the embodiment of the *'Gemeinschaft'* (Tönnies, 2001), 'Theory Y-society' (McGregor, 1960) and 'village' (Sethi *et al.*, 1986) concepts that can help us to understand Japanese society at large. The Japanese company may be taken to symbolize the very opposite of Western society, which is described as 'contractual' (Sethi *et al.*, 1986), *'Gesellschaft'* (Tönnies, 2001) or 'Theory X' (McGregor, 1960).

The feeling of mutual commitment, trust, duty and responsibility is considered as far more binding than the legal aspect of the employment contract (the employment contract is typically just a few pages long and very unspecific anyway) (Rehfeld, 1995). Therefore the employees' knowledge that it is (or was until recently) virtually impossible under the lifetime employment principle to be laid off has never translated into an incentive not to work very hard (Inohara, 1990). More specifically, lifetime employment has never been part of a legal or contractual stipulation, but has been implicitly assumed. Legally it is in fact comparatively easy for a company in Japan to lay someone off. A discharge under these circumstances, and until recently even a resignation, is perceived very negatively and raises doubts about the employee's character. Moreover as the external labour market is completely underdeveloped it is very difficult to find a job of equal standard after leaving the core workforce of a large company (Aoki, 1990).

Under lifetime employment not only the employee but also the company does its best to fulfil its part of the implicit agreement, and thus avoids laying off employees for economic reasons. Doing so would result in a substantial loss of confidence on the part of its own workforce and the public at large, and cause serious conflict with the unions. When faced with a difficult financial situation, Japanese companies therefore usually cut dividends rather than lay off employees, which is the opposite of what most American firms would do (Kono and Clegg, 2001). Corporations with a high employee turnover rate are considered incompetent, if not inhuman in Japan (Inohara, 1990). In 1990 the annual turnover rate in Japan (3.5 per cent) was lower than the monthly rate in the United States (4 per cent) (Thurow, 1993).

The lifetime employment system does not, however, mean that it is impossible to reduce the size of the workforce, and because of high labour costs many companies are currently engaged in downsizing (Shirakai, 2002). Nonetheless laying off members of the core workforce is done only as a last resort. Before that overtime is reduced, workers are transferred from one department to another or to subsidiaries (usually with lower salaries), new recruitment is suspended, pay cuts, temporary paid leave or unpaid holidays are introduced, and voluntary early retirement is offered (Locke *et al.*, 1995; Kono and Clegg, 2001). However, it is debatable whether voluntary early retirement really is voluntary. For example in order to put employees under pressure to leave, some are placed in positions where there is nothing to do. Those employees are called *madogiwa-zoku* – literally 'those sitting at the window' – because they sit all day at their desks and for lack of work look out of the window. Even the telephones are removed from some desks in order to demonstrate unmistakably that the employees should leave the firm (Sethi *et al.*, 1986). Furthermore many companies largely hire temporary workers and a few mid-career specialists rather than add new recruits to the core workforce (Takahashi, 1990). With the number of part-time and temporary workers substantially increasing in recent years and a record level of unemployment, the employment system has in fact lost its former stability to a significant degree (Rowley *et al.*, 2004).

In the absence of a *quid pro quo* relationship stipulated in detail in a contract (fair remuneration for doing a precisely defined job), recruitment is not usually aimed at finding the right person for a specific position, but at finding the right person for the company and subsequently the right job for the new recruit. Typically only graduates of schools and universities are recruited, and only once a year. Hiring mid-career employees from the external labour market is not part of the traditional system. However exceptions have always been made for a few specialists (for example in IT or R&D) (Ballon, 1992). As it is assumed that new recruits will stay in the company for their entire working life, the selection is made very carefully (MSC, 1987). In addtion, it is based primarily if not exclusively on social criteria (Inohara, 1990). Learning potential, conformity, leadership potential, loyalty and in particular the ability to fit into the team continue to be of crucial importance.

The advantages of lifetime employment have certainly been considerable under the very specific circumstances of the Japanese business model. The loyalty and commitment of employees, because they know they will spend the next 30 to 40 years with the company, are strengthened significantly and therefore positive labour relations are promoted (Bleicher, 1982; Park, 1985). Furthermore, as will be discussed in more detail in the following sections, lifetime employment can be regarded as the basis for a concern for long-term growth, intensive training, flexible job assignments, job rotation, organizational learning, the development of multiple skills, the accumulation of knowledge and planned career development (Kono and Clegg, 2001). Dore (1973) even claims that it was largely due to lifetime employment that Japan was able to surpass other industrialized countries in its stunning postwar economic development.

The disadvantages of lifetime employment, however, have become increasingly evident over the last decade. First, because of the impossibility in practice of dismissing personnel, lifetime employment has functioned without problems only in times of uninterrupted economic growth and growing demand for personnel (Sethi *et al.*, 1986). While this was the case for most of the postwar period, in the 1990s Japan not only turned from a developmental high-growth economy into a mature low-growth economy, but was also confronted, due to structural difficulties, with very low if not negative growth rates. As labour costs under lifetime employment have to be largely considered as fixed costs, they became an increasing financial burden during an economic downturn. Demographics have made the situation even worse. With the falling birth rate the average age of employees has risen, which in combination with the seniority principle has resulted in increased labour costs. Furthermore a company must not only be able to dismiss those employees who are no longer needed but also, in order to introduce new knowledge, technologies, processes and products, to hire from the external labour market the experts and specialists it requires. At a time when speed, flexibility and adaptability to major transformations in the business environment have gained more and more importance in the struggle to remain competitive, lifetime employment, with its inherent need for stability, has increasingly become a liability (Aoki, 1990). While lifetime employment can be understood as a key reason for the strength of Japanese companies in pursuing long-term growth strategies, it also accounts for their weakness in engaging quickly in major changes and restructuring. Unfortunately for the Japanese, it seems that the business environment is increasingly demanding the latter over the former.

Change, however, has not only occurred on the employers' side. A shift in the societal value system, particularly among younger people, has resulted in a growing emphasis on the work itself, in self-actualization and independence, instead of loyalty and willingness to sacrifice (Woronoff, 1992). While this behaviour is strongly criticized and stigmatized by some sections of the population, particularly the older generation, as a sign of moral decline, it is gradually being accepted by society at large. Many employees are therefore less and less willing to commit themselves to one company for their entire working life as they might find better career opportunities or higher salaries at other companies. Furthermore, while the large Japanese multinationals were until recently only matched by the elite government bureaucracy in their attractiveness as employers, smaller, flexible and innovative start-up companies are increasingly providing an interesting alternative for young, highly talented, creative and independent-minded Japanese (MSC, 1987).

All these arguments indicate a rather fundamental change in lifetime employment practices. There is indeed ample evidence of companies distancing themselves from such practices, even to the point of completely abandoning them in some cases (Ornatowski, 1998). However Kono and Clegg (2001), Matanle (2003) and Chen *et al.* (2004) observe that many companies are still reluctant to abandon fully and openly the principle of lifetime employment and therefore dispute its collapse. But even those companies that strive to uphold the principle of lifetime employment have been forced to adapt to economic necessities. Importance is given to the concept of employability, so that employees who are forced or want to leave the company have broadly applicable skills that can easily be transferred elsewhere. To this end people are increasingly being encouraged to take greater responsibility for their own careers (Chiba *et al.*, 1997), and companies are paying attention to career development and offering counselling on opportunities both within and outside the company (Kono and Clegg, 2001). Consequently, irrespective of whether or not companies are officially remaining loyal to the principle of lifetime employment, recruitment practices are becoming more flexible, individualized, open and market oriented (Whitehill, 1991; Matanle, 2003). However for many employees this break with former practices constitutes a breach of confidence, and this has negatively affected their loyalty and commitment to their company. Lifetime employment is still considered by most members of society as a much appreciated ideal (Reinhold, 1992).

It should be noted when analyzing the above arguments that, with regard both to the critique of the lifetime employment principle and to observations about its decline, not all the works cited are recent. This indicates that gradual change towards a more flexible, individualized, open and market-oriented employment model has been going on for some time. Indeed Matanle (2003, p. 101) states that 'lifetime employment, in an institutional and organizational sense at least, must be seen as a permanently evolving, responsive, and dynamic system rather than as a static phenomenon that has remained virtually unchanged throughout most of the post-war period.' Thus the changes observed today cannot be viewed only as a reaction to the current crisis in the Japanese economy and the Japanese business and management model. Rather it was well under way even during the heyday of the Japanese management model. The question, therefore, is up to what point can one speak about gradual change *within* the system (of lifetime employment) and from what point does one assume a radical change of the system *itself*? Does the traditional concept of lifetime employment still matter for Japanese companies, or are they abandoning it altogether and replacing it with a Western-style employment system?

Some additional insights into the recruitment policies of Japanese companies are provided by an empirical study of HRM practices in large corporations in Japan, the United States and Germany (Pudelko, 2000). Questionnaires were sent to the heads of the human resource departments of the top 500 companies in each of the three countries. The managers were asked to rate the HRM practices of companies in their own country on a series of items. Their answers showed that the practices used by Japanese corporations for recruiting and dismissing personnel were strikingly different from those of their German and particularly their American counterparts. Most Japanese companies largely engaged in the recruitment of new graduates to a permanent employer–employee relationship with more senior positions being filled exclusively using internal personnel (people-oriented). In contrast the American and German recruitment practices were more about finding the best qualified candidate (from within the company or externally) for a predefined position (job-oriented). While the American and German practices were found to be very similar, they both differ from the Japanese approach. Furthermore in Japan selection was based on inter-personal skills, while in the United States and Germany it was based on performance and expertise in a given area. Also here, results for the USA and Germany are very similar, while differing strongly from the Japanese. Finally, both Japanese and German companies were characterized by low labour turnover (high degree of loyalty between employer and employee), while in the American companies there was a high labour turnover (low degree of loyalty). Interestingly, here the situation in the Japanese and German companies was very similar, and both differed significantly from that in the United States. Overall these results suggest that Japanese practices for the recruitment and dismissal of personnel are, compared with those in the two Western countries, strongly determined by the lifetime employment principle. This finding supports the continuity argument rather than the change argument.

In addition to describing their own practices, the HR managers were asked whether companies in their country had (since the 1980s) oriented themselves towards particular HRM practices from the other two countries, or were likely to do so in the coming years. The results showed that the Japanese HR managers oriented themselves strongly towards the American model and expected to do so even more in the future than in the past. No other country combination received more robust results than the Japanese orienting themselves towards the Americans. Indeed the Americans had very little inclination to learn from Japan and expected to do so even less in the future than in the past. The HR managers were also asked in open questions which HR practices they were particularly inclined to adopt. In the case of practices relating to the recruitment and dismissal of personnel, the following three statements were made most often by those Japanese who wished to adopt American practices: 'turning away from lifelong employment respectively flexibility of recruitment, dismissal of personnel and change of employer'; 'recruitment of experienced specialists for specifically advertised positions' and 'managers are externally recruited and can also be laid off again more easily'. All three arguments provide clear evidence that Japanese HR managers intend to move away from the lifelong employment system and wish to adopt American-style practices.

To sum up, the survey shows that current Japanese practices for recruitment and dismissal continue to be significantly different from those in the United States and Germany and lean more towards the traditional Japanese HRM model, but that Japanese HR managers intend to move away from this model and adopt more American-style practices.

Training and development

The Japanese school and university systems are strongly geared to providing a broad general education rather than teaching specialized knowledge and skills. Consequently companies cannot assume that their new recruits will possess any job-relevant knowledge, and it is therefore their task to train these recruits. The main objective is not to produce excellent specialists but to nurture versatile generalists. In order to train and mould their employees, all large corporations have established a long-term and exhaustive employee development programme, and the larger the company the more systematic and comprehensive the training activities tend to be.

In general training commences with an introductory course that lasts several weeks or even months, in which the new recruits learn about the company, its culture, history and mission. This first stage serves more to socialize the newcomers than to provide them with training in the strict sense of the word (Inohara, 1990). Thurow (1993, p. 140) bluntly calls these 'indoctrination programmes' and compares them to the training of soldiers. This reflects the conviction of Japanese companies that spending time on attaching new employees to the organization is rewarded by strong employee commitment and willingness to make sacrifices. Socialization and integration into close networks are also primary mechanisms of control in Japanese companies, more so than formalized bureaucratic control or output control (Gamble *et al.*, 2004).

Employees are usually assigned to the HR department for a period of three to twelve months after the introductory course, during which time they have to perform rather poorly regarded jobs. Engineers might be put to work on the assembly line, and university economics graduates employed by banks might have to visit retail customers on their bicycles in order to cash cheques. It is only afterwards that career paths are differentiated according to the employees' previous education and future potential (Inohara, 1990).

Because of the low employee turnover rate, Japanese companies can invest heavily in their employees without fearing the loss of this investment. They focus particularly on the training and development of workers and managers at lower and middle levels. Training activities occur during the entire employment period and are considered an essential part of everyday work. Unlike in the West, passing a specific training programme does not justify promotion or a higher salary. Furthermore Japanese training activities take place mainly within the company and are geared to the specific needs of the company. Thus they vary from company to company.

According to Ballon (1992) the most important task of training and development is to promote collective learning in the company. The simplest way to achieve this is teamwork and the systematic sharing of work-related knowledge with colleagues. Training is therefore almost exclusively focused on gaining on-the-job experience and is carried out according to the learning-by-doing principle. Written manuals or instructions are largely unknown. Instead knowledge is passed on orally from person to person and by observation of what more experienced colleagues do. No formal training programmes exist, and neither do specific instructors (Inohara, 1990).

As noted above, training in Japanese companies is continued and general. The reason for this is that very specific knowledge and expertise are quickly outdated in a fast moving world and this renders highly specialized employees unproductive. As the discharge of such people and the recruitment of others who have the required new knowledge is not an option under lifetime employment, broad-based training is regarded as a guarantee of flexible employees with enduring value. Retraining for new jobs is a markedly different strategy from the American 'hire and fire' approach, under which employees are hired to do a specific job for which they have the necessary skills and are laid off again when their skills are not longer needed (Kono and Clegg, 2001). Training is thus to be understood as a comprehensive, continuous process in which the company invests a substantial amount of time, effort and capital in order to produce multi-skilled generalists (Aoki, 1988; Purcell *et al.*, 1998).

A further component of generalist training and development is job rotation (McMillan, 1996). Workers are frequently moved between working groups and working stations, while white-collar employees rotate between different departments and functions. Job rotation is not just a training instrument for junior staff, rather it continues up to high management levels and is less about the development of single employees than about creating a learning organization in which broadly based knowledge, understanding and experience permeate the entire organization. This can be interpreted as the basis for all *kaizen* or continuous improvement activities. Japanese companies still value job rotation and on-the-job training throughout the employee's working life, even though there seems to be a growing emphasis on off-the-job training (Koike, 1997; JIL, 1998; Rowley *et al.*, 2004). Another practice is the *sempai–kohai* relationship, in which an older and more experienced company member (*sempai*) guides and advises one or two junior employees (*kohai*) who are not direct subordinates. According to Morishima (1995b), cooperation in interdepartamental working groups, job rotation and the *sempai–kohai* relationship are the three principal means of on-the-job training and development in Japan.

Job descriptions are of little importance in Japan, unlike in the West (Inohara, 1990). Although job descriptions, particularly for blue-collar workers, do exist, they are ambiguous, meant only as broad guidelines and do not preclude significant deviations according to the company's needs (Arvey *et al.*, 1991; Morishima, 1995b). Who does what in a team is not prescribed, and as tasks often overlap they are performed by several employees collectively (Plenert, 1990; Kono and Clegg, 2001). Harmonious working relations are essential in this context. Frequent cooperation in working groups consisting of individuals from different functions increases understanding of the various perspectives of other departments (Morishima, 1995b). Acquired knowledge and skills result in a gain in productivity not only for individual employees but also for the organization as a whole (Arvey *et al.*, 1991). Next to the advantages stemming directly from the collective learning process, identification with the entire company and with colleagues and team members is strengthened, as is commitment to the company.

The basic philosophy of the Tayloristic American model is that through specialization companies can reduce the cost of workforce training to a minimum, provided the workers are closely supervised. While 100 or so different job descriptions can exist in American plants, there may be no more than seven for the same tasks in Japanese plants. This means that one

Japanese worker is capable of doing what needs to be done by 10–20 different persons in the United States. Workers not only operate machines, but also clean, maintain and – when possible – repair them. With a multi skilled workforce, flexibility increases substantially as the workers can be quickly reassigned to whatever job needs to be done at a specific moment in time. The efficiency gains obtained from this and other production process innovations have substantially increased the productivity of Japanese companies over time (McMillan, 1996). What Japanese firms have achieved in this context was once perceived in the West to be impossible: improving product quality through incremental process innovations, while at the same time reducing production costs. Not surprisingly, during the period of high economic growth in Japan these innovations were held up as key factors in the success of Japanese companies.

Quality circles (instruments of the Japanese business model about which there has been much comment) should also be mentioned in the context of training and process innovation. Working in autonomous groups, five to ten employees engage in what nearly all Japanese children learn from kindergarten onwards: to increase the collective and individual competence of everyone involved by cooperatively trying to solve a problem. This intense cooperation, however, does not preclude a competitive aspect to quality circle activities. On the contrary, as the achievements of the various quality circles are compared, not only identification with one's own circle but also competition with other circles increases. This competitiveness is a major driver of motivation and has a positive effect on active learning. For Plenert (1990) and Ballon (1992), it is not the solution to problems that stands in the foreground of quality circles, but identification with the process of finding the solution.

Japanese companies' training and development activities are often the subject of considerable praise because of their long-term orientation, comprehensiveness and positive motivational effects. Yet criticism is increasingly being expressed in this area as well. With ever faster product cycles and the growing complexity of technology there is a greater need for specialized knowledge. Japanese companies, however, have been rather reluctant to embrace training activities that are geared to specialization. After all, specialists undermine the lifelong employment principle, as with their expertise they become increasingly exchangeable among companies. This might facilitate the hiring of experts from other companies, but by the same token it presents the risk that the company's own experts might be lured away to competing firms, and this in turn makes long-term, comprehensive training a more costly and uncertain business. Moreover moving away from generalist training undermines seniority-oriented promotion and remuneration. The rather egalitarian in-house generalist career path has strengthened identification with the company and enhanced the feeling of being appreciated by the company. In contrast the presence of highly specialized and externally trained experts can disturb harmonious working relations. Yet with the decline of lifetime employment and (as will be seen) the seniority principle, more specialized training and development activities are taking place. This is supported by the gradual transformation of the attitude of Japanese employees, who are increasingly expressing their preference for specific jobs and specialized careers. More specialized skills also enhance the employee's employability, which will become more and more important as lifetime employment declines. In order to accommodate these factors, companies are beginning to gear training to employees' individual interests, preferences and talents (Leme Fleury, 1996).

Turning to empirical evidence gained from the study discussed in the previous section (Pudelko, 2000), Japanese companies stress widespread training for broadly defined tasks (the goal being to create a generalist), while the German and more so the American practices are geared towards training focused on specific knowledge for narrowly defined tasks (the goal being to create a specialist). While the American and German practices are evaluated very similarly, they both differ significantly from the Japanese ones. Furthermore, in Japan there is a clear tendency for training to be extensive and focused on the work group, while in Germany and in particular in the United States it tends to be limited and focused on the individual. Here again, American and German practices are described in a very similar way, while they both differ strongly from the Japanese ones. For the last criterion the results clearly deviate from the previous pattern of country differences: both American and Japanese companies invest much effort in moulding the employee in accordance with the company's culture, while in German companies there is little effort to do so. Thus Japan and the United States are very similar in this regard and both deviate from Germany. Overall, it should be noted that the differences among the three countries with respect to training and development are clearly less pronounced than was the case with the recruitment and dismissal of personnel. This is also reflected in the statements made by the Japanese managers on what they would like to adopt from the United States. Training and development played a comparatively insignificant role. The strongest point made was that there should be more training of specialists and less emphasis on the formation of generalists. This confirms the direction of change indicated earlier. By and large, however, in Japanese companies training and development practices seem not to be undergoing a significant transformation.

Employee appraisal and promotion

For employee appraisal three criteria can be considered relevant: performance, behaviour and potential. Comparative neglect of the first and concentration on the last two criteria have been described as characteristic of traditional

Japanese HRM (Hilb, 1985). Knowing that they will spend their entire working life in the same company, employees' continuous efforts and willingness to integrate are regarded as highly important. This explains the value that has been traditionally attached to behaviour. As for performance appraisal, it is primarily people's contribution to group objectives that is important, less so the meeting of individual objectives. Individual contributions to group objectives are seen in the context not only of meeting economic targets but also of strengthening the working morale of the entire group (Inohara, 1990). Moreover as short-term achievements might be the result of circumstances over which employees have little control, performance evaluations tend to be more oriented towards the long term. Employee appraisal is also based on more implicit, subtle and informal criteria, and a formal interview is not often part of the Japanese appraisal procedure. Less than positive evaluations might lead to the appraised losing face, and is therefore avoided. For the necessary feed-back, more indirect means of communication are chosen (Inohara, 1990; Bloom *et al.*, 1994).

The stress on group orientation should not be interpreted as meaning that the Japanese are not interested in pursuing individual careers and are strangers to interpersonal competition and rivalry. In fact, the Japanese term *risshin-shuse*, which can be translated as 'to build up one's own career', is the motto of many ambitious Japanese. Furthermore competition and performance orientation are integral to the Japanese education system, and the competitive pressure to pass the entry exams for the best universities is extreme. However the competition for promotion in Japanese companies works differently from that in Western organizations, insofar as it takes a more concealed form as group harmony officially takes precedence over everything else. Chang (1982) refers in this regard to individualism through the group.

Despite antidiscrimination laws, women are rarely recruited to the core workforce and therefore are hardly ever found in higher management positions (Arvey *et al.*, 1991; Bloom *et al.*, 1994). This is despite the fact that as many women graduate from university as men. It is still expected that women will marry after some years of employment and then commit all their time to their families, without taking up a job again, after the education of their children. Consequently companies are unwilling to invest much in the training of women. Japanese female university graduates are often highly overqualified for the jobs they perform (Inohara, 1990; Rehfeld, 1995). If they wish to pursue a career in a corporation their only option is to work for a subsidiary of a foreign company. But here too career possibilities are generally restricted to the subsidiary itself, as moving to the country where the headquarters is situated is usually not an aim. While foreign observers should always avoid pronouncing judgements on the fairness or unfairness of specific characteristics of other cultures, from a purely economic perspective the neglect of a well-educated (female) workforce has to be regarded as a substantial waste of resources, from the point of view of both the company and the entire economy.

Promotion and remuneration policies are strongly influenced by the seniority principle in the traditional Japanese HRM model. The seniority principle, together with lifetime employment and the company unions, make up the 'three pillars of Japanese HRM' (Park, 1985; Taylor, 2001.) The promotion and remuneration of employees is therefore determined less by individual performance than by length of employment. This reflects, according to Lincoln (1989), East-Asians' traditional deference to age and seniority. The rapid promotion of high performers, resulting in younger employees becoming superiors of older ones, would be viewed as unjustifiable discrimination against older and more experienced employees, and would disturb the overall harmony of the company. The seniority principle should not, as with lifetime employment, be construed as an invitation for idleness. If employees do not live up to expectations, delayed promotion (if not discharge) can result. With a change of employer not being an option under lifetime employment, the possibility of delayed promotion and therefore loss of face are strong incentives to keep one's performance in line with the expectations of superiors and colleagues (Inohara, 1990; Ballon, 1992).

As a consequence of the seniority system, young, highly motivated and outstanding employees have not been able to rise quickly through the ranks until recently. Under the seniority principle there is no fast-track career system and employees are promoted in small but steady steps. Yet in order to guarantee that important decisions are taken by competent personnel, formal hierarchical position and (informal) decision-making authority do not necessarily coincide. Young employees with leadership qualities are entrusted from early on with significant responsibilities, even though they still lack the formal recognition of a higher position in the organization. Knowing, however, that promotion to a senior management position is based on long-term evaluation, this does not (or did not) demotivate high achievers. Furthermore the seniority principle facilitates the functioning of job rotation, as the concrete task to be performed is not directly linked to a specific hierarchical position. For Japanese employees it is therefore easier to accept less attractive positions as they know that their career depends on seniority and commitment, not on their current position. Appraisal in the context of job rotation is therefore always related to the individual employee and not the job position in question. However this makes appraisal both more troublesome and potentially less objective. Hence the introduction of obligatory appraisal training programmes for managers and of grievance systems for handling complaints related to performance appraisals (Shibata, 2000).

With regard to the relative weight of the seniority principle for promotion decisions, Takahashi (1985) refers to the hierarchical level. For the lower and middle ranks seniority and commitment are the main promotion criteria, whereas for higher levels initiative and performance results are of more importance. Finally, for top management, only initiative and performance results count, with seniority being of no significance. Thus in the traditional Japanese HRM model promotion depends on a combination of seniority and appraisal of behaviour and results.

The seniority principle has often been held up as a key factor in the success of Japanese companies (Lincoln, 1989), but others have disputed this. For example Woronoff (1992) suggests that the seniority system has turned Japanese companies into bureaucratic rather than entrepreneurial organizations. Dore (1973) has come to a similar but more neutral conclusion by comparing the Japanese employee not to a bureaucrat but to a civil servant. Woronoff (1992) considers that due to automatic promotions up to a certain management level, the various hierarchies are permeated with less competent managers, who would have been filtered out under a more performance-oriented promotion system. In the case of top management there are two further problems. First, when managers finally arrive at the very top they are advancing in age, well past their most productive years and possibly out of touch with the latest trends and technologies. Second, even more worrying than the right people arriving at the top too late is the wrong people getting to the highest level. The traditional Japanese promotion system works in favour of loyal, highly motivated and efficient employees who do not rock the boat, and against those with outstanding leadership qualities who have the courage to take uncomfortable decisions. In view of the ongoing economic crisis and the arguable need for comprehensive change, the lack of leaders who are both willing and competent to embrace new management principles and implement them uncompromisingly can be perceived as one of the key reasons for the paralysis of Japanese business.

Furthermore the seniority principle depends largely on a growing economy, a constant demand for additional personnel and the need for additional management positions. However the Japan economy is not only mature but has also been in or close to recession for a long period of time, and therefore the need for more personnel and managerial positions has decreased substantially. Companies that have been confronted with a declining demand for managers but a continuing expectation by their employees that they will be promoted have introduced more and more intermediate hierarchical layers. These have little organizational effect and are merely a means to satisfy the staff. Among the consequence of this, many managers do not have a single subordinate, personnel costs have increased and the decision-making process has become less effective and more inefficient. As the overall demand for managers has declined, experts with specialized skills have become more important. Because they often have to be recruited from the external labour market at mid-career level, outside specialists have become superiors of employees who have worked as generalists at the company for many years and were counting on being promoted to the positions in question (Whitehill, 1991; Woronoff, 1992). This creates friction and is detrimental to loyalty and motivation.

Change, however, is not only initiated by companies but also sparked by employees. As companies increasingly withdraw from the practice of lifetime employment, young and highly capable employees with much sought-after qualifications are becoming more impatient and less willing to accept slow steps up the promotion and remuneration ladders. Now that they can change employers more easily they are well-placed to push for a relaxation of the rigid seniority system (Lincoln, 1989; Leme Fleury, 1996; Dalton and Benson, 2002; Rowley *et al.*, 2004). Given the current economic situation, the limit to which the seniority system can continue to function seems to have been reached, if not surpassed. Employees are increasingly opting for more specialized career paths as they provide better career opportunities, both within and outside the company. As employees gradually identify more with their specialization and less with their company, these changes are adding to their motivation (Kono and Clegg, 2001).

Several authors have reported a strong decline in the application of the seniority principle (ibid.; Ballon, 2002). However it is often overlooked that this is by no means a recent phenomenon or merely a response to the present economic situation, but rather a continuous development. Park (1985) had already found in 1985 that 96 per cent of all Japanese companies were carrying out performance evaluations, which indicated to him that promotion was by no means an automatic process guided exclusively by seniority. Instead individual performance was, in his judgement, of growing significance in terms of streamlining the corporate structure, improving corporate decision making and setting incentives for high performers. Sethi *et al.* (1986) similarly noted one year later that more competent and dynamic persons were acceding faster to key positions. Thus even during the heyday of the Japanese business model the seniority principle was already highly disputed and in decline.

The shift in the relative importance of seniority and performance is necessitating a number of further changes. First, more precise and transparent evaluation criteria are needed to measure individual performance (Sano, 1993). As employee appraisal tended to be rather subjective, additional people are now included in the appraisal process to increase objectivity (Kono and Clegg, 2001). Second, transparency and objectivity in turn require more specific job descriptions from which explicit performance criteria can be established. However this renders job rotation more difficult, and the continuing stress on team work makes the assessment of individual performance rather complicated. Ultimately these reforms risk alienating many employees who regard the changes as a unilateral cancellation of the mutual trust relationship and a betrayal of the values to which they were introduced by their company (Sethi *et al.*, 1986; Whitehill, 1991; Woronoff 1992; Sasajima, 1993).

In general observers seem to be rather unanimous in finding a weakening of the seniority principle in Japanese corporations. What remains in dispute, however, is whether the seniority principle is already a relic of the past that has been replaced by the more Western concept of individual performance, or whether it is still of some importance in promotion decisions. To gain some insight into this we shall return to the findings of the comparative empirical study conducted in Japan, Germany and the United States (Pudelko, 2000).

First, according to the Japanese HR managers questioned, Japanese promotion practices are very much half way between giving a heavy weighting to seniority and individuals contribution to collective achievements on the one hand, and giving a heavy weighting to individual achievements on the other. In comparison with all other findings on the recruitment and dismissal of personnel, training and development, employee assessment and promotion criteria as well as remuneration, the seniority principle seems to be the least oriented towards the pole representing the traditional Japanese HRM model. Given the fact that this principle was considered to be a cornerstone of Japanese management, this finding suggests a considerable change in Japanese HR practices. On the other hand, compared with companies in Germany and the United States, which stress individual achievement, Japanese companies are still more inclined towards seniority. This now gives the continuity argument some credence.

With regard to the nature of the promotion criteria, the results are even less straightforward. Promotion criteria in Japan fall in between primarily informal and non-quantifiable (behaviour-oriented) on the one hand, and primarily formal and quantifiable (results-oriented) on the other. Much the same applies to the criteria used in American and German companies.

Finally, in Japan the career path encompasses several departments and areas, while in Germany and particularly the United States it is usually confined to one department or area. Here the difference between the generalist Japanese approach based on job rotation and the specialist American and German career development is very clear, indicating a continued validity of the traditional model.

To sum up, in the area of promotion in particular the decline of the seniority principle is noteworthy, although Japanese companies still value seniority significantly more highly than their American and German counterparts.

Remuneration

When defining a remuneration model, three criteria can be used: external remuneration fairness (in relation to other companies), internal remuneration fairness (in relation to job requirements and performance) and the spread of remuneration between the highest salary and the lowest wage. Japanese remuneration practices are characterized by a low ranking in all three criteria. As the external labour market in Japan is traditionally under-developed because of the lifetime employment system there is little attention to equality of remuneration among companies. Moreover because bonus payment schemes vary markedly, salaries between companies are difficult to compare. With regard to internal fairness, the Japanese remuneration system is only loosely linked to job positions (because of job rotation) and individual performance (due to team orientation), resulting in low internal remuneration fairness (Hilb, 1985).[1]

The spread between the top salary and lowest wage in Japanese companies is very narrow compared with those in the West. If pay cuts have to be introduced, they start with the salaries of the top management (Ballon, 1992). The low income disparity between managers and workers is considered to be an important means of ensuring harmony in industrial relations and workers' identification with the company. According to Crystal (1991) the comparatively low salaries paid to Japanese managers are due to the fact that monetary incentives are relatively less important to them than recognition by colleagues with whom they have cooperated over many years. Rehfeld (1995) highlights an interesting difference from Western countries in this connection. In the West, top managers earn high salaries, gain financial independence, can buy expensive status symbols, and can change companies with ease. In contrast Japanese companies pay their top managers significantly lower salaries, which not only brings a feeling of solidarity among workers and managers but also because of the underdeveloped external labour market keeps top managers financially dependant on the company. Moreover it is the company that pays for the managers' status symbols – such as nightly outings to exclusive bars, golf club membership fees and so on – so if they lose their jobs they lose not only their salary but also a large part of their social life and ultimately their social recognition.

As in the case of promotion, remuneration in Japanese companies has traditionally been largely determined by seniority. In the first 10 to 15 years, all employees of comparable seniority receive very similar salaries, with frequent but small increases. During this period remuneration is determined by duration of employment in the company, age, education, family status and gender. Only afterwards do those who have exhibited a better individual performance quietly receive somewhat higher pay increases. This holds for both white-collar employees and blue-collar workers (Ballon, 1992). Both groups also receive similar treatment in terms of working time and annual leave. Thus equality is more pronounced than hierarchical differences (Reinhold, 1992; Itoh, 1994).

A characteristic of the Japanese remuneration system is the importance of bonuses, which are typically paid twice a year and can amount to five times the monthly salary. These can be subdivided into bonuses related to the performance of the individual employee, the working group or the company, overtime pay, and a number of supplements and social benefits. Under the seniority principle and lifetime employment, salaries and wages have largely been considered as fixed costs. It is the bonus system that has provided companies with at least some degree of flexibility.

The seniority principle has strengthened employees' attachment to lifetime employment because wages increase with tenure. As salaries are not directly related to specific job positions, job rotation is facilitated. Consequently, compensation is more linked to the individual employee than to his job (Itoh 1994). As with promotion policy, remuneration based largely on individual performance goes against the group orientation of the Japanese business model. To single out certain individuals in a team as better performers than the other team members and therefore entitled to a higher salary would ruin the harmony of the team and the egalitarian atmosphere of the company.

As mentioned above, Japanese companies offer their employees a number of social benefits. These not only meet material needs but also strengthen employees' loyalty to the company. Examples are housing subsidies, money for the education of children, payments to the widows of dead employees and even the right to burial in company-owned cemeteries. The organization of group leisure time pursuits and holdiays, the provision of company hospital care and the availability of an internal marriage brokerage service further illustrate the holistic care that Japanese companies provide for their employees (White and Trevor, 1983; Okabe, 2002). This care is often described as paternalism. Akio Morita, former president of Sony, once joked that a Japanese firm sometimes more resembles a welfare organization than a profit-seeking institution.

As noted above, under the seniority system new recruits start out on very low pay, so many continue to live with their parents as they cannot afford to rent their own accommodation. Well-educated and capable employees in particular are significantly underpaid in comparison with their contribution. Because of the inadequate pension schemes offered by Japanese companies, older people also have to live on a comparatively low income when they retire, usually at the age of 60. As a result many choose to stay on with the company after their official retirement date, or move to a subsidiary in order to liaise with former colleagues, or take a different job altogether. These after-retirement jobs are usually comparatively low paid. Given the traditional respect of age in Eastern cultures, which is also reflected in the seniority system, this seems rather odd (Woronoff, 1992). One might, however, maintain that the system is just as it benefits the middle aged who are establishing a family, buying a home and paying for their children's education. Conversely young employees who do not yet have a family and retired people whose children are economically independent need less and therefore should receive less.

In the discussion on promotion it was argued that the seniority principle is steadily declining in significance. The same argument can be applied to remuneration. As early as 1969 Abeggeln observed that Japanese companies, when determining their employees' salaries, gave more weight to qualifications, skills and performance than to seniority. Merz (1986) and Sasajimma (1993) also argued many years ago that performance was valued more highly than seniority when it came to remuneration. Furthermore, whereas salary discrepancies due to performance differences once occurred only after ten years or more with the company, now they are introduced increasingly earlier. Salaries are thus losing substantially in uniformity and calculability. As the seniority system means that older employees cost more, companies are trying to reduce the proportion of older employees (Sano, 1993; Sasajima, 1993), especially in the face of growing competitive pressure (Ornatowski, 1998; Rowley *et al.*, 2004).

Despite these changes it appears that seniority is still a factor in the determination of remuneration. Furthermore there has been little change to the rather narrow spread between management salaries and workers' wages (Kono and Clegg, 2001), so while pay differentiation based on performance differences is being introduced, it is not being taken to extremes.

With remuneration too, changes do not only occur on the company side, but also on the motivational side of the employees. While loyal, hard-working but less outstanding employees are losing out under a more performance-oriented compensation system, high performers are being better rewarded and are therefore more motivated to excel (Dalton and Benson, 2002; Rowley *et al.*, 2004). As identification with the company weakens, commitment to a specific occupation rises, and the expectation of emotional and moral reward is being replaced in some measure by the demand for a material repayment that is considered fair given the performance delivered. Employees' willingness to make sacrifices for the company (accepting jobs that are considered unattractive, long working hours, renunciation of holiday time, spending evenings with colleagues instead of the family) is gradually being replaced by a wish for fulfilment through a professional challenge in a job of their own choosing.

As with the HRM functions discussed previously, empirical evidence from the three-country survey (Pudelko, 2000) can provide some additional insights into the degree to which remuneration practices in Japanese companies have been subject to change. When asked whether their companies primarily favoured material incentives or a mixture of material and non-material incentives, the Japanese respondents stated that there was a slight preference for the latter. Given the characteristics of the traditional Japanese HRM model a much stronger orientation towards non-material incentives might have been expected, so this suggests a move towards

Western practices. The judgements of the American and German HR managers on their own respective incentives were so similar that no difference between the Western policies could be established. In response to the question of whether pay depended on individual performance or seniority the Japanese HR managers stated that the two had equal weight. As with promotion, the seniority principle is also with regards to compensation the one from all items tested which was perceived by the Japanese HR managers to be most distant from the traditional Japanese HRM practices. This suggests a major move away from this once so typical aspect of Japanese HRM. On the other hand, again as seen with promotion, the German and in particular the American remuneration practices are still significantly more oriented towards individual performance. This result now supports the continuity argument, as it highlights the (still) existing difference between Western and Japanese HRM practices. Finally, the Japanese HR managers strongly agreed that their companies were more directed towards 'little differences in pay between top-managers and average workers (less than 20 fold), as opposed to a 'very large differences in pay between top-managers and average workers'. The Germans are also leaning more towards smaller pay differences, albeit to a much lesser extent, whereas the American HR managers clearly observe very high income discrepancies between top-managers and average workers in their companies. Here, from all 12 items tested related to the four HRM functions covered in this article, the pattern of the Japanese and the American HR practices opposing each other, with Germany in the middle, is most striking.

Overall there is a clear indication that remuneration in Japanese companies is becoming increasingly differentiated, depending more and more on individual performance, although the difference between the pay of top managers and of workers remains comparatively modest.

Conclusion

The objective of this chapter has been to determine whether the Japanese HRM model has been subject to substantial change in response to the perceived crisis of the Japanese business and management models. Both the analysis of the literature and the findings of the author's empirical survey have provided strong evidence that traditional Japanese HRM is currently undergoing significant change. This transformation has a clear direction which can be summarized as a convergence towards more Western-style management practices. Another indication of this trend is the large number of HRM-related consultancies of Western origin that are currently springing up in Japan. Additional interviews conducted by the author with Japanese HR managers and HR consultants in Japan, and with HR managers of Japanese subsidiaries in the USA and Germany confirm that HRM in

Japanese companies is becoming more 'Westernized'. The interviews furthermore clearly indicated that Japanese managers almost exclusively focus on the United States when looking for inspiration from abroad.

Companies are introducing HRM practices characterized by greater market orientation and individualization and, consequently, diversity, in order to respond better to the rapidly changing external environment and to individual employee differences in terms of performance, skills, achievements and demands (see also Matanle, 2003; Watanabe, 2003). This process covers the full range of HRM functions, including the recruitment and dismissal of personnel, training and development, employee appraisal and promotion, as well as remuneration. However the overall finding of significant change towards Western practices is subject to five qualifications.

First, the move away from the traditional Japanese model towards more Western practices is by no means a new phenomenon, as the analysis of the literature has shown. More than 20 years ago studies found signs of change in a number of key areas (for example, decline of lifetime employment, seniority system and generalist career paths and rise of job mobility, performance orientation and specialist career paths.) What can be argued, however, is that the pressure for change has grown substantially during the current economic crisis.

Second, it has been established that change in the sense of 'Westernization' is not to the advantage of all company members, and consequently it has met with opposition. Broadly speaking the agents of change are often those at the very top of the hierarchy, as it is they who bear overall responsibility for the company and are under pressure to maintain or regain the company's competitiveness. Equally, supporters of change are young employees with strong potential and specialized skills who are no longer constrained by lifetime employment or the seniority system and seek a higher degree of self-actualization. Change means they can rise more quickly up the hierarchy or move to a better job in another company. Either way they will earn more money and enjoy greater autonomy. In contrast the Westernization of HR practices is meeting resistance from those who will suffer personal disadvantage from it. These are mostly middle managers who have made sacrifices for their company in the past (for example, low starting salary, slow promotion, frequent moves under job rotation) and are now counting on receiving the traditional rewards for their loyalty and hard work. Fearing that they will not be rewarded or that they might even be dismissed makes them natural opponents of change. The debate on continuity versus change is therefore not just about what is best for the company, but also a matter of what is in the interest of those directly involved and, thus, a question of internal power struggles. The more a company is subject to global competition and/or is under economic strain, the more influence the promoters of change will have. In this regard companies in protected industries, such as construction and retailing, change less than companies in sectors such as car manufacture and electronics.

Third, even assuming an irreversible trend towards a gradual individualization of Japanese society and more insistent demands for self-actualization by Japanese employees, Japanese society continues to be highly collective and therefore fundamentally different from Western societies. Despite this, the picture of Japan as a cultural island (Moss-Kanter, 1991) or as a village (Sethi *et al.*, 1986) is increasingly difficult to uphold, with Japan becoming more closely intertwined with other economies and Japanese managers being increasingly active internationally (Morgan *et al.*, 2003). Thus globalization, demographic changes, the maturing of the economy, material affluence, consumerism, a growing variety of opportunities and new ideas about modernism are challenging the Japanese system of values, needs and demands, by stressing Western concepts such as individualism, personal happiness, self-fulfilment and self-actualization. To assume, however, that Japan will follow this path to such an extent that it will eventually become Westernized would be wrong. For this, (each) society is too deeply rooted in its culture, which is far from being subject to rapid change (Hofstede, 2001). Consequently Japanese employees will continue to adhere to their roles and obligations in the complex web of group relationships that constitute the foundation of their social life. Self-actualization also has to be seen in the context of interpersonal relations and mutual obligations. Even though traditional practices such as lifetime employment and the seniority system might not offer the most individually fulfilling working life, they continue to be appreciated by many for their role in supporting relational values and the security and stability they entail. Also not to be underestimated is a certain pride in Japanese exceptionalism that would be only reluctantly abandoned in favour of the American way of life (and management). With the exception of the clear winners from change (who consequently support it) and the clear losers (who consequently reject change), the majority of Japanese employees seem to be torn between the new chance for self-realization and the economic and social risks, between participating in a global society and the loss of 'Japaneseness'. Meanwhile the 'salaryman' has lost his status as a hero of Japanese society and his certainty about his role in society. He is therefore suffering from the emotional challenge of redefining his position in the no man's land between the rigidity but stability of the past and the flexibility but insecurity of the future. Because of these ambiguities, signs of pressure for change by Japanese society should not be automatically equated with a desire to emulate Western social and cultural values and norms nor, more specifically, Western HRM practices (Matanle, 2003).

Fourth, a comparison with American and German HRM has indicated that most Japanese HR practices are still significantly different from those in the West and continue to lean towards the traditional Japanese HRM model.

Thus a complete convergence with Western management practices is by no means taking place. This indicates that even though the differences between Japanese HRM practices and those of Western countries are seeming to shrink, they nonetheless still continue to exist.

Fifth, the empirical analysis demonstrated as well that it would be erroneous to assume that there is a stark differentiation between Japanese practices on the one hand and a homogeneous block of Western (in this case American and German) practices on the other. Rather the data presented seems to indicate the existence of a continuum, with the highly individualistic American HRM model at one end, the collectivistic Japanese model at the other, and the German one in between (Pudelko, 2000). If one accepts the idea that HRM practices are at least partly defined by the specific cultural context, the existence of a continuum is supported by the findings of arguably the two most prominent authors to establish rankings for national cultures. The same pattern, with the USA and Japan in many ways at the opposite ends and Germany in the middle, can indeed be established with four out of the five of Hofstede's dimensions (individualism, masculinity, uncertainty avoidance and time perspective) and all six of Trompenaars's dimensions (universalism vs. particularism, individualism vs. communitarianism, specificity vs. diffuseness, achieved vs. ascribed status, inner vs. outer direction, and sequential vs. synchronous time) (Hofstede, 2001; Hampden-Turner and Trompenaars, 2000). More specifically, with regards to the three HRM models, in a previous publication (Pudelko, 2000) the author of this article defined this continuum using the following opposite poles: 'short-term performance efficiency based on flexible market structures and profit orientation' (USA) and 'long-term behavioural effectiveness based on cooperative clan structures and growth orientation' (Japan). The concept of a continuum suggests now that the question of continuity (of 'traditional' Japanese approaches) versus change (towards Western practices) is not a question of either/or, but a matter of degree, as Western practices also differ amongst themselves. Thus, lifelong employment might for example well be abolished as a strict system, but employment in Japan is likely to continue to be more long-term oriented than for instance in Germany, or in the USA in particular. Consequently, the continuum with the highly individualistic American HRM model, a more moderately individualistic European HRM model such as the German one, and a rather collectivistic Japanese HRM model might become shorter, but will continue to exist.

Western approaches might, in consequence, serve Japanese companies as an indicator for the direction of change; however, the extent to which this direction should be taken can only be determined under close consideration of the specific Japanese context. In other words, Western management might function as a source of inspiration, but should not be understood in any way as a blue-print to be copied (Pudelko, 2004a,b). This is even more so, as the assumption of a monolithic 'Western management model' is misleading, as has been established here. Therefore instead of focusing only on the American model, Japanese HR managers would do well to broaden their search for outside inspiration, particularly in countries that have a more partnership-oriented HRM model.

To conclude, what was once perceived as a serious challenge to the Western management model has lost much of its strength, fascination and appeal. In order for Japan to regain its competitiveness it is not a miracle that is needed, but the development of a hybrid approach between traditional practices and more Western ones which takes account of the specificities of the Japanese sociocultural context. However it is difficult at this stage to predict where this new equilibrium between continuity and change will lie.

Note

1. The term and definition of external and internal job fairness are taken from the literature and applied to the case of Japan. It should be noted, however, that it is problematic to attribute a low degree of fairness to the Japanese remuneration system according to Western standards. Japanese who value group effort more than individual performance will, for example, be hardly convinced that it is fair to pay a CEO two hundred times more than a worker (as is common in the United States), even though this might be considered fair in the West.

References

Abegglen, J. C. (1968) 'Organizational Change', in R. J. Ballon (ed.), The Japanese Employee, (Rutland, Vermont: Charles E. Tuttle).

Aoki, M. (1988) *Information, Incentives, and Bargaining in the Japanese Economy* (Cambridge: Cambridge University Press).

Aoki, M. (1990) 'Toward an Economic Model of the Japanese Firm', *Journal of Economic Literature*, 28 March, pp. 1–27.

Arvey, R. D., R. S. Bhagat and E. Salas (1991) 'Cross-Cultural and Cross-National Issues in Personnel and Human Resource Management: Where do we go from here?', in G. R. Ferris and K. M. Rowland (eds), *Research in Personnel and Human Resource Management. A Research Annual* (Greenwich, CT, and London: Jai Press), pp. 367–407.

Ballon, R. J. (1992) *Foreign competition in Japan. Human resource strategies* (London and New York: Routledge).

Ballon, R. J. (2002) 'Human Resource Management and Japan', *Euro Asia Journal of Management*, 12 (1), pp. 5–20.

Ballon, R. J. (2005) 'Organizational Survival', in R. Haak and M. Pudelko (eds), *Japanese Management – The Search for a New Balance between Continuity and Change* (Basingstoke and New York: Palgrave), 55–77.

Bleicher, K. (1982) 'Japanisches Management im Wettstreit mit westlichen Kulturen', *Zeitschrift Führung & Organisation*, 51 (7), pp. 444–50.

Bloom, H., R. Calori and P. de Wool (1994) *Euromanagement. A New Style for the Global Market* (London: Kogan Page).

Chang, C. S. (1982) 'Individualism in the Japanese Management System', in S. M. Lee and G. Schwendiman (eds), *Japanese Management. Cultural and Environmental Considerations* (New York: Greenwood), pp. 82–8.

Chen, Z., M. Wakabayashi and N. Takeuchi (2004) 'A Comparative Study of Organizational Context Factors for Managerial Career Progress: Focussing on Chinese State-Owned, Sino-Foreign Joint Ventures and Japanese Corporations', *International Journal of Human Resource Management*, 15 (4), pp. 750–74.

Chiba, H., R. Iikubo and O. Sawaji (1997) 'Salary Man Today and Tomorrow', *Compensation and Benefits*, Sept./Oct., pp. 67–75.

Crawford, R. J. (1998) *Reinterpreting the Japanese Economic Miracle* (Cambridge, Mass: Harvard University Press).

Crystal, G. S. (1991) *In Search of Excess. The Overcompensation of American Executives* (New York and London: Norton).

Dalton, N. and J. Benson (2002) 'Innovation and Change in Japanese Human Resource Management', *Asia Pacific Journal of Human Resources*, 40 (3), pp. 345–62.

Dore, R. (1973) *British Factory – Japanese Factory* (Berkeley, CA: University of California Press).

Dore, R. (1987) *Taking Japan Seriously. A Confucian Perspective on Leading Economic Issues* (Palo Alto, CA: Stanford University Press).

Dore, R. (2000) *Stock Market Capitalism: Welfare Capitalism. Japan and Germany versus the Anglo-Saxons* (Oxford: Oxford University Press).

Dore, R. (2002) 'Will Global Capitalism be Anglo-Saxon Capitalism?', *Asian Business & Management*, 1 (1), pp. 9–18.

Durlabhji, S. (1993) 'The Influence of Confucianism and Zen on the Japanese Organisation', in S. Durlabhji and N. E. Norton (eds), *Japanese Business: Cultural Perspectives* (Albany, NY: State of New York Press), pp. 57–79.

Frenkel, S. (1994) 'Pattern of Workplace Relations in the Global Corporation: Toward Convergence?', in J. Belanger, P. K. Edwards and L. Haiven (eds), *Workplace Industrial Relations and the Global Challenge* (Ithaca, NY: ILR Press), pp. 210–74.

Gamble, J., J. Morris and B. Wilkinson (2004) 'Mass Production is Alive and Well: The Future of Work and Organization in East Asia', *International Journal of Human Resource Management*, 15 (2), pp. 397–409.

Hampden-Turner, C. and F. Trompenaars (2000) *Building Cross-Cultural Competence. How to Create Wealth from Conflicting Values* (Chichester: Wiley).

Hilb, M. (1985) *Personalpolitik für Multinationale Unternehmen. Empfehlungen aufgrund einer Vergleichsstudie japanischer, schweizerischer und amerikanischer Firmengruppen* (Zurich: Verlag Industrielle Organisation Zürich).

Hofstede, G. (2001) *Culture's Consequences. Comparing Values, Behaviors, Institutions and Organizations across Nations*, 2nd edn (London and Thousand Oaks, CA: Sage).

Holland, H. M. (1992) *Japan Challenges America. Managing an Alliance in Crisis* (Boulder, CO: Westview Press).

Huczynski, A. (1996) *Management Gurus. What makes them and how to become one* (Boston, Mass.: Thomson).

Inohara, H. (1990) *Human Resource Development in Japanese Companies* (Tokyo: Asian Productivity Organization).

Itoh, H. (1994) 'Japanese Human Resource Management from the Viewpoint of Incentive Theory', in M. Aoki and R. Dore (eds), *The Japanese Firm. The Sources of Competitive Strength* (Oxford: Oxford University Press), pp. 233–64.

Japanese Institute of Labour (JIL) (1998) *Japanese Working Life Profile* (Tokyo: Japanese Institute of Labour).

Kenney, M. and R. Florida (1988) 'Beyond Mass Production: Production and the Labour Process in Japan', *Politics and Society*, 16 (1), pp. 121–58.

Kenney, M. and R. Florida (1993) *Beyond Mass Production: The Japanese System and its Transfer to the US* (Oxford: Oxford University Press).

Koike, K. (1997) *Human Resource Development*, Japanese Economy and Labour Series no. 2 (Tokyo: Japanese Institute of Labour).

Kono, T. and S. Clegg (2001) *Trends in Japanese Management. Continuing Strengths, Current Problems and Changing Priorities* (Basingstoke and New York: Palgrave).

Leme Fleury, M. T. (1996) 'Managing Human Resources for Learning and Innovation: A Comparative Study of Brazilian, Japanese and Korean Firms', *International Journal for Human Resource Management*, 7 (4), pp. 797–812.

Lincoln, J. R. (1989) 'Employee Work Attitudes and Management Practices in the U.S. and Japan: Evidence from a Large Comparative Survey', *California Management Review*, 32 (1), pp. 89–106.

Locke, R., T. Kochan and M. Piore (1995) 'Reconceptualizing Comparative Industrial Relations: Lessons from International Research', *International Labour Review*, 134 (2), pp. 139–61.

Lux, W. (1997) 'Japanese Management Evolves Again', *Management Review*, 86 (6), pp. 36–9.

Manpower Services Commission (MSC) (1987) *The Making of Managers. A Report on Management Education, Training and Development in the USA, West Germany, France, Japan and the UK* (London: National Economic Development Council and British Institute of Management).

Matanle, P. (2003) *Japanese Capitalism and Modernity in a Global Era. Re-fabricating Lifetime Employment Relations* (London and New York: RoutledgeCurzon).

McGregor, E. (1960) *The Human Side of the Enterprise* (New York: McGraw-Hill).

McLeod, R. H. and R. Garnaut (1998) (eds) *East Asia in Crisis: From Being a Miracle to Needing One?* (London: Routledge).

McMillan, C. J. (1996) *The Japanese Industrial System*, 2nd edn (Berlin and New York: Walter de Gruyter).

Merz, H.-P. (1986) *Personalpolitik japanischer Unternehmen in der Bundesrepublik Deutschland. Arbeitsbeziehungen und Manpower-Integration als Problem Transnationaler Unternehmen* (Berlin: Express Edition).

Methé, D. (2005) 'Continuity Through Change in Japanese Management: Institutional and Strategic Influences', in R. Haak and M. Pudelko (eds), *Japanese Management – The Search for a New Balance between Continuity and Change* (Basingstoke and New York: Palgrave), pp. 21–54.

Morgan, G., B. Kelley and R. Whitley (2003) 'Global Managers and Japanese Multinationals: Internationalization and Management in Japanese Financial Institutions', *International Journal of Human Resource Management*, 14 (3), pp. 389–407.

Morishima, M. (1995a) 'Embedding HRM in a Social Context', *British Journal of Industrial Relations*, 33 (4), pp. 617–40.

Morishima, M. (1995b) 'The Japanese Human Resource Management System: A Learning Bureaucracy', in L. Moore and P. Jennings (eds), *Human Resource Management on the Pacific Rim. Institutions, Practices, and Attitudes* (Berlin and New York: Walter de Gruyter), pp. 119–50.

Moss-Kanter, R. (1991) 'Transcending Business Boundaries: 12,000 World Managers View Change', *Harvard Business Review*, May/June, pp. 151–64.

Nakane, C. (1970) *Japanese Society* (Berkeley, CA: University of California Press).

Okabe, Y. (2002) 'Culture or Employment Systems? Accounting for the Attitudinal Differences between British and Japanese Managers', *International Journal of Human Resource Management*, 13 (2), pp. 285–301.

Ornatowski, G. (1998) 'The End of Japanese-Style Human Resource Management', *Sloan Management Review*, 39 (3), pp. 73–84.

Ouchi, W. G. (1981) *Theory Z. How American Business Can Meet the Japanese Challenge* (New York: Avon Books).
Park, S.-J. (1985) 'Informalismus als Managementrationalität', in S.-J. Park (ed.), *Japanisches Management in der Praxis. Flexibilität oder Kontrolle im Prozess der Internationalisierung und Mikroelektronisierung* (Berlin: Express Edition), pp. 101–18.
Pascale, R. T. and A. G. Athos (1981) *The Art of Japanese Management. Applications for American Executives* (New York: Warner).
Plenert, G. J. (1990) *International Management and Production. Survival Techniques for Corporate America* (New York: McGraw-Hill).
Pudelko, M. (2000): *Das Personalmanagement in Deutschland, den USA und Japan*. Vol. 1: *Die gesamtgesellschaftlichen Rahmenbedingungen im Wettbewerb der Systeme*; vol. 2: *Eine systematische und vergleichende Bestandsaufnahme*; vol. 3: *Wie wir voneinander lernen können* (Cologne: Saborowski).
Pudelko, M. (2004a) 'HRM in Japan and the West: What are the Lessons to Be Learnt from Each Other?', *Asian Business and Management*, 3 (3), pp. 337–61.
Pudelko, M. (2004b) 'Benchmarking: Was amerikanische, japanische und deutsche Personalmanager voneinander lernen', *Zeitschrift für Personalforschung*, 18 (2), pp. 139–63.
Purcell, W., S. Nicholas and D. Merrett (1998) *The Transfer of Human Resource Management Practice by Japanese Multinationals to Australia: Does Industry, Size and Experience Matter?*, Discussion Paper no. 5, Australian Centre for International Business.
Rehfeld, J. E. (1995) *Das Beste aus Fernost und West. Management perfekt kombinieren* (Landsberg and Lech: Verlag Moderne Industrie).
Reinhold, G. (1992) *Wirtschaftsmanagement und Kultur in Ostasien. Sozial-kulturelle Determinanten wirtschaftlichen Handelns in China und Japan* (Munich: Iudicium).
Rowley, C., J. Benson and M. Warner (2004) 'Towards an Asian Model of Human Resource Management? A Comparative Analysis of China, Japan and South Korea', *International Journal of Human Resource Management*, 15 (5), pp. 917–33.
Sano, Y. (1993) 'Changes and Continued Stability in Japanese HRM Systems: Choice in the Share Economy', *International Journal of Human Resource Management*, 4 (1), pp. 11–27.
Sasajima, Y. (1993) 'Changes in Labour Supply and their Impacts on Human Resource Management: The Case of Japan', *International Journal for Human Resource Management*, 4 (1), pp. 29–43.
Sethi, S. P., N. Namiki and C. L. Swanson (1986) *False Promise of the Japanese Miracle. Illusions and Realities of the Japanese Management System* (Boston, Mass.: Caroline House).
Shibata, H. (2000) 'The Transformation of the Wage and Performance Appraisal System in a Japanese Firm', *International Journal of Human Resource Management*, 11 (2), pp. 294–313.
Shirakai, M. (2002) 'Why Can't Japanese Multinationals Utilize both International and Local Human Resources in ASEAN? A Comparative Analysis', *Journal of Enterprising Culture*, 10 (1), pp. 23–37.
Smith, P. (1997) *Japan: A Reinterpretation* (New York: Pantheon).
Takahashi, Y. (1985) 'Merkmale des Japanischen Managements unter besonderer Berücksichtigung des Personalmanagements', in S.-J. Park and H.-P. Merz (eds), *Transfer des japanischen Managementsystems* (Berlin: Express Edition), pp. 39–60.
Takahashi, Y. (1990) 'Human Resource Management in Japan', in R. Pieper (ed.), *Human Resource Management: An International Comparison* (Berlin: Springer), pp. 211–34.

Taylor, B. (2001) 'The Management of Labour in Japanese Manufacturing Plants in China', *International Journal of Human Resource Management*, 12 (4), pp. 601–20.

Thurow, L. (1993) *Head to Head: The Coming Economic Battle among Japan, Europe, and America* (New York: Warner Books).

Tönnies, F. (2001) *Community and Civil Society* (Cambridge: Cambridge University Press).

Vogel, E. F. (1979) *Japan as Number One. Lessons for America* (Cambridge, Mass.: Harvard University Press).

Vogel, E. F. (1987) 'Japan: Adaptive Communitarianism', in G. C. Lodge and E. F. Vogel (eds), *Ideology and National Competitiveness. An Analysis of Nine Countries* (Boston, Mass.: Harvard Business School Press), pp. 141–72.

Watanabe, T. (2003) 'Recent Trends in Japanese Human Resource Management: The Introduction of a System of Individual and Independent Career Choice', *Asian Business & Management*, 2 (1), pp. 111–41.

White, M. and M. Trevor (1983) *Under Japanese Management. The Experience of Japanese Workers* (London: Heineman).

Whitehill, A. M. (1991) *Japanese Management. Tradition and Transition* (London and New York: Thomson).

Woronoff, J. (1992) *The Japanese Management Mystique. The Reality Behind the Myth* (Cambridge, Mass.: Irwin).

Yoshimura, N. and P. Anderson (1997) *Inside the Kaisha: Demystifying Japanese Business Behavior* (Boston, Mass.: Harvard Business School Press).

10
Japanese Production Management: Organizational Learning at the Confluence of Knowledge Transfer, Technology Development and Work Organization

René Haak

Introduction

For more than 20 years Japanese production management has been the subject of lively interest and debate in the West. Particularly in the 1980s and early 1990s there was a boom in studies of the secret of Japanese success. One of the best known of these was carried out by Womack, Jones and Ross in 1990. The findings intrigued legions of production scientists, management researchers and industry practitioners and had a large impact on subsequent research, on the Western view of Japanese production management and on the self-image of Japanese production managers themselves.

The researchers investigated the differences between factories in the automotive industry world-wide. Their data relates to the basic hallmarks of the production system that became known globally as lean production and with which Japanese production management in the automotive industry, particularly the Toyota production system, is equated. The researchers suggested that lean production would change the world in the same way as Fordist mass production had in the past, so that sooner or later all the major car manufacturers would be forced to adopt the Japanese system. However the existence of 'one best way' revealed itself as a myth during the 1990s. A number of Japanese car manufacturers, once the paradigms of Japanese production management, were forced to enter into partnerships with foreign companies, and in some cases the management of the Japanese company was also handed over to ensure continued competitiveness. Others, however, such as Toyota and Honda were able to maintain their world-wide leadership and continued to develop their specific forms of production management. Toyota's profits have continued to increase and it now occupies second place in the world ranking, behind General Motors and ahead of Ford.

In order to examine Japanese production management one must first ask what is meant by production management, so the development and nature of this will be analyzed in the following pages. In this chapter production management is defined as the management of manufacturing companies. This definition is based on the integrative approach to production management, where production management includes the running of production processes, quality management, logistics, maintenance, industrial engineering and procurement.

The Toyota production system, knowledge of which is essential to understanding Japanese production management, can be seen as a technology-based, comprehensive system whose primary goals are to increase productivity and reduce costs (Monden, 1983). This is achieved by reducing cycle time, increasing flexibility, reducing stock levels and shortening machine changeover times. The difference between the terms lean production and Toyota production system is that the former can be applied to any company in any branch of industry, whereas Toyota production system refers only to the production management system at Toyota, although it includes basically the same elements. According to Liker (2004, p. 7) a lean enterprise is

> the end result of applying the Toyota Production System to all areas of your business. In their excellent book, *Lean Thinking*, James Womack and Daniel Jones define lean manufacturing as a five-step process: defining customer value, defining the value stream, making it 'flow', 'pulling' from the customer back, and striving for excellence. To be a lean manufacturer requires a way of thinking that focuses on making the product flow through value-adding processes without interruption (one-piece flow), a 'pull' system that cascades back from customer demand by replenishing only what the next operation takes away at short intervals, and a culture in which everyone is striving continuously to improve.

This chapter will not discuss all aspects of Japanese production management. Rather it will highlight key developments, identify change and continuity, and describe particular characteristics. Special attention will be paid to the Toyota production system as it has made a permanent mark on Japanese production management. However it should not be thought that the Toyota production system is typical of all Japanese production management. There are different types of production system and these vary according to industrial sector.

Two central issues will be discussed. First we shall examine the key factors that have influenced the development of the principal features of Japanese production management, particularly in its most striking form: Toyotaism. Second, we shall look at whether the strength of Japanese production management, as expressed for example in the Toyota production system, is due to the fact that it is a dynamic rather than a static system, thus providing the flexibility required to ensure that the system survives in the face of rapidly changing competitive circumstances and market configurations. We shall also consider whether the Japanese production system can be viewed as a key factor in the corporate processes of learning, adaptation and improvement, that is, as the key factor in a learning organization, and whether the coexistence of change and continuity is a defining characteristic of the Japanese production system.

The early years

A look back at the development of production management in Japanese companies reveals that the global success of Japanese companies in recent decades can be linked in no small part to technology and knowledge transfer and the associated advances in organizational learning. One of the areas in which the success of Japanese production management crystallized was automation technology and the development of the autonomation system (*jidoka*) at Toyota, which will be examined in greater detail later. The successful transfer and further development of advanced automation technologies from the United States and Western Europe were important prerequisites for the emergence of a specifically Japanese system of production management, and therefore for the striking economic and technological advances made by Japanese manufacturers after World War II.

The organizational learning processes that took place in Japanese manufacturing companies as the result of technology and knowledge transfer changed their organizational and management structures and their competitiveness for ever. The development and widespread use in Japan of the automation technology that came with the new forms of production and technology management and a specific form of work organization were crucial to the rapid rise of Japanese companies after 1945.

Adopting and improving technology from the United States and Western Europe, improving productivity by means of new forms of work organization, management and staff development, a nationwide programme to improve quality (based on the thinking of the Americans Deming and Juran) and ensuring a high degree of flexibility were the key measures that enabled Japanese companies to catch up quickly with advances in organizational learning. With many Japanese companies integrated into networks of firms from various sectors (*keiretsu*) it was possible to disseminate the advances made in automation technology, quality management and production management (Asanuma and Kikutani, 1992).

At the individual level, it was the commitment and willingness to learn on the part of Japanese technicians, engineers and managers, particularly those in companies engaged in electrotechnology, mechanical engineering and machine tool building, and in laboratories undertaking research into manufacturing science, that made possible the advances in production management.

The years of reconstruction

Immediately after World War II, Japan began to build up new economic structures (Freedman, 1988) in order to reconstruct the economy (Itô, 1992). Price controls, subsidies and the allocation of resources were among the most important measures the government used to support and expand coal and steel production.

The principal factor in Japan's rapid economic development was the meteoric growth of industrial production (Tsuruta, 1988, p. 50). At its core were mass production, automation technology and specifically Japanese forms of production management (Park, 1975; Nakamura, 1996), backed by the reforms implemented during the years of the American occupation (Waldenberger, 1994, p. 23). The deconcentration measures introduced at that time disentangled the threads of capital, organization and personnel that had bound together the ten big business conglomerates (*zaibatsu*), thus creating the necessary conditions for the competition that fuelled the reconstruction and high growth phase, which lasted until the beginning of the 1970s (Beason, 1994).

Foreign demand for Japanese goods stimulated and accelerated economic development in the early 1950s (Abegglen and Stalk 1985). The development of Japanese industry was further boosted by the outbreak of the Korean War on 25 June 1950, which, together with the tension generated by the Cold War, resulted in increased demand worldwide. The large contracts with the United States had a particularly marked effect on Japanese mechanical engineering.

After a brief slowing of growth in the wake of this boom (due mainly to falling private capital investment), high growth resumed in 1956–57, when large amounts of investment were poured into heavy industry to increase production capacity and modernize and rationalize production facilities. This also required production managers to find ways of improving the quality of production and processing. The techniques developed in quality management by researchers and managers in the United States were adopted and adapted to Japanese industrial operations.

Between 1955 and 1960 real growth of GDP averaged 8.6 per cent, in 1960–65 it rose to 10.6 per cent, and in 1965–70 it peaked at an astounding 11.2 per cent (Itô, 1992; Keizai Kikakuchô, 1994). This growth was astonishing, given the extent of the destruction caused by World War II (Hemmert and Lützeler, 1994).

Up to the 1950s the branches of industry that dominated production were those which had reigned prior to the war, for example the textile industry. Thereafter assembly industries developed into mainstays of economic growth

(Waldenberger, 1996). These included car assembly, electrotechnology, mechanical engineering (particularly machine tool building) and precision engineering (Nakamura, 1996), which also became the drivers of change in Japanese production management. It was essential to coordinate the individual manufacturing stages effectively and efficiently and at the same time achieve low unit costs and high quality standards, and it was these industries that developed innovative forms of production management, with the automotive industry in the vanguard. The development of the Toyota production system played a key role here.

As a result of considerable dialogue between national and international manufacturing and production researchers and between industrial practitioners, the automotive industry and its supplier companies – in particular the manufacturers of machine tools for process technology – became both the vehicles and the engines of Japanese automation efforts (Spur, 1991). Thus the fundamental learning and transformation processes that facilitated the successful introduction of automation technology and new forms of production management took place in the assembly industries, with the automotive and electronics industries in the lead. The use of technology and new ways of organizing labour and production processes were mutually dependent.

These advances were reinforced by the Japanese state, which encouraged technology and knowledge transfers from abroad (Renkel, 1985) and provided tax breaks and cheap loans. Foreign currency was allocated specifically for the importation of raw materials and advanced machine technology. The international exchange of scientists was also supported by the state so that new knowledge could be disseminated via universities and scientific organizations, or directly to the organizations themselves. At the same time knowledge of quality management spread quickly throughout Japan and had a strong impact on production management.

The new knowledge of innovative manufacturing technology and forms of production process organization was rapidly disseminated throughout companies by quality circles, which were the instrument for organizational learning in Japanese companies. The quality circles moved learning processes and knowledge from the individual level onto a broad organizational basis. The members of the organization shared the same knowledge about production management in their company and worked together to develop the existing pool of knowledge – a key requirement for organizational learning (Ducan and Weiss, 1979; Garratt, 1990; Geißler, 1996; Hanft, 1996).

During the economic boom years, investment in Japanese industry was used primarily to rationalize and modernize production facilities. This presented challenges to management, which had to adapt constantly to changing manufacturing processes (Nihon Kôsaku Kikai Kôgyôkai, 1982). This evolutionary development of production management was given impetus by innovations in manufacturing technology and consequent changes in work organization.

The machine tool industry

The machine tool sector, as a principal supplier to assembly industries, had a key role in the development and performance of manufacturing technology and hence in production management. The Japanese automotive industry in particular profited from technological innovations made in the machine tool sector; or in other words from advances in learning in this area (Takayama, 1997). These advances were apparent in automated precision machine tools and the associated forms of production organization in car manufacture.

Immediately after World War II the impetus for growth in the Japanese machine tool industry came largely from domestic industry, as did specific technological requirements relating to production (it was not until the start of the 1970s that Western European and American companies began to purchase Japanese machine tools – Collis, 1988). In the 1950s and 1960s it was necessary to improve Japan's basic technology by importing advanced machine tools and management knowledge, which were adapted to Japanese manufacturing requirements. It was also important to pass on the new knowledge to suppliers so that they could suitably develop their technology and production methods. This 'wet nursing', which was provided by the key production companies in the conglomerates (*keiretsu*) to the underdeveloped companies supplying the Japanese mechanical engineering, automotive and electronics industries, constituted an extended form of organizational learning in production management.

In the late 1960s and early 1970s the importation of advanced machine tool technology, particularly from Western Europe and the United States, close cooperation between Japanese machine tool companies and their suppliers, and long-term collaboration with university research departments provided Japanese machine tool manufacturers with the technological capability to meet the growing demand from the national and international markets (Fischer, 1979).

Due to the economic conditions prevailing in those years, attempts at automation using conventional machine tools were aimed mainly at mass production. Automation, particularly for the users of machine tools and above all in the automotive industry, was driven by the development and widespread use of the modular construction system (Spur, 1979).

Flow lines

Flow lines consisted of linked groups of several, mostly highly productive, special-purpose machines that enabled several automated manufacturing procedures to be carried out at one station. This was associated with organizational learning, in that during the process the company adapted its technological artefacts (tacit knowledge) so that it could react appropriately to internal (for example employee training) and external (for example market demand) challenges.

In the 1950s and early 1960s Japanese industry was characterized by rigidly linked manufacturing machines and the automatic transfer of the components by feed systems with a shared control system in a cycle time that was determined by the longest work cycle (Chokki, 1986). Fixed (and later flexible) flow lines were used primarily in the car industry. Crankshafts, camshafts, valves, stub axles and transmission housing were but a few examples of components produced on fixed flow lines at that time.

The electronic control system was a crucial element of the flow line (Kennedy, 1954; Griffin, 1955), so the development of flow lines depended on advances in electrotechnology (Asanuma, 1989) and control systems became the subject of extensive research by American, West European and Japanese engineers (Spur, 1991). The main job of a control system was to repeat the same series of movements quickly and precisely so that products could be mass produced in consistent quality without human intervention (Mommertz, 1981). The control system was adapted to the technical production conditions in question, with a distinction made between mechanical, electrical, pneumatic or hydraulic control system components.

Numerically controlled machines

Whereas flow lines were used for mass and large-series production, numerically controlled machines were used mainly for made-to-order or small-series production in the late 1950s and 1960s. Previously, mechanical, electrical and hydraulic copy control systems with templates had been used for this kind of production. The introduction of numerical control technology resulted in just a few years in completely new types of machine and the technology became the engine of the entire production system (Simon, 1969), necessitating new forms of production management.

In the late 1960s and early 1970s, Japanese research and development concentrated mainly on application research and on putting the new numerical control technology to use in the processing industries. The first numerically controlled machines were deployed in mechanical engineering, in automobile production and in the electronics industry. However, it was only with growing experience and advances in problem solving and learning processes, that Japan's own discoveries of new technologies became important for production technology in Japanese companies.

Technology and knowledge transfer from Western Europe and the USA as the object and catalyst of individual and organizational learning processes in the early years of automation technology was implemented in many different ways. The Japanese mechanical engineering industry within the framework of collective strategies made intensive use of the opportunity to acquire patents and licences and to enter into co-operation agreements with leading technology companies in the mechanical engineering sector and the electronics industry (Nonaka, 1990).

Working together with European and American businesses not only facilitated technology transfer, but also made it easier for Japanese companies to enter foreign markets. Integrating Japanese scientists and engineers in international research into manufacturing technology was also crucial for the advances in organizational learning brought about by technology and knowledge transfer. To all intents and purposes Japanese management and engineers fared well with co-operative ventures. As co-operative strategies coincided with structures receptive to learning, they represented the crucial factor for successful technological and economic development in Japanese industry following World War II.

Furthermore, when entering on their career with a company, Japanese manufacturing engineers were first employed in processing where they frequently became highly qualified at user level (Koshiro, 1994). When a new employee was taken on, the part of the company in which he would work was not at that point clearly specified. He needed to be flexible enough to change direction in the company (staff rotation), as he needed to absorb new information and learn new accomplishments and skills. This is primarily individual learning in order to cope with new challenges in working in the company. Staff rotation takes place in formal management systems and tried and tested bureaucratic structures. This form of learning is a long way from organizational learning unless the employee shares the knowledge he or she acquired in the previous position with the new group (participative learning) and according to Ducan and Weiss (1979) creates a basic prerequisite for organizational learning – developing a knowledge base shared with other members of the organization.

Since the mid 1960s, the impact of automation, computer technology (NC and CNC technology), flexibilization and decentralization of manufacturing processes has lead to a fundamental change in the way industrial businesses work and in individual and organizational learning processes. Japanese production management has also undergone radical changes. The new forms of operation which became more important in Japanese industry at that time were those which aimed to reduce the functional division of work by integrating tasks (Spur, 1994).

With computer support in the factory, particularly with the use of CNC machines, there have been new opportunities for work system design since the end of the 1970s and beginning of the 1980s. It only became possible to establish different forms and varieties of group work as rational alternative forms of organizing labour in Japanese factories, or to be more precise in automated manufacturing processes, with the wider use of computer-assisted manufacturing equipment. Technological changes and individual and organizational learning processes have been mutually dependent. Job enlargement, job enrichment and change of job location could be realized simultaneously as a principle of design as illustrated by the development of the Toyota production system.

The Toyota production system

The Toyota production system, which combines advanced automation technology and forms of organization, is an expression of both learning through technology and knowledge and the process of continuous improvement of structures and systems referred to as the corporate philosophy of kaizen. The term 'Toyotaism', which is heard frequently in the context of discussions about Japanese production management and which is equated with the Toyota production system, has established itself mostly as the opposite, but sometimes as an extension of or complement to 'Western Taylorism' and 'Fordism' in scientific discussion and in industrial practice.

Similarly to Fordism, the Toyota production system is used mainly in large companies which have concentrated on mass production. The distinguishing feature of Toyotaism is lean production (Clark *et al.*, 1992; Jung, 1992; Boesenberg and Metzen, 1993; Scherm and Bischoff, 1994; Freyssenet *et al.*, 1998; Durand *et al.*, 1999; Liker, 2004). The economic success enjoyed by many Japanese manufacturing companies in the 1970s and 1980s introduced the concept of lean production in the 1990s which is frequently seen as the antithesis to Fordism, to mass production as practised in the West.

Alongside these two central basic concepts of Fordism and Toyotaism, there are many different peculiarities and specific ideas in Japanese production management which reveal themselves in the different ways in which technology is implemented, in the organization of production management and in the self-image of Japanese industry. In the following I will present and discuss the most important basic concepts and forms of organization including production management at Toyota, as the Toyota production system had a considerable impact on the development of production management in Japan itself. Nevertheless, it should not be assumed that the manifestation of production management at Toyota is that of the whole of Japan, even though Toyotaism has made a deep impression on the form of production management in other industry sectors.

Work system design

Engineers and managers at Toyota were not the first to apply themselves to the question of how to organize work systems in the production process. There have been many scientific examinations of work systems design issues, particularly that of work organization since the middle of the 19th century. However, the findings by economic and production scientists and by managers with an interest in the design of work systems had a considerable impact on the form and implementation of production management at Toyota.

In other words, to understand the development and the current production management situation at Toyota and from that understand the key elements of Japanese production management it is necessary to review the defining concepts of production organization. We must also consider manual production, Taylorism and Fordism, which influenced the shape of Toyotaism. Despite all the reservations regarding simplification of this kind, it is first necessary to sketch out an outline of the organization of production, both to highlight the necessity of a differentiated view and also to illustrate the main influences on the Toyota production system. It is not sufficient to fall back on the study by Womack, Jones and Ross (1990) although with its international comparison it made a key contribution to the understanding of the special productive capability of the Toyota production system and opened up a perspective of the specifics of Japanese production management via the concept of lean production in the Western world.

The factory as a whole system

The Toyota production system has made its mark on industrial practice and on manufacturing science research in places other than in Japan. It embodies in lean production a corporate approach and a basic company strategy that view the factory as a whole system, as a work system overlaying the single work station and the workshop. Essentially, Toyotaism concerns the developmental mainstays of production management: manufacturing technology and work organization. It tries, whilst avoiding any form of waste, to combine the benefits of manual production – Taylor's central interest in rationalization – with the advantages of mass production (Fordism).

As Toyotaism became more widespread, internal and external production logistics (just-in-time) took up a key position for corporate success along with work organization and manufacturing technology (autonomation, *jidoka* in Japanese). Toyota people usually explain just-in-time and *jidoka* as the twin pillars of the Toyota Production System (Ohno, 1978; Nihon Noritsu Kyokai, 1978; Monden, 1983) and do not highlight the work organization system specifically, although it plays a large part in the success of the Toyota Production System.

The term *jidoka* can be translated as autonomation. This term includes on the one hand the concept of automation and on the other that of autonomous monitoring for defects and elimination of their causes. In automated work processes, a defect or poor quality can cause the machines to come to an immediate standstill. Work can only continue when the cause of the problem has been removed. If one work stage is interrupted, the whole production system can come to a stop, as the constraints of kanban only allow minimum interim stocks. In some cases there are no interim or buffer stocks. Therefore the production workers have to be in a position to find the defect as soon as possible and take the appropriate steps towards fixing it to minimize production down time. For example, all the work places are supplied with light indicators called *andon* which call the workers allocated to that particular production section to help. The potential for disruption to the production system resulting from autonomation, quality assurance and cost reduction has also earned Toyotism the name 'management by stress' (Parker and Slaughter 1988). Furthermore, social pressure on less productive employees in the group can cause problems for the productivity and motivation of the group members. From the point of view of the learning organization, that is looking at autonomation from the aspect of learning theory, stress within a certain context (taking into account intensity, time period, the constitution of the individual, social norms) can however promote learning.

Lean production was developed for the manufacture of passenger cars in the Toyota's factories and is used primarily in the automobile and the automobile supply industry. It did not remain limited to Japan: it has proved an effective structure for production in other economies and achieved considerable productivity and quality effects (Schmitt, 1998; Yui, 1999).

The lean production approach originated with Eiji Toyoda and Taiichi Ohno. In a well-known study by the Massachusetts Institute of Technology, which was published in 1990 under the title *The Machine that Changed the World*, Toyota's factors for success are named as technology leadership, cost leadership and time leadership.

In their comparative study, the authors find the main factor for success in Japanese companies is a different system of production from that practised in European and American companies: lean production. In their view, lean production combines the advantages of manual production with those of mass production, whilst avoiding the high costs of the former and the inflexibility of the latter. On the one hand, many multi-skilled workers work in groups, as is the case in manual production; on the other, large volumes of standardized parts are produced with the aid of flexible automated machinery – similarly to mass production (Womack *et al.*, 1990).

The findings of the international comparison made in this study between mass and lean production are summarized in the following list of lean production features:

- Fewer defects in car manufacture.
- The manufacturing process is much faster.
- The repair area in the company is smaller.
- The stocks held by the company are smaller.
- The majority of employees work in teams.
- The workers frequently change their job within the company in the production area.
- The workers offer more suggestions and are trained for longer.
- The organizational structures are flatter.

Essentially, the key factor is organizational learning, which manifests itself as the result of the advances in manufacturing technology and in work organization, improved product quality and careful use of resources. Other features of this organizational learning system are low warehouse stocks, shorter product development times and low staffing levels and, especially at Toyota, involving assembly workers in the permanent quality control system and the continuous process of improvement (*kaizen*) (Shimizu, 1988). As a result, production errors fell dramatically and costly post-processing was minimized.

Kaizen

Kaizen can be interpreted as the Japanese management philosophy which involves every employee in achieving the goal of continuous improvement of structures and systems (Hayashi, 1991; Jürgens, 1991). The starting point for this philosophy is the knowledge that each business is confronted with many problems which can be solved by establishing a company culture with two main features: each employee can with impunity point out errors and identify problems, and solutions for the weaknesses identified are found by the employees of the organization working together (Yamashiro, 1997; Imai, 1993).

Continuous improvement of structures and systems uses a systematic procedure based on Deming's PDCA cycle (Plan, Do, Check, Act). The PDCA cycle is used in Japanese companies to initiate, track and review improvements. Approaching the matter systematically, the cycle begins with the planning phase (Liker, 2004). For example, the area earmarked for improvement is discussed in the work group and the most important findings and the biggest obstacles are identified. Then the current situation is analysed. In order to proceed efficiently, the problem under investigation is defined and described precisely. To identify causes, relevant data is collected from the production workers. A quantitative base of data is indispensable for identifying clearly the potential for improvement and defining appropriate interim goals and actions. This is also a requirement for making the targeted improvements unmistakably visible to all the employees in the course of the improvement process.

In the do phase of the improvement cycle, the actions selected are carried out. This does not mean however that it is impossible to return to the plan phase if necessary, in order to gather more information and review the actions. Defining the actions is only the first step on the way to achieving the improvement of the production systems and structures.

In the check phase that follows, the effects of the planned actions are analysed. An investigation is carried out into whether and how the goals defined in the planning phase can be achieved. The results are monitored, documented and illustrated in the activity catalogue. Regular monitoring reveals whether the goals have been achieved. If this is not the case, then investigations are carried out into why the undesirable deviations occurred. Even failures hold important information for shaping the improvement process.

The last phase of the cycle – act – serves to review the previous phases and to record the experiences made during the process, by standardizing successful factors and making them obligatory for other employees in the company, and to initiate follow-up activities, from which targets for subsequent improvements can be set up. If the cycle is carried out sequentially as it is intended to be, the problems under consideration are increasingly limited as knowledge and experiences from the previous cycles can be applied.

The newly created standards or rules set up by the *kacho* or *bucho* (in some Japanese companies by the *kakaricho* or *kumicho*) as results are not set in stone. The aim of the standard is to create a basis for further improvement, but also to encourage confidence in consistent quality, to create a solid basis for worker education and training and to remove product liability problems (Suzuki, 1994). The old standard is only replaced when a new one is defined in the course of the improvement process. The role of the *kakaricho* or the *kumicho*, the immediate supervisor, who does not work in production with the other employees is to find new templates for standards on the basis of the daily production data and to push through improvement measures together with expert kaizen teams, who are assembled specifically for the problem situations, or with work groups. The PDCA cycles running on the different levels of the company can be integrated both upwards and downwards in the hierarchy. This creates multifunctional project teams primarily in the area of product development or in production process innovation. Problems which cannot be dealt with on one level of the company or in a functional area are referred to the next highest level or to a level with the specific subject knowledge, as are faults in the production process, so that precisely the knowledge required for solving the problem can be applied. In this context, the integrated PDCA cycle can also be understood as a process of organizational learning, in which subject knowledge and experience can be gathered on an individual basis and made available through the improved standards to be worked with throughout the company.

Avoiding waste

A central concern of *kaizen* is to eliminate or avoid waste of all kinds in the company. Frequently, waste in a company is not perceived because it is associated with processes that have developed historically and new, simpler options are not even considered. Seven areas with the potential for waste have been identified in the production area. The most important area is overproduction where a larger volume is manufactured than is required by the internal or the external customer. Unnecessary process stages are created with this kind of waste with serious consequences, as overproduction in its turn can cause a number of different types of waste. The just-in-time system developed by Toyota and product control with the *kanban* system have provided a remedy in this situation.

Overproduction leads to more work-in-progress. This represents waste as it requires space, incurs storage costs, requires to be searched, makes additional movement of materials necessary and, above all, conceals problems in the production process (e.g. machine downtime) or unstable processes. Also, any form of transport is classified as waste in the Toyota production system, as material transport does not in itself add value. Work stations placed at distance from each other result in additional costs for the transport of work-in-progress. The turnaround time of the product or the workpiece is longer, thus increasing the job time calculated for the manufacturing process. One outcome of big buffer inventories and lengthy transport are waiting and idle periods. This form of waste results in an unbalanced utilization of workers and machines.

Waste in the manufacturing process is frequently a result of the previously listed types of waste. However, there is also waste in the manufacturing process if there is a simpler or faster way to carry out a certain production task. This waste is caused by ambiguous instructions, lack of ability, skill or knowledge on the part of the employees or by too many unnecessary inspections. One of the basic premises of *kaizen*, that the manufacturing process can always be improved, is that unnecessary motion should be avoided, by reducing the number of movements in the work flow by changing the work systems (e.g. avoiding long distances, repeated refamiliarization due to too many unnecessary interruptions). Defects, the seventh waste area, arise frequently due to inattention or lack of concentration. Defects in their turn also cause other kinds of waste, such as the same work having to be carried out twice or more, or long idle or waiting times.

Employees – the source of improvement

One of the basic convictions of *kaizen* is that nobody knows a work station as well as the employee who works there in the production process day in, day out. For this reason, the aims of *kaizen* and hence the lean production philosophy as embodied by the Toyota production system are to increase productivity and employee motivation by eliminating waste within the framework of a systematic and consistent operation.

How should waste be eliminated from the work environment? This is one of the central issues of *kaizen* and therefore one of the fundamental issues for Japanese production management. In other words, how can the knowledge, the experience, the skills and the expertise of the workers be used to create the most effective work system? The 5S process can be applied to the whole company or focus on just one work station. The core of the 5S process to combat waste can be understood as follows:

1. *Seiri*: the employee needs to decide which tools and accessories are required at the work station.
2. *Seiton*: the employee needs to put the tools and accessories he thinks he requires in order so that they are at hand in the right place at the right time when he needs them for his work.
3. *Seiso*: the employee needs to keep the workstation clean; that is, clean and take care of the orderly workstation and the tools and accessories.
4. *Seiketsu*: the employee must observe standards, rules and regulations; he must turn instructions into rules.
5. *Shitsuke*: the employee must observe all the points listed and to improve on them continuously.

The 5S process is not a fashionable trend in management science. It originated in the Japanese manufacturing industry and forms a central part of Japanese production management. One can posit the theory that the 5S process forms part of the self-image of a Japanese production manager in any industry sector. The central question from a business management point of view is: what are the benefits of continuously maintaining and improving the work environment? The answer is quite easy: it creates more time for the value added process or time can be better utilized.

Tools for solving problems

Through *kaizen*, tools have been developed for solving problems which are intended to enable continuous improvement in the interests of the customer. Quality assurance, just-in-time, automation, extensive product monitoring, *kanban*, suggestion schemes, and much more are linked together under the *kaizen* 'umbrella' (Nonaka and Takeuchi, 1997; Sebestyén, 1994). First and foremost, *kaizen* encourages process-oriented thinking, as it is mainly corporate processes that are to be improved to allow goals to be reached more efficiently (Matzky, 1994). Following Argyris and Schön (1999), this process-oriented thinking is equivalent to organizational learning. Implementation of the *kaizen* philosophy and its tools places the organization in a problematic situation. For example, the employees in a multifunctional project group (Hyodo, 1987) find after systematic investigation that there is a discrepancy between the results they expect from their actions and the actual outcome of the actions. The employees examine the matter and try to rearrange their activities so that their actions and results are again congruent (Nonaka and Takeuchi, 1997). Following Argyris and Schön's (1999) concept of the learning organization, the organization members' theory-in-use is modified if the discoveries leading to the solution of the problem are fixed in company-specific artefacts such as a change in the manufacturing organization and in new work programmes. The result of these modifications is that the organization has learnt.

A key element of this problem solving process specified in the *kaizen* philosophy which can find negative deviations (performance gaps) is repeated analysis of an existing set of facts (Nonaka and Takeuchi, 1997). Looking at the company to find the causes of problems and the reasons for performance gaps and identifying solutions is the core thinking behind *kaizen.* Continuous improvement of the processes means that all the members of the company are constantly learning so that they can on the one hand react flexibly to permanently changing challenges and on the other improve on the existing situation more and more. *Kaizen* is quite different from traditional methods of business rationalization as it is not a matter of large-scale innovation but of small, but continuous improvement.

Working in groups

In order to diffuse the philosophy of continuous improvement further throughout the company, product teams on the level of work organization and personnel management were put together under the leadership of Taiichi Ohno. In these product teams, each member was able to carry out all the stages in production. The group members were supposed to distribute the work in the group themselves and discuss and agree with each other on the ways to optimize the production process (Hyodo, 1987; Nonaka and Takeuchi, 1997; Ernst, 1999).

Group work organization was seen above all as communication and dialogue to improve the group members' performance. Rotation within the jobs allocated to the group played a key role in employee training. The rotation plans were compiled on a daily basis by the supervisor and planned to allow weaker group members to improve their skills and to make provision for more effective employees to be kept on standby for when production was disrupted.

This form of work organization has cost cutting (avoidance of waste) and productivity increase as its foremost goals; employee training is seen as the tool that will achieve the goals. Training group members is important in planning for and working with a work force that is as flexible as possible. However, note here that there are groups of employees (such as short-term workers, new recruits, or employees from other areas) who are not considered for participation in these job rotation schemes. It also takes some time before work experience is sufficient to allow group members to be included in the rotation scheme.

The existing training and problem solving potential of employees deployed in the context of wide-ranging improvement activities also form a key source of information for creating adaptable work systems. The structural integration and harnessing of individual knowledge gained through experience is a comprehensive program which runs on all levels of the company. For production, these are quality circles, suggestion schemes and improvement measures at the individual worker level. All these activities are supported by work groups, teams of experts or individuals.

The just-in-time system

On a concrete level – the flow of parts in the production process – Ohno developed the well-known just-in-time system, which is represented in the literature in many different and occasionally contradictory ways. The determining features are group technology, the kanban system, short set-up times, harmonization of the production process and quality assurance (Görgens, 1994).

This astonishingly simple and economically so promising idea was that in each stage of the process only as many parts are produced as necessary to cover the immediate requirements of the next manufacturing stage. Empty containers are returned to the previous processing stage which is the automatic signal to produce more parts (Ohno, 1988). Essentially, this just-in-time system is oriented towards intracompany and intercompany processes. A just-in-time system would not be thinkable without the conscious implementation of collective strategies in the organization. Toyota undertook to guarantee its suppliers a certain volume of orders over a certain period and furthermore, was prepared to share with them the profits achieved with the cost savings if the partner adopted the Toyota production system – in this particular case the just-in-time principle of pulled material flow.

Teams of design and production engineers

Another modification to work organization which affected the whole production process at Toyota was the grouping together of design and manufacturing engineers in teams and the encouragement given to group-based success. Learning and knowledge boundaries within the organization were abandoned and the knowledge available on different hierarchical levels and the associated methods for solving problems were put on a broader plane. As a result of this change to work organization, development time for new car models fell dramatically and product quality again improved. This structural change also represented a considerable advantage from the marketing policy point of view. It was possible to respond more quickly to changes in customer requirements and penetrate a number of niche markets intensively and at a low cost.

Organizing a team as an independent and accountable business unit initiates learning where performance gaps are identified and makes knowledge available so that team members can carry out their work. Each team member has the ability to carry out many, in some cases different, types of work within the group and the resulting redundancy creates a very flexible company (Hyodo, 1987).

With shared knowledge bases, organization as a team forms the basis and is a catalyst for organizational learning in Japanese companies (Ducan and Weiss, 1979).

Quality management

In Japanese manufacturing companies, quality is at the centre of the product and process-oriented efforts towards improvement and innovation integrated in the *kaizen* company philosophy. Economic success only comes when the customer is convinced of the quality of the product. The high quality of Japanese products and the quality management systems in Japanese businesses are considered exemplary today.

Originally the development of production-oriented quality procedures derives from American ideas and industrial applications (Deming circle and quality control). The process of continuous improvement is based on the PDCA cycle which was developed in the 1950s by W. Edwards Deming, an American. Following World War II, these American achievements were methodically developed into total quality control in Japan and then developed further to the total quality management of today. Quality circles are a central core element of the total quality management system (Goetsch and Davis 2003). These quality circles, which are held regularly and are supported by engineers can also be seen as a central element of the learning organization as they identify performance gaps and lead to a review of the way the organization works.

Before World War II, the emphasis in Japan was on (final) inspection, which in line with Taylorism, was carried out by a dedicated quality control department. American influence after World War II brought the introduction of statistical quality control (1946). The modern Japanese concept of quality circles therefore has its roots in the period shortly after World War II. 1946 saw the foundation of the Union of Japanese Scientists and Engineers, which promoted the development of quality control in Japanese manufacturing businesses considerably. In the 1950s, on the initiative of the Japanese Union of Scientists and Engineers the idea of systematic quality assurance was brought to Japan.

It was American quality experts who shaped the eventually independent quality system in Japan. In the years 1950–52 Deming held a series of lectures on the subject of 'Statistical quality control' (inspection during production). Joseph M. Juran emphasized in his seminars (1954) the role that top and middle management should play in quality control. Armand V. Feigenbaum, who invented the term (total quality control), extended responsibility for quality to all areas of the company. Quality no longer meant the elimination of defective products but that they were avoided from the beginning by monitoring the process. These methods were developed further in Japan. One of the most important representatives of the Japanese movement was Kaoru Ishikawa, who extended quality management to include social aspects. Another step forward was taken by Masaaki Imai, who postulated that continuous improvement of processes to raise the standard of all output would be a recipe for success in Japanese quality management.

These efforts resulted in 1962 in the first official registration of a quality circle. At the beginning of its development, the quality circle was originally a learning group which then gradually addressed itself to solving problems with practical application of techniques it had learnt. Japanese production management moved further and further away from traditional inspection-oriented quality control and developed quality procedures for use within the production process and within product development.

Today, this idea is also applied to suppliers and other business partners who play their part in the value added process. Whilst quality control originally focussed on production and other technical areas in the company, efforts are made far beyond that nowadays.

The core idea of the quality circle is that problems are most likely to be identified and eliminated where they occur. Using this approach, production employees are supposed to identify the weak points in their day-to-day work and find the solution themselves. The primary goal of the quality circle is to improve the quality of the product and the process.

Quality circles have two main aims:

- To optimize manufacturing processes and work flow using the employees' knowledge and experience.
- To improve job satisfaction and motivation with regular group meetings which also improve company-internal communications (knowledge transfer, exchange of experience, transparency).

Conclusion: *kaizen* – the core of Japanese production management and the embodiment of organizational learning

Organizational learning processes have been made possible by the transfer of knowledge and technology (for example, automation technology and the autonomation system at Toyota) and frequently form the basis for the development of systems (for example NC and CNC-technology and manufacturing applications), which in their turn enable organizational learning by modifying the knowledge base (knowledge linked to the technology, for example, manufacturing processes) in the organization.

Organizational learning in production through the company-wide and cross-company process of continuous improvement (*kaizen*) is one of the main characteristics of Japanese manufacturing companies, a key hallmark of Japanese product management. The endeavour to achieve a zero-fault strategy in Japanese production plants as part of the total quality management system, which means that a defective part is not only rejected but that the cause of the error is also removed, is an expression of kaizen and as such an expression of the fundamental thinking by Japanese production management.

In response to the technical problems with products and production which arose in the interplay between American, Western European and the

Japanese' own methods and applications, the continuous improvement system today concentrates on production, but as a management concept includes all the activities and employees throughout the whole company. This means that Japanese production management can be considered the management of the process of continuous improvement which forms the basis of the way manufacturing companies are run.

For instance, Japanese production workers, marketing experts and design engineers actively co-operate in groups to identify problems, find solutions and develop better technology in order to eliminate performance gaps they have identified. The improvements they work out apply not only to their particular working group but also become valid for other working groups via a central integration and co-ordination mechanism; works management for example.

The improvement becomes obligatory for all the members of the organization, becomes a new standard and a long-term theory-in-use also for employees new to the company. The search for improvements to products, processes and systems applies not only to the company itself, but as part of a collective strategy creates a bridge to intercompany co-operation (for example, involving supplier companies).

The high degree of standardization in the formal management systems of Japanese companies brings about successful learning in groups which benefits the whole organization, that is, it enables organizational learning. This knowledge is also passed on to or shared with other companies via the collective strategies (collaborating companies, value added partnerships, alliances, supplier networks). New knowledge circulates through companies in the same networks very quickly. The highly-regarded *kaizen* concept, the Japanese leadership philosophy which still remains valid even under the currently prevailing low growth conditions, has proven to be an effective method for learning particularly in the area of production and enables progress in a combination of individual, organizational and interorganizational learning.

Japanese production management is associated with specific forms of work organization (for example, group work, team organization), of logistics and quality (for example, just-in-time, *kanban*, quality circles), of manufacturing processes (high-tech manufacturing systems, NC and CNC systems, autonomation), of personnel deployment (for example, job rotation) and of education. Its main characteristic overall is that it has been strongly moulded by the Toyota production system and is expressed in the philosophy of continuous improvement.

References

Abegglen, J. C. and G. Stalk (1985) *Kaisha: The Japanese Corporation* (New York: Basic Books).

Adler, P. S. (1988) 'Managing Flexible Automation', *California Management Review*, 30(3) pp. 34–56.

Argyris, C. and D. A. Schön (1978) *Organizational Learning. A Theory of Action Perspective* (Reading, Mass.: Addison-Wesley).

Argyris, C. and D. A. Schön (1999) *Die lernende Organisation* (Stuttgart: Klett-Cotta).

Asanuma, B. (1989) 'Manufacturer–supplier Relationships in Japan and the Concept of Relation-specific Skills', *Journal of the Japanese and International Economies*, 3, pp. 1–30.

Asanuma, B. and T. Kikutani (1992) 'Risk Absorption in Japanese Subcontraction. A Microeconomic Study of the Automobile Industry', *Journal of the Japanese and International Economies*, 6, pp. 1–29.

Beason, R. and D. E. Weinstein (1994) *Growth, Economies of Scale, and Industrial Targeting in Japan (1955–1990)*, Harvard Institute of Economic Research Discussion Paper 1644 (Boston, Mass.: Harvard Institute of Economic Research).

Behrendt, W. K. (1982) 'Die frühen Jahre der NC-Technologie: 1954 bis 1963', *Technische Rundschau*, 19, pp. 19–21.

Boesenberg, D. and H. Metzen (eds) (1993) *Lean Management. Vorsprung durch schlanke Konzepte* (Landsberg: Verlag Moderne Industrie).

Brödner, P. (1991) 'Maschinenbau in Japan – Nippons Erfolgskonzept: so einfach wie möglich', *Technische Rundschau*, 37, pp. 54–62.

Chalmers, J. (1986) *MITI and the Japanese Miracle. The Growth of the Industrial Policy, 1925–1975* (Stanford, CH: Stanford University Press).

Champy, J. and M. Hammer (1994) *Business Reengineering – Die Radikalkur für das Unternehmen* (Frankfurt and New York: Campus).

Chokki, T. (1986) 'A History of the Machine Tool Industry in Japan', M. in Fransman (ed.), *Machinery and Economic Development* (New York: St Martin's Press), pp. 124–52.

Clark, K. B., T. Fujimoto and E. C. Stotko (eds) (1992) *Automobilentwicklung mit System. Strategie, Organisation und Management in Europa, Japan und USA* (Frankfurt am Main: Campus-Verlag).

Collis, D. J. (1988) 'The Machine Tool Industry and Industrial Policy 1955–1988', in M. E. Spence and H. A. Hazard (eds), *International Competitiveness* (New York: Center of Business and Government, John F. Kennedy School of Government, Harvard University), pp. 75–114.

Ducan, R. B. and A. Weiss (1979) 'Organizational Learning: Implications for Organizational Design', in B. W. Staw (ed.), *Research in Organizational Behavior*, vol. 1, pp. 75–123.

Durand, J.-P., P. Stewart and J. J. Castillo (eds) (1999) *Teamwork in the Automobile Industry. Radical Change or Passing Fashion*? (Houndsmill: Palgrave Macmillan).

Ernst, A. (1999) 'Personnel Management of Japanese Firms and Information Flows', in Albach, H., U. Görtzen and R. Zobel (eds), *Information Processing as a Competitive Advantage of Japanese Firms* (Berlin: Edition Sigma), pp. 239–53.

Fischer, W. (1979) *Die Weltwirtschaft im 20. Jahrhundert* (Göttingen: Vahlen).

Ford, H. (1922) *My Life and Work* (New York: Doubleday & Page).

Freedman, D. (1988) *The Misunderstood Miracle – Industrial Development and Political Change in Japan* (Ithaca, NY: Cornell University Press).

Freyssenet, M., A. Mair, K. Shimizu and G. Volpato (eds) (1998) *One Best Way? Trajectories and Industrial Models of the World's Automobile Producers* (Oxford and New York: Oxford University Press).

Fujimoto, T. (1994) *Buhin Torihiki Kankei to Suparaiyâ Shisutemu* (Parts Transaction Relationships and the Supplier System), Discussion Paper Series 94-J-19, Research Institute for the Japanese Economy (Tokyo: University of Tokyo Press).

Fujimoto, T. (1996) *An Evolutionary Process of Toyota's Final Assembly Operations. The Role of Ex-post Dynamic Capabilities*, Discussion Paper Series 96-F-2, Research Insitute for the Japanese Economy (Tokyo: University of Tokyo Press).

Fujimoto, T. (1999) *The Evolution of a Manufacturing System at Toyota* (Oxford and New York: Oxford University Press).

Fujimoto, T., S. Sei and A. Takeishi (1994) 'Nihon Jidôsha Sangyô no Supuraiyâ Shisutemu no Zentaizô to sono Tamensei' (The Whole Picture of the Supplier System of the Japanese Car Industry and its Diversity), *Kikai Keizai Kenkyû*, 24, pp. 11–36.

Fujimoto, T. and A. Takeishi (1994) *Jidôsha Sangyô 21 Seiki e no Shinario* (Scenario for the Car Industry in the 21st Century) (Tokyo: Seisansei Shuppan).

Furin, W. E. and T. Nishiguchi (1990) 'The Toyota Production System. Its Organizational Definition in Japan', *Keizai Kenkyû*, 42 (1), pp. 42–55.

Garratt, B. (1990) *Creating a Learning Organisation. A Guide to Leadership, Learning and Development* (Cambridge: Director Books).

Geißler, H. (1996) 'Vom Lernen in der Organisation zum Lernen der Organisation', in T. Sattelberger (ed.), *Die lernende Organisation: Konzepte für eine neue Qualität der Unternehmensentwicklung* (Wiesbaden: Gabler), pp. 79–95.

Goetsch, D. L. and S. B. Davis (2003) *Quality Management; Introduction to Total Quality Management for Production, Processing, and Services* (Upper Saddle River, NJ: Prentice-Hall).

Görgens, J. (1994) *Just in time Fertigung. Konzept und modellgestützte Analyse* (Stuttgart: Schäffer-Poeschel).

Griffin, G. C. (1955) 'Maschinensteuerung – die Grundlage der Automatisierung', *Machine Shop Management*, 16, pp. 46–50.

Haak, R. (2001a) 'Innovationen im Werkzeugmaschinenbau – Ein Überblick über die Frühphase der japanischen und deutschen Fertigungsautomatisierung', *Japan Analysen und Prognosen*, 175 (Munich: Japan-Zentrum der Ludwig-Maximilians-Universität).

Haak, R. (2001b) 'Technologie und Management in Fernost- Ein Blick auf die Frühphase der japanischen Automatisierungstechnologie', *Zeitschrift für wirtschaftlichen Fabrikbetrieb*, 96 (5), pp. 274–80.

Haak, R. (2002) 'Japanische Zuliefernetzwerke in der Globalisierung', *Zeitschrift für wirtschaftlichen Fabrikbetrieb*, 97 (3), pp. 133–6.

Haak, R. (2003a) 'A new theoretical approach to internationalisation strategies: First thoughts about a metastrategy', *Innovation: Management, Policy and Practice*, 5 (1), pp. 41–8.

Haak, R. (2003b) 'Japanisches Produktionsmanagement – Organisationales Lernen als strategischer Erfolgsfaktor', *Zeitschrift für wirtschaftlichen Fabrikbetrieb*, 98 (7–8), pp. 67–73.

Haak, R. (2004a) 'Japanese Supplier Network System in Transition – Survival Strategies', *Innovation: Management, Policy and Practice*, 6 (1), pp. 45–9.

Haak, R. (2004b) *Theory and Management of Collective Strategies in International Business – The Impact of Globalization on Japanese–German Business Collaboration in Asia* (Basingstoke: Palgrave).

Hanft, A. (1996) 'Organisationales Lernen und Macht – Über den Zusammenhang von Wissen, Lernen, Macht und Struktur', in G. Schreyögg and P. Conrad (eds), *Wissensmanagement* (Berlin and New York: de Gruyter), pp. 133–62.

Hayashi, S. (1991) *Culture and Management in Japan* (Tokyo: University of Tokyo Press).

Hemmert, M. and R. Lützeler (1994) 'Einleitung: Landeskunde und wirtschaftliche Entwicklung seit 1945', in *Die japanische Wirtschaft heute*, 10, pp. 23–44.

Hirsch-Kreinsen, H. (1989) 'Entwicklung einer Basistechnik. NC-Steuerung von Werkzeugmaschinen in den USA und der BRD', in K. Düll and Lutz, B. (eds), *Technikentwicklung und Arbeitsteilung im internationalen Vergleich* (Munich: Hanser).

Hirsch-Kreinsen, H. (1993) *NC-Entwicklung als gesellschaftlicher Prozeß. Amerikanische und deutsche Innovationsmuster der Fertigungstechnik* (Frankfurt and New York: Campus-Verlag).

Hitachi Seki (1991) Hitachi Seki Kabushiki Kaisha: hito ni yasashii gijutsu – Chie to sôi no 55 nen – Sôritsu 55 shûnen (Hitachi Seki Co. Ltd. Human Being Orientied Techology: 55 years Expierence and Creativity (Tokyo: Hitachi Seki).

Hoffmann, J. (1990) *Erfolgsbedingungen des Innovationsprozesses der numerisch gesteuerten Werkzeugmaschine in Japan* (Berlin: TU IWF).

Hyodo, T. (1987) 'Participatory Management and Japanese Workers' Consciousness', in J. Bergmann and S. Tokunaga (eds), *Economic and Social Aspects of Industrial Relations. A Comparison of the German and the Japanese Systems* (Frankfurt and New York: Campus-Verlag), pp. 261–70.

Imai, M. (1993) *Kaizen* (Frankfurt am Main: Ullstein).

Itô, T. (1992) *The Japanese Economy* (Cambridge, Mass., and London: MIT Press).

Jung, H. F. (1992) 'Lean-Management. Arbeitswelt und Unternehmensethik in Japan', in *Lean-Management. Ideen für die Praxis* (Nuremberg: WiSo-Führungskräfte-Akademie), pp. 102–30.

Jürgens, U. (1991) *Kaizen – die Organisation von Verbesserungsaktivitäten zwischen Industrial Engineering und Qualitätszirkelaktivitäten* (Berlin: Wissenschaftszentrum Berlin).

Jürgens, U. (1994) 'Lean Production', in H. Corsten (ed.) *Handbuch Produktionsmanagement* (Wiesbaden: Gabler), pp. 369–79.

Jürgens, U., T. Malsch and K. Dohse (1989) *Moderne Zeiten in der Automobilfabrik. Strategie der Produktmodernisierung im Länder- und Konzernvergleich* (Berlin, Heidelberg and New York: Springer).

Keizai Kikakuchô (1994) *Kokumin keizai keisan nenpô* (Annual report on the National Accounts), (Tokyo: Keizai Kikakuchô keizai Kenkyujo), pp. 46–7.

Kennedy, P. (1954) 'Automatic Controls Take Over in Automotive Manufacturing', *Automotive Industry*, 111, pp. 62–7, 138–44.

Kief, H. B. (1991) 'Von der NC zur CNC: Die Entwicklung der numerischen Steuerungen', *Werkstatt und Betrieb*, 124 (5), pp. 385–91.

Koshiro, K. (1994) 'The Employment System and Human Resource Management', in K. Imai and R. Koyama (eds), *Business Enterprises in Japan – Views of leading Japanese Economists* (Cambridge, Mass., and London: MIT Press), pp. 247–49.

Liker, J. K. (ed.) (1997) *Becoming Lean: Inside Stories of U.S. Manufactures* (Portland, Or. Productivity Press).

Liker, J. K. (2004) *The Toyota Way* (New York: McGraw-Hill).

Matzky, U. (1994) 'Das Management des kontinuierlichen Verbesserungsprozesses in der japanischen Automobilindustrie', in Ostasiatisches Seminar der Freien Universität Berlin (eds), *Soziale und Wirtschaftliche Studien über Japan/Ostasien*, Occasional Paper 91 (Bulin: Free University of Bulin).

Mommertz, K. H. (1981) *Bohren, Drehen und Fräsen. Geschichte der Werkzeugmaschinen* (Hamburg: Reinbek bei Hamburg).

Monden, Y. (1983) *Toyota Production System* (Norcross, Ga.: Industrial Engineering and Management Press).

Nakamura, K. (1993) *Subcontracting System and Segmented Labour Market in Japan* (Tokyo: Musashi Universtity).

Nakamura, T. (1996) *Lectures on Modern Japanese Economic History 1926–1994* (Tokyo: Universtiy of Toyko Press).

Nihon Kôsaku Kikai Kôgyôkai (1982) *Haha-naru kikai: 30 nen no ayumi* (The Mother of Machines: Thirty Years of History), (Tokyo: Nihon Kôsaku Kikai Kôgyôkai).

Nihon Noritsu Kyokai (1978) *Toyota no Genba Kanri* (Tokyo: Nihon Noritsu Kyokai).
Nonaka, I. (1990) 'Redundant, Overlapping Organization: A Japanese Approach to Managing the Innovation Process', *California Management Review*, 32 (3), pp. 27–38.
Nonaka, I. and H. Takeuchi (1997) *Die Organisation des Wissens. Wie japanische Unternehmen eine brachliegende Ressource nutzbar machen* (Frankfurt am Main and New York: Campus-Verlag).
Ohno, T. (1988) *Toyota Production System: Beyond Large-Scale Production* (Cambridge: Productivity Press).
Park, S.-J. (1975) 'Die Wirtschaft seit 1868', in H. Hammitz (ed.), *Japan* (Nuremberg: Glock & Lutz), pp. 123–44.
Park, S.-J. (ed.) (1985) *Japanisches Management in der Praxis: Flexibilität oder Kontrolle im Prozess der Internationalisierung und Mikroelektronisierung* (Berlin: Express Edition).
Parker, M. and J. Slaughter (1988) *Choosing Sides: Union and Team Concept* (Boston: South End Press).
Pfeiffer, W. and E. Weiß (eds) (1990) *Technologie-Management* (Göttingen: Vandenhoeck & Ruprecht).
Reingold, E. (1999) *Toyota: People, Ideas, and the Challenge of the New* (London: Penguin).
Renkel, H.-P. (1985) *Technologietransfer-Management in Japan. Gründung, Innovation und Beratung* (Cologne: Eul).
Scherm, M. and P. R. Bischoff (1994) 'Lean Management – stereotype Sichtweisen japanischer Unternehmensphänomene', in M. Esser and K. Kobayashi (eds), *Kaishain. Personalmanagement in Japan. Sinn und Werte statt Systeme, Psychologie für das Personalmanagement* (Göttingen: Verlag für Angewandte Psychologie), pp. 100–7.
Schmitt, W. W. (1998) *Management japanischer Niederlassungen. Strukturen und Strategien* (Bonn: Institut für Wissenschaftliche Publikationen).
Schröder, S. (1995) *Innovation in der Produktion* (Berlin: IPK Berlin).
Sebestyén, O. G. (1994) *Management-Geheimnis Kaizen. Der japanische Weg zur Innovation* (Vienna: Wirtschaftsverlag Ueberreuter).
Shimizu, T. (1988) 'Japanisches Management', in W. Busse von Colbe, K. Chmielewicz, E. Gaugler and G. Laßmann (eds), *Betriebswirtschaftslehre in Japan und Deutschland. Unternehmensführung, Rechnungswesen und Finanzierung* (Stuttgart: Poeschel), pp. 173–91.
Simon, W. (ed.) (1969) *Produktivitätsverbesserungen mit NC-Maschinen und Computern* (Munich: Hanser).
Smitka, M. (1991) *Competitive Ties: Subcontracting in the Japanese Automotive Industry* (New York: Columbia University Press).
Spur, G. (1979) *Produktionstechnik im Wandel* (Munich and Vienna: Hanser).
Spur, G. (1991) *Vom Wandel der industriellen Welt durch Werkzeugmaschinen* (Munich and Vienna: Hanser).
Spur, G. (ed.) (1994) *Fabrikbetrieb. Handbuch der Fertigungstechnik* (Munich and Vienna: Hanser).
Spur, G. (1998a) *Technologie und Management. Zum Selbstverständnis der Technikwissenschaften* (Munich and Vienna: Hanser).
Spur, G. (1998b) *Fabrikbetrieb* (Munich and Vienna: Hanser).
Spur, G. and F.-L. Krause (1997) *Das virtuelle Produkt* (Munich and Vienna: Hanser).
Spur, G. and D. Specht (1990) *Die Numerische Steuerung – Fallstudie einer erfolgreichen Innovation aus dem Bereich des Maschinenbaus* (Berlin: Akademie der Wissenschaften zu Berlin).
Staehle, W. (1999) *Management* (Munich: Vahlen).

Suzuki, Y. (1994) *Nihon Teki Seisan Shisutemu to Kigyo* (Sapporo: Hokkaido Daigaku Tosho Shuppan Kai).

Suzuki, Y. (2004) 'Structure of the Japanese Production System: Elusiveness and Reality', *Asian Business & Management*, 3, pp. 201–19.

Takayama, K. (1997) 'Machine Tool Industry', in Ifo Institute for Economic Research and Sakura Institute of Research (eds), *A Comparative Analysis of Japanese and German Economic Success* (Tokyo: Sakura Institute of Research), pp. 427–40.

Taylor, F. W. (1903) *Shop Management* (New York: Harper & Brothers).

Taylor, F. W. (1911) *The Principles of Scientific Management* (Westport, Conn.: Greenwood Press).

Toyoda, E. (1987) *Fifty Years in Motion* (Tokyo: Kodansha International).

Tsuruta, T. (1988) 'The Rapid Growth Era', in R. Komiya, M. Okuno and K. Suzumura (eds), *Industrial Policy in Japan*, Orlando, Fl.: Academic Press), pp. 49–87.

Vestal, J. E. (1993) *Planning for Change. Industrial Policy and Japanese Economic Development 1945–1990* (Oxford: Oxford University Press).

Waldenberger, F. (1994) 'Grundzüge der Wirtschaftspolitik', in Deutsches Institut für Japanstudien (ed.), *Die japanische Wirtschaft heute* (Munich: Iudicium), pp. 23–44.

Waldenberger, F. (1996) 'Die Montageindustrien als Träger des japanischen Wirtschaftswunders. Die Rolle der Industriepolitik', in W. Schaumann (ed.), *Gewollt oder geworden? Planung, Zufall, natürliche Entwicklung in Japan* (Munich: Iudicium), pp. 259–71.

Waldenberger, F. (1998) 'Wirtschaftspolitik', in Deutsches Institut für Japanstudien (ed.), *Die Wirtschaft Japans. Strukturen zwischen Kontinuität und Wandel* (Berlin: Springer), pp. 19–54.

Womack, J. P., D. T. Jones and D. Ross (1990) *The Machine that Changed the World* (New York: Rawson).

Womack, J. P. and D. T. Jones (1996) *Lean Thinking: Banish Waste and Create Wealth in Your Corporation* (New York: Simon & Schuster).

Yamashiro, A. (1997) *Japanische Managementlehre, Keieigaku* (Munich: Oldenbourg).

Yui, T. (1999) 'Japanese Management Practices in Historical Perspective', in D. Dirks, J. F. Huchet and T. Ribault (eds), *Japanese Management in the Low Growth Era. Between External Shocks and Internal Evolution* (Berlin, Heidelberg and New York: Springer), pp. 13–18.

Part III
Conclusion

11

Continuity versus Change: The Key Dilemma for Japanese Management

Markus Pudelko

In recent years there has been an abundance of testimonials on the relative decline in competitiveness of the Japanese economy and the Japanese management model. Many of these reports suggest that the only way for Japan to regain its competitiveness is to adopt management practices from the business model that currently, due to its alleged superiority, seems to be the focus point of global convergence: the Western, or more specifically, the Anglo-Saxon model. Indeed, it seems that the majority of management scholars are advising Japan to adopt certain key characteristics of the Anglo-Saxon model, and in many ways these are the opposite of those of the traditional Japanese system. This includes a comparatively stronger focus on the following:[1]

- Market regulation (instead of governmental guidance).
- Shareholders' interests (instead of employees' interests).
- Capital markets (instead of bank loans).
- Constant profits (instead of long-term market growth).
- Corporate strategies (instead of operational effectiveness).
- Differentiation from competitors (instead of imitation of best practices).
- Radical change (instead of incremental steps towards improvement).
- Open, global and geocentric approaches (instead of insular, domestic and ethnocentric ones).
- Flexible transnational alliances and supply chains (instead of rigid domestic *keiretsu* structures).
- Proactive top management (instead of delegating decision making to middle management).
- Willingness to abandon prior decisions and ongoing activities and to embrace new ones (instead of perfecting old decisions and activities).
- Transparency in corporate governance and financial markets (instead of a 'behind closed doors' insider system).
- Clear accountability and responsibility (instead of vague responsibility sharing).

- Flexible labour markets (instead of lifetime employment).
- Performance (instead of seniority).
- Diversity of knowledge, originality, creativity and individuality (instead of homogeneity, *status quo*, conformity and collectivism).

What seems to have been all but forgotten in the current debate on Japanese management is, however, that no more than 20 years ago many commentators were giving rather pessimistic prognoses of the future of American management and suggested an orientation towards certain aspects of the Japanese business model. Paradoxically, looking at the above list, their advice frequently went in the opposite direction by stressing:

- Closer business–government cooperation to define and develop new markets (instead of relying exclusively on market forces).
- Retention of companies (instead of breaking them up after unfriendly takeovers and selling the parts for the benefit of shareholders).
- Increase of the debt to equity ratio in order to become more independent from the moods and short-term orientation of capital markets (instead of having to produce good financial results every quarter to keep investors satisfied).
- Long-term development of market share in order to drive out competitors (instead of focusing on short-term profits).
- Close cooperation in long-term relationships with suppliers (instead of frequently changing partners for the sake of short-term cost reduction).
- Wealth creation through improving operational effectiveness (instead of redistributing wealth by buying and selling off parts of companies).

So how has the United States achieved economic growth and increased its competitiveness since the 1990s, while Japan has found itself with a stagnating economy and companies that are struggling for survival? Did American companies follow the advice to adopt aspects of the Japanese business model, while the Japanese somehow deviated from the path that only a short time ago had led to so much success? Most certainly not. In some selected areas American managers might well have been inspired by Japanese management practices (improving operational effectiveness in production processes, quality orientation, strengthening the commitment of employees, team orientation), but overall the US economy regained its competitiveness by drawing on its traditional strengths. As for the Japanese business model, the current criticism is not that Japanese companies somehow forgot about their traditional strengths and became less efficient in what they previously did well, rather it is that they have continued to adhere to management practices that are increasingly ineffective. It is therefore suggested here that what has changed fundamentally over the last two decades is not so much the actual (American or Japanese) management practices but the global business environment, which ultimately determines whether or not management practices are successful. In other words the characteristics, and therefore the inherent strengths and weaknesses of the American and Japanese (or any other) management models, have remained quite stable over time; what has changed is the relevance of the various strengths and weaknesses. The reason for the overall stability of national management models is suggested here to lie in their deep embeddedness in their particular socio-cultural context. Unfortunately for Japan, the global business environment has changed in such a way that the inherent strengths of its management model have lost much of their significance over the last two decades, while its weaknesses have increased in importance. Conversely the inherent strengths of the American management model have become more relevant, while its weaknesses have declined in significance. Several developments in the business environment can be highlighted to substantiate this claim.

First, with the globalization of markets what matters now is less the pooling of specific domestic productive forces in order to manufacture goods to be exported overseas, but more the integration of national productive forces into a network of transnational value chains, strategic alliances and newly merged and acquired companies in order to tap global expertise and manufacture close to the markets one is serving. Open, global and geocentric approaches (such as the American one) have consequently become more successful and insular, domestic and ethnocentric ones (such as the Japanese) have not.

Second, competition has become more intense as the former communist countries have entered the global economy. Countries that focus on differentiated, sophisticated, high value-added products and services that are difficult to copy (such as the United States) have a better chance of avoiding competition from these new entrants than countries that concentrate on operational effectiveness, which is easier to copy (such as Japan).

Third, as business clients and consumers grow increasingly more sophisticated, information on their specific demands becomes more dispersed and fragmented, and therefore more difficult to gather or predict. Consequently economies that put their trust in market forces (the United States) have an advantage over those which rely more on government forecasting and planning and on close government–business cooperation (Japan).

Fourth, as societies become more affluent they tend to become more individualistic and materialistic. This translates into a move away from collective and partnership-oriented solutions towards more individualistic ones. Remuneration, pension and social security schemes are areas in which more individualized solutions are being sought globally. This trend benefits countries that already have an individualistic and more materialist culture (the United States), but creates insecurity, confusion and friction in more collectivistic countries that are having to undergo significant change (Japan).

Fifth, with expansion of materialism and individualism, economies increasingly favour the shareholder value model over the more multidimensional and collectivistic stakeholder model. Countries that have been shareholder oriented for a longtime (the United States) already have profit-oriented companies and (at least in principle) transparent and shareholder-friendly corporate governance models, accounting standards and regulatory environments, while others (Japan) have to undergo fundamental changes to accommodate the increased importance of shareholder value.

Sixth, the competitive environment is becoming increasingly dynamic and characterized by disruptive and non-linear innovation processes. Economies that embrace creativity, originality, unconventional solutions, radical changes, risk taking, corporate restructuring and creative destruction (the United States) are consequently in a stronger competitive position than economies that are more *status quo* oriented (Japan).

Seventh, new industries are becoming increasingly important (software, communications, biotechnology). Countries that excel in the breakthrough innovations that characterize these industries (the United States) have an advantage over those whose strength lies more in incrementally perfecting products manufactured by mature industries (Japan).

Eighth, industries such as IT and communications have not only become increasingly important in terms of their relative share of wealth creation, but also their products have facilitated dramatic gains in the organizational efficiency of unrelated industries. Countries that have fully embraced dramatic organizational changes (the United States) have improved their performance substantially, while those which have been more reluctant to do so (Japan) have become less competitive.

Finally, with growing affluence the importance of services increases relative to manufacturing. Countries with long-standing strengths in service industries such as finance, consulting, communications and entertainment (the United States) are benefiting from this development while manufacturing-oriented countries (Japan) are suffering.

These examples support the argument that changes in the global competitive environment are detrimental to the traditional Japanese management model but play in favour of the American one. Overall, globalization has taken away much of the stability that shielded the Japanese economy and allowed for an insular and ethnocentric management approach. Because of its *status quo* orientation the Japanese management model has been unable to adapt quickly and radically to fundamental changes in the global business environment. Moreover developments that are specific to the Japanese macroeconomic context have further weakened the sustainability of traditional Japanese management:

- Japan's high-growth economy has become one of virtually no growth.
- The Japanese management model is based not only on economic but also on demographic growth. However the Japanese population is declining dramatically.

- With the crisis in the financial sector after the bursting of the 'bubble economy', banks became very reluctant to issue new loans, thus impeding growth.
- While 'me too' strategies based on improving operational efficiency were appropriate in the period of high growth, now that the economy is stagnant or only growing slowly they cannot guarantee survival.
- With the breaking up of the bank lending system, foreign investors have substantially increased their share of Japanese companies and are now demanding the adoption of global (or better, Western) business standards.

Having established the underlying reasons for the problems of the Japanese management model, some thoughts on the future of Japanese management are required. As already mentioned, numerous observers have pointed out the need for major change if Japanese companies are to regain their former competitiveness. Given the transformation of the business environment, this call for change has struck a chord and accordingly many fundamental changes to Japanese management practices have been introduced over the last decade. However there is a danger of repeating the mistake made some 20 years ago: extrapolating current trend into the future and neglecting the possibility of yet another paradigm shift in the business environment that might completely upset the rules of the game all over again. Indeed two decades ago many predicted that the Japanese economy would continue to grow and the US economy would continue its relative decline. What was overlooked at the time was the possible transformation of a rather stable business environment (favourable to Japan) to a substantially more dynamic one (favourable to the United States). Consequently, who can say whether the changes now taking place will continue with the same scope, depth and speed? The current phase of major innovations characterized by technological breakthroughs (a strength of the United States) could be followed by a phase in which these innovations will have to be fine-tuned through incremental process innovations (a strength of Japan). In addition the current restructuring, global strategic alliances, large-scale mergers and acquisitions and so on might prove to be more difficult to manage than expected. With the new megastructures in place, national and organizational cultural differences might render day-to-day operations more complex and complicated than anticipated. Divestures and a shift of attention from sophisticated transnational strategies to operational effectiveness could be the result. This would certainly play in favour of the traditional Japanese strengths.

It is not intended here to make firm predictions for the future. The only purpose of the scenario outlined above is to warn against a linear extrapolation of current trends into the future, and against ignoring the possibility of non-linear ruptures taking place in the future.

Having made this argument, one should not come to the erroneous conclusion that Japanese managers just need to wait for the strengths of the Japanese management model to become relevant again. Even if the current phase of major restructuring is at some point followed by a fine-tuning phase, it will still have to be initiated in the first place, and here Japan still seems to have a backlog. The key questions for the future of the Japanese management model, therefore, are as follows: is Japanese management finding a new balance between continuity of traditional practices and change, to meet the demands of the global business environment? What will this new balance be? Will inspiration from foreign management models play a part in it? Figure 11.1 provides an overview of the major driving forces for both continuity and

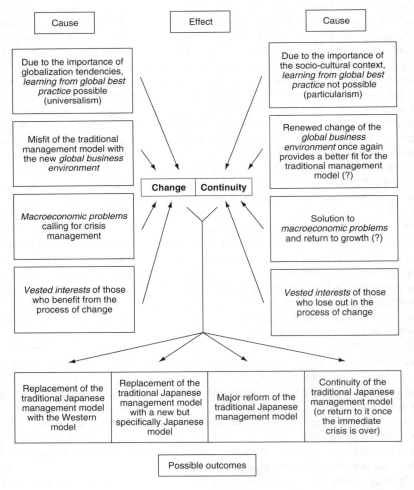

Figure 11.1 Causes, effects and possible outcomes of change and continuity in the Japanese management model

change and the possible consequences this might have for the Japanese management model.

As can be seen, four opposing pairs of driving forces for change and continuity have been identified. These relate to the following issues: learning from best practice, the global business environment, macroeconomic problems and vested interests.

Because of the increasing competition in the global economy, Japanese companies are under growing pressure to learn from management practices that have proved to be highly successful, no matter where these practices originated. Proponents of what might be called the universalism (or convergence, or culture-free) approach claim that human needs, technology and economic systems throughout the world are converging, thus necessitating the convergence of management practices towards global best practices. In this sense globalization is functioning as a driving force for change, and some argue that even cultural differences are declining. Affluence and material independence frequently result in the individualization of societies, and that also includes more collectivist societies such as that of Japan. On the other hand management models are not only embedded in but are also substantially defined by their particular socio-cultural contexts. Indeed disciples of the particularism (or divergence, or culture-specific) approach stress that convergence towards global best practices is rendered impossible by cultural differences, and given the importance of the socio-cultural context, even the notion of global best practices is misleading. As for the alleged convergence of national cultures, this is considered to exist only very superficially, and at a more fundamental level the differences persist. As societies and cultures are perceived to be quite stable and not subject to dramatic change, those who focus on the socio-cultural context tend to stress the continuity argument.

It has already been established that the traditional Japanese management model is not well suited to the current global business environment, which is characterized by disruptive and non-linear innovation processes. This has prompted calls for the model to be adapted to the requirements of that environment. If, on the other hand, the business environment were to change again and in a way that was beneficial to the traditional model, this would strengthen the argument for maintaining the traditional model (stressing for example, stability and incrementalism). However as discussed previously, this is just one of several possible scenarios.

For more than a decade Japan has been experiencing a major macroeconomic crisis, characterized by two mutually reinforcing negative phenomena: low (or even negative) growth and deflation. This has put additional pressure on companies to take substantial measures to increase their competitiveness, which would ultimately help to break the vicious cycle of low growth and deflation. There are currently some encouraging signs that Japan may finally be emerging from its lengthy economic crisis, although it is too early to judge whether the current developments really do indicate a sustainable improvement. If a crisis (such as a recession) is a driver of change, the overcoming of a crisis (such as economic recovery) may well reduce the pressure for change. A genuine and sustainable solution to the current macroeconomic problems could therefore result in a return to traditional management practices. An amelioration of the macroeconomic situation could even mean that some of the current transformations will be reversed. However this is purely hypothetical at this point as the growth path of the Japanese economy is very difficult to predict.

Finally, irrespective of the overall positive effects change may have, some players will particularly benefit from the current transformation. These are mainly young, flexible, specialized, high-potential, high-performing individuals who identify more with the job they do than with the company they work for. With the decline of lifetime employment they can change companies more easily if they find better career opportunities elsewhere; with the decline of the seniority principle they can gain faster promotion and increase their salaries if they perform well; and with the decline of job rotation and the generalist career path they can specialize in the area in which they are most interested. The advocates of change also include foreign investors who would like to see a performance and profit orientation taking root in Japanese management. Another group who favour change are career-minded Japanese women, who still have hardly any career opportunities. With all the transformations currently taking place in Japan, in this respect, however, little change can be observed. On the other hand, the traditional Japanese management model is to the advantage of certain groups of people who wish to preserve their status and therefore object to change. This applies mainly to middle-aged male members of the core workforce of large Japanese companies who were hired under the principles of lifetime employment, seniority and job rotation. They started out with very low salaries, received steady but slow promotions and small pay increases and were required to change jobs (and possibly locations) frequently within the company. After years of hard work and sacrifice they are now counting on receiving their reward in the form of job security, automatic promotion to managerial positions and constant pay increases. However with the declining importance of lifetime employment, the seniority principle and the generalist career path they might be passed over for promotion and pay increases in favour of younger, more productive high performers, or might even lose their jobs. Hence they are natural opponents of change. Furthermore, members of the bureaucracy tend to favour the maintenance of the traditional system as they do not want their influence on the business sector to diminish. They also wish to retain the possibility of their moving into the private sector for a high salary under the *amukadari* system. Finally the Liberal Democratic Party – the political embodiment of the 'old system' – and uncompetitive business sectors that have benefited from government subsidies, such as construction and retailing, prefer the continuation of the traditional model.

Having discussed four driving forces for change and four directly opposing forces that encourage continuity, it is now of interest to consider which might ultimately prevail. Four potential outcomes for Japanese management can be distinguished.

If, at one extreme, the forces of change triumph over those of continuity, comprehensive replacement of traditional Japanese management principles with Western ones could result, as it is the West (or more specifically the Anglo-Saxon countries) that is currently setting the standards for successful management. As a consequence the strategies listed at the start of this chapter would be implemented in Japan in a similar way as in the West. This potential outcome is based on the universalist concept that in a globalized world the margin for culture-specific solutions is becoming increasingly smaller, and the need to adopt best practices, no matter from where they originate, is becoming ever more pressing.

The next potential outcome also implies fundamental changes to the Japanese management model, although this scenario is somewhat less radical than the previous one. It entails replacement of the traditional model with a new, but still genuinely Japanese model. Inspiration might well come from Western management principles, very much along the line of the first set of bullet points listed above. However, this would not be in the form of a one-to-one adoption of those policies, but of an adaptation to the Japanese socio-cultural context. Other sources of inspiration might be Japanese companies that to date have been viewed as rather unconventional. Sony is an obvious example, as are some innovative start-up companies. Interestingly, many of the unconventional but successful Japanese companies are located away from the economically dominant metropolitan areas of Tokyo and Osaka. For example Kyoto, which used to host few company headquarters, is now home to many thriving young firms. Geographical distance from the strongholds of traditional management practices can apparently be helpful in finding new approaches.

The third potential outcome is adaptation of the traditional Japanese model to the new business environment. This would involve a further weakening of the *keiretsu* system, of government–business cooperation, of finance being provided by the main bank and so on, although these would continue to exist and play some role in Japanese management.

The fourth and final outcome would be for no major change of the management model to take place. This obviously does not imply a completely static model, as during the heyday of Japanese management there was also constant adaptation to changes in the business environment. However these adaptations took place *within* the management model and did not result in a change of the model itself. A slight variation of this outcome is that the changes made might be reversed when the overall economic situation improves. With the weakening of the *keiretsu* system, and in particular the dependence on the main banks, some of the former jewels of Japanese industry, such as Nissan and even Mitsubishi Motors for a while, have come under the *de facto* control of foreign competitors. This was once completely unthinkable and therefore constitutes a major change. With a return to competitiveness and improvement of the overall economy, it is not inconceivable that a joint effort by the government bureaucracy, the main banks and the Japanese managers of those companies will try to regain (domestic) control.

Having described these four possible outcomes, we must now ask where in the spectrum ranging from wholesale change to continuity will Japanese management (re)position itself? This is not a question of selecting one choice over the others, as different aspects of different management outcomes from complete adoption of Western policies to the continuation of traditional concepts are possible. For most aspects of management, complete convergence with the Western model is likely to be the exception rather than the rule. With regard to the overall socio-cultural context, convergence tendencies seem to be at a rather superficial level, so that it would be naïve to expect a profound Westernization of Japanese society. Because of Japanese socio-cultural particularities, many management practices that have been highly effective in Western countries would not work in Japan.

A look at past history can help to put the claim for the convergence of Japanese management practices towards Western management principles into context. Looking at the Meiji restoration of 1868, one might argue that the transformations Japan forced itself to undergo in subsequent years in order to avoid dependence on the Western powers was one of the most comprehensive cross-cultural learning processes in modern history. During that time Japan turned from a mainly feudal and completely self-isolated rural society into the first non-Western industrialized country. It adopted from Europe many aspects of state bureaucracy, military organization, technology, industry, commerce, education and the law. Seventy-seven years later, under its first ever occupation by a foreign nation, Japan undertook another wave of major reforms. For example it borrowed constitutional and public law from the Americans, plus many aspects of popular culture. In the realm of management, the focus on quality enhancement, propagated by Deming, is an often cited case of Japan adopting a concept that originated in the United States. However in each of these two crucial phases of Japanese history – the Meiji restoration and the American occupation – learning never meant outright copying but careful adaptation to the very specific circumstances of Japanese culture and society. As one slogan said during the Meiji period: 'Western technology, Japanese spirit'.

These two adaptation phases resulted in what was later described as the first management model to present a thorough challenge to Western management principles. So, if these two major Westernization processes resulted in what is today known as 'the Japanese management model', who is now to say that the difficulties Japan is currently facing are so fundamental that they will force it to abandon its own methods and replace them with Western ones? And to put Japan's current problems into perspective; even after ten years of suffering a stagnant economy Japan is still the second most important economic power in the world. In comparison, in 1868 Japan was facing economic colonization by Western powers and in 1945 the country was occupied for the first time in its history of more than 2000 years and was under foreign military rule. Consequently to expect Japanese management to conform to Western principles is to fall into the trap encountered by many chroniclers of historical developments: that of overestimating the impact of (recent) change in history and underestimating the tenacity of continuity.

At the opposite extreme, the continuation of all aspects of the traditional management model is equally unlikely. The overall drivers of change are of such significance that there will be little scope for limited readjustments within the confines of the traditional model. Moreover some of the changes that are currently taking place in Japan, such as the growing flexibility of the labour market, the increase in direct financing, the stronger profit orientation and so on, are so fundamental that they seem to be largely irreversible. In addition, globalization means that insular and ethnocentric management approaches are no longer an option.

What seems likely, therefore, is a combination of the two possibilities depicted in the centre of Figure 11.1. Many aspects of Japanese management have already changed (or can be expected to change) to such a degree that they constitute a true paradigm shift. For example there has been a move away from the institutionalized seniority system towards performance-related pay and promotion. This shift can be regarded as so significant that one might well speak of the imminent replacement of the old system by a new one. There are, furthermore, clear signs that Western, and here in particular American, management functions as a role model for Japanese companies. The definition of what performance actually means for the evaluation of Japanese employees, however, can only be provided by taking into account the Japanese socio-cultural context. Given the collectivist nature of Japanese society, the performance criteria must consider individuals' contribution to group objectives, a longer-term commitment to the company and pursuit of longer-term objectives than would be the case in Western companies.

In other areas of Japanese management, reforms have taken place (or are expected to take place) *within* the traditional system, with no wholesale shift from one system to another. For example companies are embracing corporate strategies to a significantly higher degree, particularly in order to differentiate themselves more from their main competitors. It would be wrong to expect, however, that Japanese firms will stop paying attention to operational effectiveness and best practice in process innovation for the sake of strategic concerns. There is strong evidence for a culture based specific strength of Japanese companies to pursue operational effectiveness, and it would be foolish to give up this competitive advantage.

Any changes within a management system often necessitate coordinated modifications in other areas of the system. At the moment, however, it seems that changes within the Japanese management model are being made in isolation from each other. This is causing inconsistencies, friction and frustration, as employees are often confronted with contradictory messages. The success of the Japanese management model until the early 1990s was largely due to the fact that it was self-contained, possessed an inherent as well as a self-reinforcing logic, and its various components complemented and mutually supported each other. It was, in other words, in a state of a stable equilibrium. However because of mainly exogenous but also endogenous shocks this equilibrium could not be maintained, and now the model is in a state of flux. Therefore, the challenge is to integrate both change and continuity, so that the management model can enter into a new state of stable equilibrium in which it is not only coherent and consistent in itself, but also well attuned to the global economy and the domestic socio-cultural context.

Note

1. It should be noted that even though the factors inside and outside the brackets are conceptual opposites, they are not mutually exclusive. Therefore in practice they are a matter of degree, not of 'either or'.

Index

Note: all entries refer to Japan unless otherwise indicated.